The Economist

GUIDE TO THE EUROPEAN UNION

OTHER TITLES FROM
THE ECONOMIST BOOKS

The Economist Desk Companion
The Economist Economics
The Economist Guide to Economic Indicators
The Economist Numbers Guide
The Economist Style Guide
The Guide to Analysing Companies
The Guide to Business Modelling
The Guide to Financial Markets
The Guide to Management Ideas
The Dictionary of Economics
The International Dictionary of Finance
Business Ethics
E-Commerce
Improving Marketing Effectiveness
Managing Complexity
Measuring Business Performance
Successful Innovation
Successful Mergers

Pocket Accounting
Pocket Advertising
Pocket Director
Pocket Economist
Pocket Finance
Pocket International Business Terms
Pocket Internet
Pocket Investor
Pocket Law
Pocket Manager
Pocket Marketing
Pocket MBA
Pocket Money
Pocket Negotiator
Pocket Strategy

Pocket Asia
Pocket Europe in Figures
Pocket World in Figures

The Economist

GUIDE TO THE EUROPEAN UNION

Dick Leonard

8th edition

THE ECONOMIST IN ASSOCIATION WITH
PROFILE BOOKS LTD

Published by Profile Books Ltd
58A Hatton Garden, London EC1N 8LX

First published in 1988 as *Pocket Guide to the European Community*;
reprinted 1988; revised editions 1989, 1992, 1994

Typeset in EcoType by MacGuru
info@macguru.org.uk

Printed in Great Britain by
St Edmundsbury Press, Bury St Edmunds

A CIP catalogue record for this book is available
from the British Library

ISBN 1 86197 419 1

For information on other Economist Books, visit
www.profilebooks.co.uk
www.economist.com

Contents

List of tables

List of figures

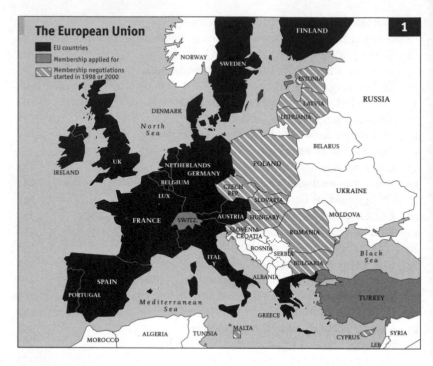

Membership   Applications for membership

1958	Belgium	1987	Turkey
	France	1990	Cyprus
	Germany[a]		Malta
	Italy	1992	Switzerland[b]
	Luxembourg	1994	Hungary
	Netherlands		Poland
1973	Denmark	1995	Bulgaria
	Ireland		Estonia
	United Kingdom		Latvia
1981	Greece		Lithuania
1986	Portugal		Romania
	Spain		Slovakia
1995	Austria	1996	Czech Republic
	Finland		Slovenia
	Sweden		

---

a East Germany joined as part of unified Germany in 1990.
b Not currently (2002) being proceeded with.

Introduction

Over 45 years after the signing of the Treaty of Rome, the European Union has established itself as a major force in the world, and its activities now impinge more and more on the lives of the citizens of its different member states. Yet the extent of public knowledge of the EU has lagged some way behind.

Many excellent books have been written about the EU. The majority of these have been addressed to specialists, or are concerned with one particular aspect of the Union's role. The purpose of this book is rather different. It is addressed specifically to lay people, and is intended to give a simplified account of the origin, history, institutions and functions of the Union in a form accessible to the intelligent reader with no previous knowledge of the EU.

The book is divided into five parts. Part I contains an account of the origins of the EC, followed by a historical account of its development up to and after the appointment of a new commission headed by Romano Prodi in September 1999. Part II describes in some detail the institutions of the Community, such as the European Commission, the Court of Justice, and so on. Part III deals with its competences, from agriculture to technological research. Part IV considers some specific problems, including enlargement and the continuing difficulties which the UK has experienced in adapting to EU membership, and concludes with an assessment of future prospects. Part V contains a series of appendixes which provide reference material on the Union and its institutions. Lastly, there are suggestions for further reading for those who wish to pursue the subject further.

The source of most of the figures and much of the factual information contained in this book is the European Commission. Permission to reproduce this information is gratefully acknowledged, as is the help of Leo Cendrowicz in preparing this eighth edition.

I would like to dedicate this book to the memory of Dr Gertrud Heidelberger, my mother-in-law, an indomitable lady who represented all that is best in European culture.

Dick Leonard, Brussels, October 1999

Notes

European Union or European Community?

In this book the terms European Union (EU) and European Community (EC) are often used interchangeably. Strictly speaking, the EC was incorporated into the EU in November 1993, when the Maastricht treaty came into force, but it continues to refer to the core of Union activities, for which the European Commission shares responsibility with the Council of Ministers, the European Parliament and the Court of Justice (see Part III). Other activities of the Union, notably foreign and security policy and the co-ordination of police and judicial affairs, are organised on an inter-governmental basis.

Currency

All sums of money referred to in this book are denoted in ecus, the European currency unit, whose value was based on the weighted average of a "basket" of the currencies of the member states, or in euros (€), whose value is the same. The euro is the new currency unit which replaced the national currencies of the 12 member states participating in the single European currency in January 2002. The fixed exchange rates of these currencies against the euro are shown on page 137. On July 15th 2002 the euro was worth £0.64, DKr7.43, SKr9.24, US$1.0024 and ¥116.22.

1

THE BACKGROUND

1 The origins

Hitler was the catalyst

Adolf Hitler was the main catalyst of the European Community, although none of its leaders would readily admit him as a founding father. Like Charlemagne and Napoleon before him, Hitler brought together, by the sword, virtually the entire land area of the original EEC, destroying in the process the self-confidence of the nation states from which it sprang.

These were recreated in 1945, but no longer saw themselves as autonomous actors on the world stage. The governments of the three smallest – the Netherlands, Belgium and Luxembourg – decided in 1944, before the liberation of their territories had been completed, that their economic futures were inextricably intertwined. The Benelux Union came into force on January 1st 1948 as a customs union, with the intention of progressing to a full economic union at a later stage.

The Marshall Plan

The United States and the Soviet Union each gave the nations of Western Europe a strong shove in the direction of unity, one with apparently benign, the other with malign intentions. The Organisation for European Economic Co-operation (OEEC) was set up in 1947 in order to divide up among the member states the flow of US aid under the Marshall Plan. The aid programme was completed over three years, but the OEEC continued as a forum for promoting economic co-operation and freer trade among West European countries. It later widened its membership to include all the advanced industrial nations of the non-communist world, and changed its name in 1961 to the Organisation for Economic Co-operation and Development (OECD).

Fear of the USSR ...

If the United States, partly no doubt through self-interest, had contributed hope, the Soviet Union contributed fear. Its brutal suppression of the countries of Eastern Europe, culminating in the communist takeover of Czechoslovakia in February 1948, forced several West European countries to come together for self-preservation. As early as March 17th 1948 the Treaty of Brussels was signed, providing for a 50-year agreement between the UK, France, Belgium, the Netherlands and

Luxembourg known as the Western European Union (WEU). This provided "for collaboration in economic, social and cultural matters and for collective self-defence". In practice the WEU was largely superseded by the creation of NATO in 1949, although it remained in existence and its five original members were joined by West Germany and Italy in 1954.

... and Germany

Fear of the Soviet Union in the post-war years was matched by fear of Germany, which had tried to overrun Western Europe in the second world war, and had also fought three ferocious wars with France over a period of 70 years. How to prevent a recurrence of these wars in the future occupied many minds in Western Europe, as elsewhere in the world, in the immediate post-war period. Two possible solutions presented themselves. The first was to ensure that Germany should not only remain divided (which the division of Europe between East and West seemed likely to secure, in any event), but that it should also be reduced to a permanent state of economic backwardness. Apart from intrinsic improbability, this solution had the serious disadvantage of conflicting with another West European priority: resisting the advance of Soviet communism. This pointed to the need not only for a German military contribution to western defence, but also for a strong economy which would help to satisfy the rapidly rising material expectations of West Europeans. It was this consideration which tipped the balance decisively towards the second proposed solution to "the German problem". This was that Germany (or West Germany at least) should be linked so organically with its neighbours, and that the link should appear so evidently in the self-interest of both Germans and all the other nationalities, that another war between the nations of Western Europe would become impossible.

Monnet's decisive role

The continental country most resistant to this concept was France, and it was fortunate that the most clearsighted and persuasive advocate of this approach was a Frenchman, Jean Monnet. If Hitler provided the impetus towards European unity, Monnet was indisputably its principal architect.

He had a remarkable career, almost all of it devoted to international co-operation of a genuinely practical kind. Originally a salesman in the UK for his family firm of brandy distillers, he spent the first world war as a temporary civil servant co-ordinating the contributions of the French and UK economies to the joint war effort. Between the wars he acted as deputy secretary-general of the League of Nations, but in 1939 he was recalled to resume his role as an Anglo-French co-ordinator. It was his plan for a Franco-UK Union which Churchill put forward in 1940 in a vain attempt to forestall the French surrender to the Germans. Monnet spent the rest of the war years in London and Washington, once again co-ordinating the economic warfare of the allied nations.

He returned to France as a member of de Gaulle's government, and subsequently became head of the French planning organisation. In 1950 his moment of destiny came: it was his proposal that paved the way for the Franco-West German reconciliation which has been the essential condition for all subsequent progress towards European unity. The occasion was the Franco-West German dispute over the Saarland, which was largely fuelled by French fears that if its iron and coal industries were integrated with those of the rest of West Germany it would once again dominate the economy of Europe. France had tried unsuccessfully to annex the Saarland, which was overwhelmingly German in population, and, as in the post-1919 period, this attempt had poisoned relations between the two countries.

The Schuman plan

Monnet succeeded in capturing the ear of the French foreign minister, Robert Schuman, a man whose own personal history (as an Alsatian born in Luxembourg) had predisposed him to the advantages of European integration. Monnet's proposal, which was put forward by the French government as the Schuman Plan, was that the West German and the French coal and steel industries should be placed under a single High Authority which should supervise their development. "The solidarity between the two countries established by joint production will show that a war between France and Germany becomes not only unthinkable but materially impossible," Schuman said in launching his plan on May 9th 1950.

Other European countries were invited to join the plan, which was instantly accepted by Chancellor Konrad Adenauer on behalf of the West German government, which rightly saw it as the way to rejoin the European comity of nations on equal terms. Italy and the Benelux countries also quickly responded, and the Treaty of Paris (see page 37), signed on April 18th 1951, formally established the European Coal and Steel Community (ECSC), which came into being on August 10th 1952. Jean Monnet was its first president.

The UK stands aloof

One notable absentee was the UK, which had been invited to join but declined to do so after giving the matter little serious thought. The decision was taken by Clement Attlee's Labour government, but was confirmed by the Conservative government under Winston Churchill, elected in October 1951. The UK did not then regard itself primarily as being a European nation, and adopted a superior attitude to the new organisation, as evidenced by the private remark of Churchill to his doctor in January 1952, "I love France and Belgium, but we must not allow ourselves to be pulled down to that level."[1]

The absence of the UK facilitated the construction of a community that was different from the many other international organisations established during this period, such as the Council of Europe, the North Atlantic Treaty Organisation (NATO) or the General Agreement on Tariffs and Trade (GATT). Each of these bodies established a permanent secretariat; however, there was no question of it having any more than an administrative role. Decision-making was reserved for meetings of representatives of each of the member states. The ECSC was unique in being provided with a supra-national High Authority which was given wide powers to determine the direction of two key industries throughout the member states. There was provision for a Council of Ministers, a purely advisory Assembly (or indirectly elected Parliament) and a Court of Justice, but the High Authority was, and was intended to be, the main organ of decision-making.

The constitution of the ECSC, as spelled out in the Treaty of Paris, closely reflected the views of Monnet, who wrote in his memoirs of the necessity of providing a firm institutional base to give effect to political intentions: "Nothing is possible without men: nothing is lasting without institutions."[1] He had intended that the ECSC would be paralleled by a common European defence force, which would supersede national armies and facilitate the rearming of West Germany without creating a specifically West German force. The same six governments – France, West Germany, Italy, Belgium, the Netherlands and Luxembourg – signed a treaty in May 1952 providing for the creation of a European Defence Community (EDC), for this purpose, but the French National Assembly in August 1954 declined to ratify the treaty.

Towards an economic community

The failure of the EDC had two significant consequences. West German rearmament proceeded on a national basis, and West Germany was admitted as a full member of NATO in October 1954. For his part, Monnet concluded that the path towards European unity lay through economic rather than military co-ordination. When his first term of office as president of the High Authority came to an end, in February 1955, he declined to accept a further term. Instead, he left to head a high-powered pressure group, the Action Committee for the United States of Europe (ACUSE), which included leading figures from the Socialist, Christian Democratic and Liberal parties of all the six member states.

ACUSE did not have to wait long for the first fruits of its activities. The foreign ministers of the Six met in Messina in June 1955 and appointed a committee under the chairmanship of the Belgian foreign minister, Paul-Henri Spaak, to investigate establishing a common market. This committee produced a report which was the basis of the Treaty of Rome, signed on March 25th 1957, establishing the European Economic Community (EEC). A separate treaty, signed in Rome on the same day, established the European Atomic Energy Community (Euratom). All six parliaments ratified the treaties, which came into effect on January 1st 1958, with a West German, Walter Hallstein, as first president of the EEC Commission.

The EEC's constitution paralleled that of the ECSC, but the supra-national element was significantly less. The EEC Commission, which was the counterpart of the High Authority, had substantially less power, and the Council of Ministers substantially more, than under the Treaty of Paris. In the early years of the EEC this difference was hardly apparent, as the confident and decisive Hallstein dominated the development of the Community. But in 1965–66 his authority was successfully challenged by France's President Charles de Gaulle (see page 11), and he subsequently resigned. None of his successors has wielded as much power as he had done, and since his departure the supremacy of the Council of Ministers (the representatives of the different member states) over the supra-national commission has been evident.

Amalgamation

The three communities – the ECSC, Euratom and the EEC – were formally amalgamated on July 1st 1967. They became jointly known as the European Community (EC), or sometimes the European Communities, although the abbreviation EEC remained in common use to denote the combined organisation.

Note

1   Alfred Grosser, *The Western Alliance: European-American Relations since 1945*, London, Macmillan, 1980, pages 121 and 102.

2 Evolution – 1958–2002

DeGaulle + Adenauer

The EEC might have broken up during its first year of operation. On June 1st 1958, five months after its foundation, General Charles de Gaulle became prime minister (and subsequently president) of France. His followers had bitterly opposed its creation; however, de Gaulle saw it as a useful means of extending French influence, and during his early years in power he encouraged its development.

Three months after coming to power he had a momentous meeting with the West German chancellor, Konrad Adenauer, which, in the words of a French historian, Alfred Grosser, turned out to be a case of "love at first sight".[1] Grosser quotes de Gaulle as writing in his memoirs: "From then until mid-1962, Konrad Adenauer and I were to write to each other on some 40 occasions. We saw each other 15 times … we spent more than 100 hours in conversation." From this mutual attraction sprang an enduring alliance which has proved to be the mainspring of the Community ever since. It was formalised in the Franco-West German Treaty of January 22nd 1963, which provided for the co-ordination of the two countries' policies in foreign affairs, defence, information and cultural affairs.

This co-ordination has been spasmodic, but whenever France and West Germany have acted together within the Community their influence has been enormous and they have generally been able to achieve their objectives. Where they have not done so, the Community has drifted and has found it difficult or impossible to agree on a course of action. For many years West Germany, although the stronger of the two powers economically, was content to play a subordinate role. When West German leaders' views differed from those of France, they were often willing to defer to their partners, or at least refrain from carrying their opposition to extremes.

An encouraging start

With the background of the Franco-West German entente, the benefit of strong economic growth in all six member states and the enthusiastic encouragement of the United States, the Community got off to a tremendous start in the first years after 1958. Intra-Community trade leapt ahead, increasing by 28.4% annually during the first ten years of the EEC, and the average increase of imports from third countries was 10%.

The timetable for removing all internal tariffs and quota restrictions was originally intended to be completed in successive stages by December 31st 1969. It was, however, twice accelerated, and the process was completed 18 months ahead of schedule, on July 1st 1968. Simultaneously with the removal of internal tariffs, a common external tariff was erected, based on an average of the duties previously levied by the member states, with some downward adjustment. This, too, was completed 18 months early, and the Community collaborated with the United States in the Kennedy round of the GATT, which resulted in a further 35% cut, on average, in its external tariff.

The other economic objective spelled out in considerable detail in the Rome treaty was the development of a common agricultural policy (CAP), based, however, on protectionism rather than free trade. In fact the two major prongs of the EEC were widely regarded as offering quid pro quos to West Germany and France. Free trade for industry accorded with the interests of West German manufacturers, and a guaranteed market for agricultural produce with those of French farmers. Despite the provisions in the Rome treaty, the CAP proved much more difficult to launch than the customs union, but in January 1962, after what a commission publication describes as "lengthy and often bitter negotiations and the longest negotiating marathon in the Community's history",[2] the Council of Ministers adopted the basic regulations for a common market in agriculture.

Foreign policy gap

The economic progress made by the Six (as the founder members of the Community were known) soon showed up a glaring omission in the Rome treaty, in that no mention was made of political co-operation. At a summit meeting in February 1961, the heads of government of the Community agreed that a political union should be set up between the Six. A committee chaired by a French politician, Christian Fouchet, produced two successive plans to bring this into effect. But neither the Fouchet Plan nor the Second Fouchet Plan was approved, owing to a basic difference between the larger and smaller member states. The larger states, particularly Gaullist France, thought that they should effectively direct the foreign policy of the Six. The smaller Benelux countries, on the other hand, fearing the prospect of domination, wanted a more equal say. In the end nothing came of the proposal, except that the heads of government agreed to hold regular meetings for general political consultation. Despite this decision, no further summit was held until six years later, and it was only after December 1974, when the European Council (see page 59) was formalised, that the heads of government began to meet regularly on a three times a year basis (reduced to twice a year in 1986).

Other European countries began to take note of the economic success of the Community. Greece and Turkey both applied to become associated states during 1959, while the UK government, whose earlier attempt to negotiate a wider free trade area within the OECD had ended in failure, became alarmed at the prospect of being left out in the cold. It took the initiative in organising the European Free Trade Association (EFTA), which linked it much more loosely with six of the smaller West European states. Together with Austria, Denmark, Norway, Portugal, Sweden and Switzerland,[3] it signed the Stockholm Convention, establishing EFTA, on January 4th 1960.

The UK knocks at the door

Yet no sooner had this Convention been signed than the UK government, led by Harold Macmillan, reappraised its position once again and decided that EFTA was much too small a grouping to meet its trading interests (it had a combined population of no more than 90m compared with 170m in the Six). In July 1961 the UK applied for full membership of the EEC, and was followed shortly afterwards by Ireland, Denmark and Norway.

The application was welcomed by five of the Six, but it soon transpired that President de Gaulle was lukewarm if not actually hostile to the entry of an "Anglo-Saxon" nation. Detailed accession negotiations began in November 1961, but soon became bogged down as the UK negotiators strove, perhaps ill-advisedly, to achieve a mass of detailed concessions on agriculture, Commonwealth trade and future relations with the other EFTA countries. Meanwhile, de Gaulle bided his time, but in January 1963, following Macmillan's Nassau agreement with President Kennedy on the supply of Polaris missiles which confirmed the French president's view that the UK's links with the United States took priority over any European commitment, he promptly vetoed the UK application at a press conference in Paris. The other three applicant countries accordingly withdrew their own applications.

The other five members states were aghast at the French action, but were unwilling to bring matters to a head. The EEC without the UK was a misfortune, in their view; without France it would be an impossibility. So they reluctantly acquiesced in de Gaulle's action, and only one week later the Franco-West German Treaty was signed. Three years later a UK Labour government, under Harold Wilson, made a renewed attempt to secure entry, but once again de Gaulle applied a veto, and once again his EEC partners submitted to his will.

Hallstein versus de Gaulle

At the head of the European Commission during the first nine years was Professor Walter Hallstein, formerly a close aide and confidant of Adenauer, whose name was previously associated with the so-called Hallstein doctrine, under which West Germany refused to have diplomatic relations with any government which recognised the East German regime. Hallstein had been the leader of the West German delegation to the Schuman Plan conference in 1950, and he enjoyed a large fund of French as well as West German goodwill at the outset of his presidency which greatly helped him to keep up the momentum. After several years, however, the gap between his own beliefs in a supra-national Europe and the more nationalistic approach of President de Gaulle became more and more apparent, and it was probably only a matter of time before a clash would occur.

The occasion might have been a difference over foreign policy or the rejection of UK membership. In the event, it was the decision-making process within the Council of Ministers which led to the break. During the early years of the Community most decisions within the council needed to be taken, under the terms of the Rome treaty, by unanimity. From 1966 onwards, when the transitional period came to an end, a wide range of decisions should have been reached by qualified majority voting. President de Gaulle was not willing to contemplate the possibility of France being outvoted on major issues and when, in June 1965, France found itself in a minority of one against commission proposals on the financing of the CAP, the provision of its own financial resources and extending the budgetary powers of the European Parliament, he refused to allow decisions to be taken. For the next six months France boycotted all meetings of the Council of Ministers, and its "empty chair" policy was not abandoned until January 1966, when the so-called Luxembourg compromise (see pages 55–6) was reached. This effectively gave all member states a right of veto when their "very important interests" were concerned. Not long afterwards Hallstein, who rightly concluded that the Luxembourg compromise had severely undermined the role of the commission as the principal initiator of policy, submitted his resignation.

The transformation of farming

One of the most profound changes within the Community during the 1960s and 1970s was the transformation of its agriculture. Not only did productivity and production shoot up, making the Community more than self-sufficient in most temperate products, but the number of people working on the land fell sharply, from 15.2m in 1960 to 5.8m in 1984 in the original six member states. The process would have gone even further if the Mansholt Plan, named after Dr Sicco Mansholt, the agricultural commissioner and later president of the commission, had been adopted. This plan, put forward in 1968, would have provided generous financial inducements for increasing the size of holdings, mechanising farming operations and taking some 5m ha of poorer land out of cultivation. A much watered down programme was eventually approved by the Council of Ministers in 1972, but unfortunately it did nothing to cure the emerging problem of structural surpluses nor to lighten the burden on the Community's funds of production guarantees.

Another significant development was the conclusion, in 1963, of the Yaoundé Convention, signed in the capital of Cameroon with 18 African states which were former dependent territories of EEC member states. The convention provided for the duty-free access of all their exports, except for certain products covered by the common agricultural policy, and for financial aid to be provided through the European Development Fund and the European Investment Bank. The first Yaoundé Convention was replaced in 1969 by Yaoundé II, and subsequently by four successive conventions bringing in many of the developing countries of the Commonwealth, signed at Lomé (Togo) in 1975, 1979, 1984 and 1989 (see Chapter 35). Lomé IV, signed by 70 African, Caribbean and Pacific states (the ACP states), continued the programme until 2000, when it was replaced by the 20-year EU–ACP Agreement, signed in Cotonou (Benin) by 78 ACP states and the 15 states of the EU.

An EC summit conference at The Hague, in December 1969, marked an important step forward. The conference finally approved the proposals for financing the common agricultural policy, the creation of the Community's own financial resources (see pages 93–4) and the extension of the European Parliament's budgetary powers, which had earlier been blocked by France. It agreed that the Community should proceed to the establishment of an economic and monetary union to be completed by 1980 (which proved to be a wildly over-optimistic target date), and it commissioned a report on ways of improving foreign policy co-ordination between member states. This report, written by Belgian diplomat, Etienne Davignon (later an influential commissioner), was approved ten months later. Since then the foreign ministers of the member states have met "in political co-operation" at frequent intervals, as have senior officials of the different foreign ministries, the idea being to discuss and if possible harmonise foreign policy opinions and activities (see Chapter 36).

Enter Denmark, Ireland and the UK

France – Pompidou
Ger – Willy
Brandt

President de Gaulle's resignation in 1969, followed by his death the following year, removed the main obstacle to UK accession. His successor, Georges Pompidou, was less inflexible and the new West German chancellor, Willy Brandt, strongly urged him to agree to an enlargement of the Community. The Danish, Irish, Norwegian and UK governments all renewed their applications and, after much hard bargaining, treaties of accession were signed in Brussels on January 22nd 1972. Norway narrowly rejected the treaty terms (by 53% to 47%) in a referendum in September 1972, but the other three countries formally became members on January 1st 1973.

Denmark and Ireland also held referenda on EC accession, which produced majorities in favour of, respectively, 83% and 63%. The UK did *UK –* not initially do so, although the issue of accession was highly divisive. *Heath* The prime minister, Edward Heath, pursued the objective of UK membership with great determination, and succeeded in rallying a large majority of the Conservative Party behind him. The Labour Party, however, was badly split on the issue, with the majority coming down decisively against. A defiant minority of 69 Labour members of Parliament, led by Roy Jenkins, insisted on voting against a three-line whip, in favour of the terms that Heath had negotiated, in a House of Commons vote in October 1971. The Labour Party subsequently resolved to hold a retrospective referendum on continued UK membership if it won the next general election.

The government of Harold Wilson, which came to power in 1974, first as a minority government, later with a tiny majority, fulfilled this undertaking in June 1975 after having "renegotiated" the terms of entry. The main change secured was the institution of a "corrective mechanism" which was intended to prevent excessive UK contributions to the EC budget. The mechanism was later to prove inoperative, but the referendum produced a decisive vote (67%) in favour of continued UK membership, and it seemed as though the controversy was at an end.

Denmark and the UK left EFTA on their accession to the EC, but were not required to sever their trading links, as the remaining members of EFTA negotiated industrial free trade agreements with the Community and formed a sort of "outer ring", sharing in the benefits of tariff-free trade, except for agricultural produce, without having to accept any of the obligations of EC membership.

Problems of enlargement

The 1973 enlargement, which increased the Community's membership from six states to nine, and its population from 191m to 255m, was expected to give it a fresh wind and enable it to develop further and faster during the 1970s. These hopes were largely unfulfilled. In part, this was because the enlarged EC lacked an agreed programme for its medium-term development, which the Rome treaty, with its precise timetable for progressing to a customs union and its outline of the basic constituents of a common agricultural policy, had provided in the first years of the Community. Moreover, the nine members formed a less cohesive grouping than the original six, and the persistence of hostility to the EC among large sections of the population in the UK and Denmark made it difficult for these two countries to accommodate themselves to the essential process of compromise and "give and take" that the smooth operation of the Community required.

The biggest blow to the Community's development, however, was undoubtedly the prolonged economic recession which followed the Yom Kippur war of 1973, and the consequent quadrupling of petroleum prices. All the member states suffered from mounting inflation and unemployment, and most of them saw their balance of payments slide into severe deficit. Moreover, efforts to co-ordinate energy policies of the member states proved elusive, as did attempts to find a common economic strategy to enable the Community to hoist itself out of the recession. The member governments all felt constrained, to varying degrees, to implement austerity policies in their own countries, and it became increasingly difficult to persuade them to release resources for the introduction of new common policies under the aegis of the Community.

Yet at the Paris EC summit in December 1974 agreement was reached on the establishment of the European Regional Development Fund (ERDF, see pages 169–72), whose purpose was to help close the gap between the most disadvantaged and the more favoured regions within the Community. Although the ERDF provided assistance to all the

— European Regional Development Fund

member states, its main beneficiaries during its first ten years of operations were the UK, Ireland and Italy.

The European Council

The same summit conference took three other important decisions. It resolved that henceforth the heads of government should consult among themselves much more frequently, and instituted the European Council (see Chapter 6), which should meet three times a year and consider important foreign policy questions as well as the affairs of the Community. It decided that the European Parliament should be elected by direct universal suffrage from 1978 onwards (later postponed until 1979). And it appointed Leo Tindemans, the then Belgian prime minister, to compile a report on European union by the end of 1975.

Tindemans duly reported one year later, proposing a series of measures, including a common foreign policy, an economic and monetary union, European social and regional policies, joint industrial policies as regards growth industries, policies affecting EC citizens and a substantial reinforcement of Community institutions. The report was discussed on several occasions by the European Council but no action was taken on it, an outcome which reflected the general lowering of the horizons of West European leaders so far as European union was concerned.

The appointment of Roy Jenkins as president of the commission, for four years from January 1977, was seen as a most encouraging development. A senior political figure, who had been deputy leader of the Labour Party as well as chancellor of the exchequer and home secretary, he had (together with Edward Heath) been the most energetic and consistent campaigner for UK adhesion to the EC. His admirers from many member states hoped that his arrival in Brussels would give the Community the added momentum which the enlargement four years earlier had failed to provide.

Jenkins proved a resourceful and diligent president but, partly because of lack of support from the UK government, first under James Callaghan and then under Margaret Thatcher, his presidency did not quite match up to expectations. He did, however, have two undoubted achievements to his credit. He established the right of the president of the European Commission to attend the annual Western economic summits as the representative of the Community, despite stubborn resistance from President Valéry Giscard d'Estaing and only lukewarm support from Callaghan. He was also one of the architects of the

European Monetary System (EMS, see pages 128–9), which came into effect in March 1979.

stabilized currency rate

The European Monetary System

The European Monetary System (EMS) has compensated, to some extent, for the failure of the earlier aspiration to achieve a full economic and monetary union by 1980. Based on a European currency unit (the ecu), the EMS comprises an exchange and intervention mechanism, credit facilities and a vehicle to ease the path of the less prosperous Community countries. Proposed by Jenkins in a speech in Florence, it was taken up by the West German chancellor, Helmut Schmidt, who, in conjunction with Giscard d'Estaing, was able to secure its acceptance by the European Council during three successive meetings in 1978. Despite the UK's refusal to join its exchange rate mechanism during its first 11 years, it was credited with having done a great deal to dampen down currency fluctuations and to encourage co-operation in financial policies between member states.

International trading relations developed continuously through the 1970s. The centrepiece was the Tokyo round of GATT negotiations between the European Community and 99 other participants. Given the background of world recession and rising unemployment (which had already reached 10m in the Community as a whole, and was subsequently to rise to 16m), the results of the round were remarkable, leading as they did to further cuts in customs duties, averaging about one-third, which came into effect from 1980.

The Community greatly extended its network of bilateral trade and aid agreements with developing countries. Agreements with the Maghreb countries (Tunisia, Algeria and Morocco), signed in 1976, were followed by others with the Mashreq countries (Egypt, Syria, Jordan and Lebanon) in 1977. An agreement had been reached with Israel in 1975, and one with Yugoslavia was concluded in 1980, which enabled the Community to implement a global Mediterranean policy. In Asia more limited agreements were made with Sri Lanka (1975), Bangladesh and Pakistan (1976), and India (1981), while a co-operation agreement was reached with the five ASEAN countries in 1981.

In Latin America agreements with Uruguay (1973), Mexico (1975) and Brazil (1980) were followed by a co-operation agreement with the five-nation Andean Pact in 1983. The third Lomé Convention, concluded in December 1984, covered trade with 66 African, Caribbean and Pacific countries, and provided aid worth 8,500m ecus for the period 1985–90 (see Chapter 35).

Attempts to secure a framework for the expansion of trade with communist countries made little progress. Talks with Comecon, the Soviet-dominated organisation for economic co-operation, continued from 1977 to 1980 but no agreement was reached, and the dialogue was only resumed in 1986, following Gorbachev's rise to power. Trade agreements were, however, concluded with China and Romania, and sectoral agreements with some other communist states (see pages 105–6).

Greece enters the Community

Meanwhile, further enlargements of the EC appeared on the agenda when three countries which had recently emerged from dictatorial or military rule applied to become full members. Greece tabled its application in 1975, and Portugal and Spain in 1977. The negotiations with Greece proceeded relatively smoothly, partly because the Greek government took the view that it had to secure entry at all costs and therefore did not haggle much over the terms, taking the view that its bargaining power would be greatly increased once it was inside the Community. It duly became a member on January 1st 1981.

The negotiations with Spain and Portugal were much more difficult, and not only because these two countries adopted a more stringent negotiating stance than Greece. There was far more opposition from within the Community itself, particularly in France, to their accession, largely because farmers in southern France, and also in Italy and Greece, feared competition from their Spanish rivals. There was a lively apprehension that France would again veto a membership application, and although this did not happen, President Giscard d'Estaing, in 1980, deliberately set out to slow down the negotiations.

Although Giscard d'Estaing played a negative role in this context, his overall influence on the Community was a positive one. Throughout his seven years as president he worked in close partnership with the West German chancellor, Helmut Schmidt, with whom he shared a considerable commonality of views, despite their different political backgrounds. Able to converse freely to each other in English, they sat side by side at meetings of the European Council and were often able to steer it in the direction in which they both wanted to go. In so far as anybody provided leadership to the Community during those seven years it was Schmidt and Giscard.

In 1981–82 both lost power and their successors, who were François Mitterrand and Helmut Kohl, signally failed to reproduce the Schmidt–Giscard relationship. Accordingly a vacuum appeared at the apex of the Community, and for several years it drifted helplessly, seemingly unable to tackle the mounting problems that it faced. A contributory factor was that Jenkins's term as president of the commission ended at about the same time, and his successor, a Luxembourger, Gaston Thorn, carried insufficient weight to be able to fill the gap.

A maze of problems

As the 1980s began, the Community was faced by a series of distinct problems which became increasingly entwined as the years went by; no solution was found until 1984. The issues were as follows.

- The prospect of disproportionately high UK payments to the budget.
- The threatened exhaustion of budget resources, allied to the need to curb the amount spent on the cap.
- The need to reform the Community's institutions in order to speed up decision-making and to make them more accountable.
- The need to respond to the technological challenge of the US and Japan if Europe was not to become an industrial backwater.
- The need to remove internal barriers within the Community.
- The enlargement negotiations with Spain and Portugal.

The UK budget problem for several years proved the most intractable, partly because of the personalities involved, including Margaret Thatcher, whose combativeness was an unwelcome revelation to her fellow heads of government. The fact that the UK was liable to pay an unacceptably high net contribution, once its transitional stage had come to an end, came to light during the closing months of James Callaghan's Labour government in 1979. The basic reason for this was that despite indications given during the negotiations and renegotiations for membership, agriculture continued to take the lion's share of the Community's budget. As a large importer of food, the UK was paying a disproportionately high amount in import levies, but as a small food producer it was getting much less than its proportionate share back in payments under the CAP.

When Mrs Thatcher became prime minister in 1979 she took an extremely robust line in defence of UK interests, and managed to obtain from the other member states in May 1980 a temporary agreement limiting UK contributions for 2–3 years while a longer-term solution was sought. An unfortunate by-product of Mrs Thatcher's hard-hitting campaign was to rekindle anti-EC feeling within the Labour Party, whose annual conference in 1980 passed a resolution calling for UK withdrawal. Under the leadership of Michael Foot, this then became part of Labour's manifesto for the 1983 general election.

The search for a long-term solution went on until 1984, practically monopolising the agenda of several meetings of the European Council before a settlement was reached, which, in the opinion of many, could have been obtained a great deal earlier if cooler counsels had prevailed.

Budgetary crisis

The UK budget dispute inevitably got bound up with the looming crisis in the general budgetary affairs of the Community, in that its "own resources" were proving inadequate to meet the many demands on its budget. The proceeds of customs duties and agricultural levies were declining each year, and the day was fast approaching when the EC's only other resource – a maximum take equal to a 1% rate of VAT throughout the Community – would be exhausted. The member states were divided between those that were prepared to raise the VAT limit and those (including especially the UK) that were more interested in budget-cutting, particularly in the large part of the budget (around 70%) devoted to agriculture.

Those that wished to expand the budget pointed to the desirability, which the commission was repeatedly asserting, of a major expansion of Community expenditure on technological research to enable European firms to obtain a share in world markets that would otherwise be monopolised by US and Japanese suppliers of "third industrial revolution" products. In parallel with this was a growing realisation that, in order to compete at all, Western Europe must turn itself into the "common market" it was supposed to be, and rid itself of the innumerable barriers to free trade which still existed a quarter of a century after the Community had been established.

Progress towards removing these barriers in the internal market was being thwarted by the failure of the Council of Ministers to agree on a vast number of proposals for liberalisation which had been tabled over the years by the commission. The backlog, largely resulting from the council's unwillingness to apply the majority voting rules of the Rome treaty, acted as a spur to proposals to speed up and democratise the decision-making process which emanated, in particular, from the European Parliament. Lastly, frustration was growing dangerously in both Spain and Portugal at the slowness of their entry negotiations, and there was a widespread feeling within the Community itself that these two newly democratic countries were not receiving the encouragement that they deserved.

Mitterrand's initiative

Like his predecessors, as president of France François Mitterrand eventually made his own considerable mark on the history of the EC. After all the above-mentioned problems had been incessantly argued for several years, to no measurable effect, he apparently determined that solutions to several of them should be reached during the course of the French presidency of the Council of Ministers, in the first half of 1984. In order to achieve this he had to rise above narrow French interests, so far as Spanish entry and the size of any budget rebate for the UK was concerned. This he succeeded in doing, and at the Fontainebleau summit, in June 1984, agreement was reached on the UK budget issue, on increasing the Community's own resources, on restraining agricultural spending and on clearing the way for the admission of Spain and Portugal.

The settlement for the UK was based on a yearly rebate of 66% of the difference between its VAT contribution and its share of EC expenditure. In exchange for this, Mrs Thatcher agreed that the general limit of VAT contributions should be raised from 1% to 1.4%. It was also agreed that in future agricultural spending would rise in each year by a smaller proportion than the overall rise in expenditure, which should have meant that the percentage of the budget devoted to the CAP would decline year by year.

The 1992 programme

A year later, at the Milan summit, progress was made on two other issues: a seven-year timetable was agreed for removing 300 barriers to the internal market (see Chapter 16); and it was agreed to hold an intergovernmental conference to discuss amendments to the Rome treaty and other ways of speeding up and democratising the decision-making process. This led to the Single European Act, adopted in Luxembourg in December 1985 and implemented, after ratification by all 12 national parliaments (which involved referenda in Denmark and Ireland), in July 1987 (see page 39).

The programme for the completion of the EC's internal market became known either as the 1992 programme or, in some member states, the 1993 programme. The ambiguity arose from the target date of December 31st 1992 by which time all 300 measures were intended to be implemented. The original idea came from Jacques Delors, but credit for the detailed planning and the enthusiastic way in which the programme was launched should go to the then UK commissioner for internal market affairs, Lord Cockfield. Despite initial scepticism, it soon became clear that the programme would be substantially completed within the timetable laid down and that it would bring considerable economic benefits to all the member states. Beyond this, it gave a new sense of purpose to the Community and helped to create the atmosphere in which further initiatives to broaden and deepen the EC appeared both practical and desirable. By the end of December 1992 almost 95% of the programme had in fact been legislated.

Meanwhile, agreement was reached on launching several EC research programmes (see Chapter 21), as well as the Eureka programme which also involved several non-EC European countries, although the budgets agreed for them were substantially less than the commission would have liked. It seemed that the EC had woken from its slumbers, and at last was tackling the most urgent problems on its agenda. Unfortunately, however, new obstacles arose to imperil some of the agreements reached. The Spanish and Portuguese entry negotiations were successfully terminated, but at the last moment their ratification was put in doubt by a stratagem of the Greek government. It refused to endorse the entry terms unless Greece received more economic aid from the Community. Greece was eventually bought off by the institution of the Integrated Mediterranean Programmes (see page 176), which provided for 6,600m ecus to be spent over seven years. Most of this sum has been applied to the modernisation of the Greek economy, but Italy and southern France have also been beneficiaries.

Enter Spain and Portugal, and a new budget crisis

No sooner had Spain and Portugal taken their places in the Community in January 1986 than the budgetary measures agreed at Fontainebleau began to come unstuck. In the face of falling world prices, and the steep decline in the value of the dollar in 1986 and 1987, the cost to the EC of export refunds for its food exports rose dramatically. It became politically impossible to adhere to the guidelines for agricultural expenditure, and within a year of the VAT limit being raised from 1% to 1.4% the available funds for the Community budget were once again exhausted. By the beginning of 1987 it was clear that the Community would face a budget deficit for the year of 5 billion–6 billion ecus, with agricultural expenditure greatly exceeding the planned appropriations, and with no prospect in sight of reconciling the EC's political and financial objectives within the existing budgetary framework. Under the leadership of Jacques Delors the commission then produced a programme which became known as the "Delors package", designed to put the funds of the Community on a more assured basis, while reinforcing control over farm spending and releasing resources for priority objectives including, especially, research and the expansion of the so-called structural funds (the regional and social funds and the guidance section of the EAGGF4), which the commission argued should be doubled, in real terms, by 1992.

A new beginning

It took three meetings of the European Council to reach agreement on the Delors package, partly because of the reluctance of Margaret Thatcher to accept proposals for controlling future expenditure which she regarded as less than watertight, and partly because of her determination that any new basis for budgetary contributions should include arrangements for abating the UK share which would be at least as generous, and as secure, as those agreed at Fontainebleau in 1984. Finally, however, at an emergency summit meeting in Brussels in February 1988, she agreed with the other 11 national leaders on proposals largely based on those put forward by Delors one year earlier.

The Brussels agreement meant that the Community could make a new start. A new budget limit was set at 1.2% of the total GNP of the Community, equivalent to 1.9-2.0% of VAT contributions as calculated on the previous basis. This enabled a budget of 43.8 billion ecus to be agreed for 1988, compared with actual expenditure of 37 billion ecus the previous year. By 1991 the budget had increased to 55.6 billion ecus. Under the agreement reached, a fourth resource based directly on the national share of GNP was added to the three main existing sources of revenue. The Fontainebleau agreement, under which 66% of the UK's net contribution is refunded, was written into the new dispensation.

The other main features of the agreement were that the structural funds were to be doubled, in real terms, by 1993, with more focus on economically backward areas, while much stricter control was to be applied to agricultural spending. In future this was not to grow by more than 74% of the annual growth rate of GNP, and so-called "stabilisers" would be applied progressively to reduce the level of subsidy for products in excess supply. Moreover, "set-aside" payments would be made to encourage farmers to take less fertile land out of production.

EMU back on the agenda

With this settlement under their belts, the EC leaders felt free to seek to revive the dormant project for economic and monetary union. At the Hanover summit of June 1988, which reappointed Jacques Delors for a further two years from January 1989, a committee was set up under his chairmanship with a mandate to study and report on means of preparing for monetary union. The summit noted that progress made towards achieving the 1992 programme for completing the internal market was now "irreversible" and that the Single European Act had succeeded in its objective of speeding up decision-making. At the subsequent Rhodes summit, in December 1988, it was noted that almost half the legislation involved in the 1992 programme had been adopted by the Council of Ministers, and the meeting reasserted the importance of the social aspects of the single market. The commission drew up proposals for a Community charter of fundamental social rights, which it hoped to have approved at the Madrid summit in June 1989. In the meantime, however, the Community had been treated to yet another example of UK reluctance to commit itself to progress towards closer European integration. The new crisis, if crisis it was, was caused by Mrs Thatcher's strident attack on the European Commission during a highly publicised speech to the College of Europe at Bruges in September 1988, accusing it of accumulating power for its own sake and of trying to create an "identikit European personality".

Mrs Thatcher's speech (which was widely characterised as "Gaullist") was followed by a deliberate policy of nit-picking over commission proposals, which was ill-received not only in other member states but in the UK as well, particularly when it was perceived as directly contrary to specific UK interests. One such case was the rejection, on legalistic grounds, of the Lingua programme of support for foreign language teaching, of which the UK was likely to be the principal beneficiary. Mrs Thatcher's campaign, which clearly embarrassed several of her own ministers, reached its climax in the third election to the European Parliament in June 1989 when, on her initiative, the Conservative Party's appeal was couched in narrow nationalistic terms.

The poor showing of the Conservatives in that election, and the strong support received both by the Labour Party and the Greens, seems to have had a chastening effect on the UK prime minister. This certainly appeared to be the case at the Madrid summit, which followed one week later. The main item on the agenda was the report of the Delors Committee on monetary union. This committee, composed mainly of the 12 central bankers of the member states, had proposed a three-stage process, leading to full currency union and a European system of central banks. It was agreed that the first stage, which involved all 12 member states adhering to the exchange rate mechanism of the EMS, should begin on July 1st 1990 while preparations should be made for an inter-government conference which would prepare the two subsequent stages and agree necessary amendments to the Rome treaty. While predicting that the UK would vote against the holding of such a conference, but would nevertheless go along with it, Mrs Thatcher acquiesced in these decisions and confirmed that the UK would join the exchange rate mechanism once certain conditions had been met. She declined, however, to endorse the Social Charter approved by the other 11 leaders, which was signed by them later in the year.

Downfall of communism

Meanwhile, momentous changes were occurring in Eastern Europe which were to have a profound effect on the European Community. By the summer of 1989 both Poland and Hungary were well on the way to a peaceful transition from communism to democracy, and in the following months hardline communist rule crumbled in East Germany, Czechoslovakia, Bulgaria and, after violent resistance, in Romania. The newly liberated states instinctively looked to the Community not only as a source of economic assistance, but also as a potential guarantor of their democratic development.

The Community responded with emergency aid and loans to Poland and Hungary, and at the Western economic summit in July 1989, the European Commission was asked to co-ordinate a much wider Western aid operation involving 24 donor nations (the members of the OECD). This programme was later opened up to include Czechoslovakia, Bulgaria, Romania and Yugoslavia, and all of these countries signed trade and co-operation agreements with the EC, as did the Soviet Union itself in December 1989.

A similar agreement was negotiated with the communist government of East Germany, but before it came into effect Germany was united on October 3rd 1990. Six months before, the EC heads of government, at an emergency summit in Dublin, agreed that, subject to transitional arrangements, the territory of the former German Democratic Republic should be integrated into the Community without any revision of the treaties, as soon as unification was legally established. So East Germany joined the EC, as part of the Federal Republic, without any of the long-drawn-out negotiations which had preceded earlier enlargements of the Community.

Central and Eastern Europe

No such quick transition awaited the other countries of Central and Eastern Europe, although all their leaders, including those of Yugoslavia and, in early 1991, of Albania, declared that their long-term objectives would be membership of the Community. Instead, ten-year association agreements, involving trade concessions, financial assistance and co-operation over a wide range of activities, were signed with Poland, Hungary and Czechoslovakia in December 1991. These agreements specifically acknowledged that the countries involved would eventually be eligible for full membership. Negotiations for similar agreements followed soon after with Romania, Bulgaria, Albania and the three Baltic states of Estonia, Latvia and Lithuania, whose independence was recognised in September 1991. By early 1994 so-called Europe Agreements had been signed with each of these countries, as well as the Czech Republic and Slovakia, to replace the earlier agreement reached with Czechoslovakia. Ukraine signed a partnership agreement with the EU in March 1994, by which time negotiations were well advanced for comparable agreements with Russia and the former Soviet republics of Belarus, Kazakhstan and Kirgizstan. Unlike those with East European countries, these agreements do not hold out the prospect of eventual membership. By contrast, this was implied in a Trade and Economic Co-operation Agreement signed with Slovenia in April 1993. Comparable agreements may well be offered to the other former Yugoslav republics as soon as a secure peace is established.

The EC was, in fact, deeply involved almost from the outset in trying to achieve a peaceful settlement to the warfare which broke out following the declaration of independence by Slovenia and Croatia in June 1991. The European Council, meeting in Luxembourg on June 28th–29th, immediately dispatched a team of foreign ministers to try to arrange a ceasefire, and subsequently a peace conference opened in The Hague, under EC auspices, in September 1991 under the chairmanship of Lord Carrington, a former UK foreign secretary. Teams of EC monitors were sent to Yugoslavia to see that the ceasefire was respected. It held in Slovenia but not in Croatia, where over a dozen further ceasefires broke down, a third of the country was overrun by Serbian forces and the federal Yugoslav army, and great death and destruction was caused before, following diplomatic intervention by the UN, a peace of exhaustion set in, reinforced by the arrival of a large UN peace-keeping force in March 1992. This was the first time that the EC had attempted to play an international mediating role beyond its own boundaries. Later in 1992 a similar scenario was played out in Bosnia-Hercegovina, although the EC role was more marginal and the UN intervened, if ineffectively, at an earlier stage.

The EC was heavily engaged in humanitarian aid and in monitoring activities, but the major role of attempting to contain the conflict was undertaken by NATO, at the request of the UN. It was, however, only after the decision to use decisive air power against the Bosnian Serbs, in August 1995, that an end to hostilities was achieved, leading to the signing of the Dayton peace agreement. The EU assumed the predominant role in providing reconstruction aid, and was directly involved in providing a temporary administration for the town of Mostar, the scene of bitter conflicts between Croats and Muslims. Similarly, following the Kosovo conflict in 1999, the EU, in co-operation with the World Bank, undertook the major financial responsibility for rebuilding the shattered territory, establishing the European Agency for Reconstruction, which assumed direct control of the construction effort.

The EC also became involved in Western efforts to provide material assistance to the former Soviet Union. Already in June 1990 the EC heads of government had asked the commission to consult with the Soviet government and to prepare proposals for short-term credits and longer-term support for structural reform. In December 1990 aid programmes of 750m ecus for food and 400m ecus for technical assistance during 1991 were approved, although the latter programme was temporarily suspended as a protest against Soviet repression in the Baltic states.

After the unsuccessful coup in August 1991 a more extensive aid programme was initiated, which, following the dissolution of the Soviet Union in December 1991, was widened to include assistance not only to Russia but also to all the other former Soviet republics. Six of these claim to be European states: Armenia, Azerbaijan, Belarus, Georgia, Moldova and Ukraine. Several have already indicated an interest in eventual membership of the EU, but none is likely to be a viable candidate until well into the next century, although most of the other states of Central and Eastern Europe seem likely to qualify by 2002 or even earlier.

Meanwhile, the EC had taken the initiative in setting up the European Bank for Reconstruction and Development (EBRD), with an initial capital of $10 billion subscribed by 40 countries. Its purpose is to help the former communist countries to develop into free-market economies (see page 83).

Inter-governmental conferences

The rapid completion of German unification proved possible only because other states were convinced of West Germany's peaceful intentions and the solidity of its democratic institutions. Nevertheless, Chancellor Helmut Kohl, who took the lead in pushing the process through, was convinced that only if a unified Germany was firmly entrenched in a more democratised European Community would it be acceptable to its neighbours. Accordingly, on the eve of the Dublin EC summit of April 1990, in conjunction with France, the German government launched an initiative to ensure that new and decisive steps should be taken towards closer European unity. The following June a further summit meeting in Dublin agreed to establish a second inter-governmental conference (IGC), to run parallel with that on economic and monetary union (EMU), to recommend changes which would lead to "political union" within the Community. It was agreed that both the conferences would be convened in December 1990, with a view to completing their work in time for the member states to ratify their proposals by the end of 1992.

Although all the member states agreed to the establishment of the two IGCs, it was evident that the UK government, still led by Margaret Thatcher, was the least enthusiastic and was unlikely to accept the far-reaching proposals for change which other member states, with France and Germany in the lead, were putting forward with increasing urgency. Although Mrs Thatcher finally agreed in early October 1990 to let the pound enter the exchange rate mechanism of the EMS, 11 and a half years after it was first established, her hostility towards EMU remained unabated. Three weeks later, at a summit meeting in Rome, she was outvoted by 11 to 1 on the starting date for the second stage of EMU. Her intemperate reaction to this rebuff triggered the challenge which led to her replacement as prime minister by John Major at the end of November.

Major lost no time in mending fences with his fellow EC leaders at the second Rome summit, which followed on December 14th–15th 1990. It was then that the two IGCs, which were manned respectively by the finance and foreign ministers of the 12 member states, were formally convened. As their work proceeded over the following months it became evident that there was no longer a serious risk of the UK being totally isolated in both conferences. It seemed more likely that compromises would be reached, involving rather slower progress towards EMU than had originally been proposed, while the changes effected by political union would be less radical than France and Germany had been seeking.

Maastricht treaty

So it proved when the European Council met at Maastricht in December 1991 to consider a draft treaty based on the work of the two IGCs. After two days of hard bargaining the Treaty on European Union was approved, but only after John Major had insisted on two opt-out clauses so far as the UK was concerned. The practical effect of these opt-outs may not be great, but they symbolised once again that the UK, or at least the UK government, still did not feel thoroughly at ease within the European family.

The Maastricht treaty is described in some detail in Appendix 8, and is discussed in Chapters 18, 23 and 36. It undoubtedly represented the most important development in the EC's history since the signing of the Treaty of Rome. Not only did it set out a detailed timetable for achieving economic and monetary union, at the latest by 1999, and provide for the development of common foreign and defence policies, but it also introduced a new concept of EC institutions. A protocol signed by 11 member states, from which the UK excluded itself, opened the way to the implementation of Social Charter legislation in those 11 countries. Lastly, the treaty committed the EU to establish a further IGC conference in 1996 to review the working of the Maastricht changes and to set the ground rules for the Union well into the 21st century.

Question marks began to appear against the Maastricht treaty in June 1992, when a referendum in Denmark narrowly went against ratification (50% to 49.3%). Although a further referendum in Ireland, later the same month, produced a strong majority in favour, the alarming prospect arose that French voters would turn the project down in a closely contested ballot in September 1992. Although closer European integration was widely supported in France, there was a serious risk that voters would take the opportunity to administer a rebuff to the unpopular Socialist government which had, quite unnecessarily, called the referendum. In the event a narrow majority (51.05% to 48.95%) approved the treaty.

There were also serious difficulties in securing ratification in the UK, where the prime minister, John Major, had great trouble in overcoming opposition within his own Conservative Party. As he was unwilling to renounce the opt-out that he had secured on the Social Charter, he was unable to count on consistent support from the opposition Labour and Liberal Democratic parties to get the treaty through the prolonged procedures required for ratification by the House of Commons. After considerable delays, which tried the patience of the UK's European partners, the ratification bill was finally approved by the House of Commons on May 20th 1993, and by the House of Lords on July 20th, enabling the UK instrument of ratification to be deposited in early August.

Nine months earlier, at the Edinburgh summit in December 1992, concessions had been made to the Danish government enabling Denmark to opt out of a single European currency, on a similar basis to that agreed for the UK, and a number of other – largely cosmetic – interpretations of the treaty were agreed in order to encourage Danish voters to reconsider their earlier rejection. Consequently, in a further referendum in May 1993, the Danes approved the treaty by 56.7% to 43.3%.

There was yet another delay when German opponents of the treaty sought a ruling declaring it incompatible with the German constitution, despite its having been adopted by an enormous majority in the German Parliament. This attempt was overruled by the German Constitutional Court on October 12th 1993, and the German instrument of ratification was deposited on the same day. This removed the last obstacle, and the treaty finally came into force on November 1st 1993, ten months later than planned. Since then the European Community has been generally known as the European Union (EU).

The difficulties over securing ratification in Denmark, France, Germany and the UK were widely seen as a demonstration that EC political leaders had moved too far ahead of public opinion in their own countries in deciding to push ahead towards closer European integration. The former UK prime minister, Margaret Thatcher, characterised it as a "treaty too far". There was some force in this criticism, and it is true that public knowledge of the provisions of the Maastricht treaty was not extensive, but it is more likely that the undoubted tailing off of enthusiasm for the EU was owing to three other factors. These were the economic recession, which struck virtually all European countries, though with varying force, between 1990 and 1994; turmoil in the currency markets which led to UK and Italian withdrawal from the exchange rate mechanism in September 1992, and the abandonment of the narrow bands within the ERM ten months later; and dismay at the apparent failure of EU efforts to bring peace to former Yugoslavia.

New enlargement

In January 1995 three of the EFTA countries – Austria, Finland and Sweden – became full members of the EU. This was the culmination of a process which began with the launching of the 1992 programme in 1985. All seven EFTA countries, anxious not to be excluded from the development of a single market of more than 370m people, sought means by which they could share in the expected benefits. On the initiative of Jacques Delors, the EC offered to negotiate to set up a European Economic Area (EEA), which would permit the EFTA states to join in the 1992 programme at the price of accepting many of the obligations of the EC member states.

The EEA treaty was signed in 1992, but was rejected in a referendum in Switzerland. When it finally came into force in January 1994 it included only Iceland, in addition to Austria, Finland, Sweden and Norway, which were already well advanced in negotiations for full membership of the EU. The door was left open for Liechtenstein to join at a later date, when it had revised its economic relationship with Switzerland. Switzerland had also applied for full membership, but its application was held in abeyance following the referendum decision on the EEA. The four other applicant states completed their negotiations in March 1994, and the membership terms were approved later in the year in referenda in Austria, Finland and Sweden, permitting the three countries to take their place in the Union. The referendum in Norway produced a negative result, and Norwegians will remain outside the Union for the foreseeable future, although they remain members of the EEA.

The prospect is, however, that the Union will take in up to a dozen new member states in the early years of the 21st century. No sooner had the negotiations with the EFTA states been concluded than Hungary and Poland tabled applications to join. They were followed over the next two years by Romania, Bulgaria, Slovakia, the Czech Republic, Slovenia and the three Baltic states. Cyprus and Malta had already applied some time earlier, and at the European Council meeting in Madrid in December 1995 it was agreed that negotiations with all 12 states could begin within six months of the conclusion of the intergovernmental conference that opened in Turin in March 1996 and completed its work at Amsterdam in June 1997. Meanwhile, the newly elected Labour government in Malta announced that it would not proceed with its application.

In May 1995 the commission issued a White Paper setting out detailed guidelines for the applicant states regarding the modifications in their economies and in their legal and administrative systems that would be required for them to qualify for membership. It was also made clear that the introduction of a free market, and firm guarantees of democratic and human rights, would be necessary conditions for their admittance. Shortly after the Amsterdam summit, the commission recommended that membership negotiations should begin in March 1998 with six of the candidate members – Cyprus, the Czech Republic, Estonia, Hungary, Poland and Slovenia. The remaining applicants, it advised, had not yet fulfilled the conditions necessary for talks to begin, but they should continue to be assisted in their preparations and the position should be kept under continuous review. The Luxembourg summit, in December 1997, accepted this recommendation, but decided that all 11 applicants (plus Turkey) should be invited to annual European conferences, the first to be held in March 1998. The Turkish government, which was offended that, unlike the other five candidates (Bulgaria, Latvia, Lithuania, Romania and Slovakia), it had not been given an assurance of eventual membership, decided to boycott the conference.

Negotiations with the six favoured candidates duly commenced in March 1998, and in February 2000 with the remaining five plus Malta. Meanwhile, at the Helsinki summit in December 1999, the status of Turkey as a valid candidate was finally recognised, although negotiations would not begin until certain pre-conditions had been met. By the summer of 2002, negotiations with ten of the 12 active candidates – all but Bulgaria and Romania – were sufficiently advanced to give a reasonable hope that they would be concluded by the end of the year, with the prospect of membership on January 1st 2004.

Turin inter-governmental conference

The inter-governmental conference that opened in Turin in March 1996 was originally conceived as a review conference on the operation of the Maastricht treaty. Long before it met, however, it became clear that its agenda would be far wider than anticipated. The IGC would have to make a fundamental reassessment of the institutional arrangements of a Union originally designed for six members, now enlarged to 15, with the prospect of increasing to 27 or more over the next decade. In particular, it needed to examine the following questions.

- ◪ Should there be more majority voting in the Council of Ministers, given the increasing difficulty of obtaining unanimity with an ever-increasing membership?
- ◪ Should there be a reweighting of votes in the Council of Ministers to safeguard against the possibility of the larger member states being outvoted by combinations of small countries whose collective population was far smaller? Should there, in particular, be a firming up of the provisions for a blocking minority?
- ◪ How large should the commission be in future, and should every member state, however small, continue to be entitled to have a commissioner?
- ◪ Should powers under Pillar Three (on justice and home affairs) continue to be dealt with on an inter-governmental basis rather than coming under the jurisdiction of all the EU institutions?
- ◪ How could the common foreign and security policy, under the inter-governmental Pillar Two, be made more effective?

As the IGC got under way, it was clear that there were significant differences between the member states on all of these issues. In particular, the interests of the larger and smaller states were seen to conflict, but it was also evident that there was a strong will to succeed and to reach a consensus on all the principal issues. There was, however, one notable exception: the then UK government had set its face against any increase whatever in the EU's powers and was adamantly opposed to any increase in majority voting. The IGC, which might otherwise have been expected to conclude in the spring of 1997, was consequently stalled. The other member states agreed informally among themselves to wait until after the UK general election on May 1st 1997 to see whether the new government would be more willing to reach a compromise agreement with its partners.

UK isolation ended by Blair's election

The unco-operative attitude of the UK government in the IGC was the culmination of a series of events which had progressively alienated the UK from the European mainstream. The events of the Thatcher period have already been recounted, but – despite the early hopes that the Major government would heal the rift – the reverse seems to have occurred. At the root was the difficulty that John Major experienced in getting his own Conservative MPs to back the ratification of the Maastricht treaty. This led him to the conclusion that only by adopting an increasingly hostile attitude to his EU partners could he hope to contain the pressure from the growing number of Eurosceptics within his own party. This was a serious misjudgement. Every concession he made to their demands only whetted their appetite to ask for more, while progressively undermining the influence that the UK government could exert within the EU.

Some of Major's actions were patently irrational. At the Corfu summit in June 1994, he vetoed the nomination (supported by all the other member states) of the Belgian prime minister, Jean-Luc Dehaene, to become president of the commission in succession to Jacques Delors. This he justified on the grounds that Dehaene was a European federalist who wanted to turn Europe into a super-state. However, a few weeks later he agreed to the appointment of the Luxembourg prime minister, Jacques Santer, who publicly stated that his own views were identical to those of Dehaene. Then in April 1996 he adopted a policy of non-co-operation in the Council of Ministers (reminiscent of de Gaulle's "empty chair" tactic 30 years earlier), under which his ministers vetoed virtually every proposal under consideration – even those the UK itself had put forward. This was in a vain attempt to force the EU to lift its ban on UK beef exports. The UK government abandoned this self-defeating tactic after six weeks, but continued its generally negative attitude until May 1st 1997, when it went down to a heavy electoral defeat. The newly elected Labour government immediately announced a "fresh start" in relations with the EU, and this enabled the inter-governmental conference to complete its work amicably, and its recommendations were duly adopted at the Amsterdam summit in June 1997. The treaty which was signed, however, was a modest document and agreement was postponed on important institutional questions which needed to be resolved before the entry of the new candidate states from central and eastern Europe. These included the weighting of votes in the Council of Ministers, the size of the commission and the extension of qualified majority voting to all but the most important issues. A further IGC was held during 2000, and agreement was eventually reached at a lengthy and notably ill-tempered summit at Nice in December 2000.

Economic and monetary union

Meanwhile, it became increasingly likely that the third stage of economic and monetary union (EMU), leading to a single currency, would start as planned on January 1st 1999, and that a majority of member states would participate. At the Madrid summit, in December 1995, it was agreed that the new currency would be called the euro and that it would be of equal value to the European currency unit (ecu), based on a basket of national currencies and used to calculate payments within the EU's budget. A year later, at the Dublin summit, a stability pact was agreed, designed to ensure that the countries which satisfied the criteria for entry into EMU would continue to do so thereafter. Finally, as described on pages 135-7, the special EU summit, held in Brussels on May 1st-2nd 1998, approved the recommendations of the commission and the European Monetary Institute that 11 of the 15 member states should join the third stage of EMU, and participate in the single currency, from January 1st 1999. Greece was excluded because of its failure to meet the Maastricht criteria, and the UK, Denmark and Sweden declined to join - largely for political reasons. The UK government indicated that it was in principle in favour of joining, but would not do so until after a referendum was held. The summit also appointed Wim Duisenberg as the first president of the European Central Bank, which replaced the European Monetary Institute on June 1st 1998.

On December 31st 1998 the Ecofin council agreed the fixed rates of exchange against the euro for the 11 participating national currencies (see page 137). From January 1st 1999 the euro became operational for banking purposes, and in January 2001 Greece was the twelfth country to join the euro-zone. Exceptional care was taken to prepare for the introduction of euro notes and coins in January 2002 and the withdrawal of national currencies in the succeeding month. In the event, the operation was extremely successful, passing off with hardly a hitch (see pages 137-8).

Resignation of Santer Commission

In December 1998 the first shots were fired in a developing row between the European Parliament and the commission, which led to the latter's resignation four months later. The Parliament refused to approve the final accounts of the 1996 budget because of concerns about fraud, mismanagement and cronyism, allegedly involving several commissioners, notably Edith Cresson, the former French prime minister, who was responsible for research and education. To head off a possible vote of censure, Jacques Santer agreed to the appointment of a five-member independent committee to audit the work of the commission. The five "wise men" produced a report within five weeks, as requested by the Parliament. It strongly criticised Mrs Cresson for appointing a dentist friend to a fictitious job and for her lax management of the Leonardo vocational training programme, but made only minor criticisms of other commissioners. Despite having turned up little in the way of active corruption, however, the report contained the stinging phrase "it is becoming difficult to find anybody who has even the slightest sense of responsibility".

Parliament did not have the power to censure individual commissioners, and Mrs Cresson refused to resign or, indeed, offer any sign of contrition nor did Santer take it upon himself to demand her resignation. Within a day or two of the report's appearance it became clear that the Parliament would be able to muster the necessary two-thirds majority to require the dismissal of the entire commission, and in anticipation of this all 20 members submitted their resignations on March 11th 1999. Two weeks later the EU heads of government, meeting in Berlin, nominated a former Italian prime minister, Romano Prodi, to succeed Santer, but it was only in September that the European Parliament voted to appoint him and a new team of commissioners, which included only four survivors from the Santer commission, to serve out the remaining four months of Santer's term and then another five years until January 2005.

New budget perspective

The other main business at the Berlin summit was to settle the budget perspectives for the EU for the seven-year period 2000–06. The newly elected German chancellor, Gerhard Schröder, had hoped to secure a major cut in his country's budget contribution to the EU, which largely exceeded that of all the other 14 member states combined. In the end, however, in the interest of getting a general agreement he settled for only marginal relief, and the annual British rebate (strongly criticised by the other member states) remained intact (see page 99) The agreement reached should enable EU activities to expand at a modest rate during the seven years, while providing a package of pre-accession aid to the candidate countries in Central and Eastern Europe, some or all of which should secure EU entry by 2006.

The convention on EU reform

There had been a great deal of dissatisfaction with the handling of the 2000 Nice summit, where Jacques Chirac, the French president, had been severely criticised for his overbearing and maladroit chairmanship. This had led to the adoption of what many considered to have been botched conclusions, particularly concerning several provisions of the Nice treaty, which were perhaps responsible, at least in part, for its rejection by Irish voters in the June 2001 referendum. There was also concern about increasing evidence of public disenchantment with the EU, which had been manifested by the record low turnout in the European Parliament elections of 1999. Largely at the behest of the German government, it was therefore decided that a further IGC should be held in 2004. This should consider a wide range of possible future reforms, including a constitution which would replace, or supplement, the Treaty of Rome and the subsequent amending treaties, and which would be a simplified document that ordinary citizens could understand.

At the Laeken summit in December 2001, it was decided that the IGC should be preceded by a convention, whose 105 members should include not only national governments, but also MPs and MEPs, as well as representatives of the 12 candidate states currently negotiating membership and of the other EU institutions. Voluntary organisations were given facilities to feed ideas to the convention, which would be presided over by Valéry Giscard d'Estaing, a former French president. The convention started meeting in February 2002 and was asked to conclude its deliberations by the end of the year, giving a further year in which its recommendations could be widely discussed in advance of the IGC itself. This process should lead to the largest shake-up in the history of the EU, coinciding with the probable adhesion of ten new member states.

Notes

1 Alfred Grosser, *op. cit.*, page 189.
2 Steps to European Unity, *European Documentation*, 1985.
3 The UK, Denmark and Portugal subsequently left EFTA on joining the EC, but Finland, Iceland and Liechtenstein became EFTA members.
4 The European Agricultural Guidance and Guarantee Fund.

3 Treaties

The Treaty of Rome

The bible of the European Community, which provides the ultimate authority for the greater part of its decisions and responsibilities, is the Treaty of Rome, signed on March 25th 1957 by representatives of Belgium, France, West Germany, Italy, Luxembourg and the Netherlands. It was actually only one of two treaties signed in Rome by the same signatories on the same day; the other established Euratom, the European Atomic Energy Community. Six years earlier on April 18th 1951 the six countries had signed the Treaty of Paris, setting up the European Coal and Steel Community (ECSC).

The Treaty of Rome is a bulky document comprising 248 articles and an additional 160 pages of annexes, protocols and conventions. The first four articles, quoted here in their entirety, define the purposes of the European Economic Community, and the principal institutions to be created to ensure their achievement.

Article 1 By this Treaty, the HIGH CONTRACTING PARTIES establish among themselves a EUROPEAN ECONOMIC COMMUNITY.

Article 2 The Community shall have as its task, by establishing a common market and progressively approximating the economic policies of Member States, to promote throughout the Community a harmonious development of economic activities, a continuous and balanced expansion, an increase in stability, an accelerated raising of the standard of living and closer relations between the States belonging to it.

Article 3 For the purposes set out in Article 2, the activities of the Community shall include, as provided in this Treaty and in accordance with the timetable set out therein:

(a) the elimination, as between Member States, of customs duties and of quantitative restrictions on the import and export of goods, and of all other measures having equivalent effect;

(b) the establishment of a common customs tariff and of a common commercial policy towards third countries;

(c) the abolition, as between Member States, of obstacles to freedom of movement for persons, services and capital;

(d) the adoption of a common policy in the sphere of agriculture;

(e) the adoption of a common policy in the sphere of transport;

(f) the institution of a system ensuring that competition in the common market is not distorted;

(g) the application of procedures by which the economic policies of Member States can be co-ordinated and disequilibria in their balances of payments remedied;

(h) the approximation of the laws of Member States to the extent required for the proper functioning of the common market;

(i) the creation of a European Social Fund in order to improve employment opportunities for workers and to contribute to the raising of their standard of living;

(j) the establishment of a European Investment Bank to facilitate the economic expansion of the Community by opening up fresh resources;

(k) the association of the overseas countries and territories in order to increase trade and to promote jointly economic and social development.

Article 4

1. The tasks entrusted to the Community shall be carried out by the following institutions:

- an ASSEMBLY
- a COUNCIL
- a COMMISSION
- a COURT OF JUSTICE

Each institution shall act within the limits of the powers conferred upon it by this Treaty.

2. The Council and the commission shall be assisted by an Economic and Social Committee acting in an advisory capacity.

Articles 5-248   These articles deal with the following areas.

- 5–8: the setting up of the Community during a transitional period of 12 years.
- 9–11: free movement of goods.
- 12–29: the establishment of a Customs Union.

- 30–37: the elimination of quantitative restrictions.
- 38–47: provisions for agriculture.
- 48–73: the free movement of persons, services and capital.
- 74–84: the requirements for a common transport policy.
- 85–102: competition policy, taxation and the approximation of laws.
- 103–116: economic and trade policy.
- 117–128: social policy.
- 129–130: the establishment of a European Investment Bank.
- 131–136: the association of overseas countries and territories.
- 137–198: the composition and powers of the various Community institutions.
- 199–209: financial provisions.
- 210–248: the legal personality of the Community, the admission of additional members, the setting up of the institutions and various miscellaneous points. Article 240 states that "The Treaty is concluded for an unlimited period". The treaty came into effect on January 1st 1958.

Other treaties

A number of other treaties, protocols and conventions have been signed by the member states over the years, which supplement the original provisions of the Treaty of Rome. The most important of these are as follows.

1 The treaty amalgamating the three European Communities (ECSC, EEC and Euratom), signed in Brussels on April 8th 1965, usually known as the EC treaty.
2 The treaty concerning the admission of Denmark, Ireland, Norway and the UK, signed in Brussels on January 22nd 1972. (Norway subsequently declined to ratify this treaty after a referendum.)
3 Equivalent accession treaties with Greece, signed in 1980, with Spain and Portugal, signed in 1985, and with Austria, Finland, Sweden and Norway, signed in 1994. (Norway again failed to ratify.)
4 The Single European Act, signed in 1986 which, among other provisions, amended several articles of the Treaty of Rome regarding voting procedures in the Council of Ministers, while somewhat enlarging the legislative powers of the European Parliament. The main objective was to facilitate the adoption of the programme of nearly 300 measures to complete the Community's internal market (see Chapter 16). These were the first substantial amendments to the Treaty of Rome in its first 30 years in operation.

The three pillars of the European Union — 2

THE EUROPEAN UNION

THE EUROPEAN COMMUNITY	COMMON FOREIGN AND SECURITY POLICY	JUSTICE AND HOME AFFAIRS
institutions and legislative procedures		asylum policy*
agricultural policy		immigration*
the internal market		the fight against drugs
environment		police co-operation
citizens' rights		etc
economic and monetary union		
regional policy		
etc		

*Transferred to Pillar One under the Amsterdam treaty.

5 The Treaty on European Union, otherwise known as the Maastricht treaty, agreed in December 1991 and signed in February 1992. This was a much more thorough-going revision of the Rome treaty, comprising two major sets of provisions: those aiming at the establishment of an economic and monetary union (EMU), at the latest by January 1st 1999; and those defined as steps towards the achievement of a political union, involving common foreign and defence policies. Other provisions extended or defined more precisely the Community's competences in other policy areas and amended the powers of various EC institutions. The treaty established three pillars for the European Union. Pillar One embraced the three existing European Communities treaties (the ECSC, EC and Euratom). Pillar Two contained new provisions on a common foreign and security policy (CFSP), and Pillar Three provided for co-operation between the member states on justice and home affairs. Pillars Two and Three are not subject to the EC institutions and are organised on an inter-governmental basis (see Figure 2). This treaty is summarised in Appendix 8.

6 The Treaty of Amsterdam, agreed in June 1997 and signed in October 1997, which came into effect after ratification by all the contracting parties on May 1st 1999. This was largely a tidying-up exercise, transferring much of the decision-making under Pillar Three to Pillar One, improving the arrangements for the Common Foreign and Security Policy, bringing the Protocol on Social Policy and the Schengen Agreement into the EC framework, extending the powers of the European Parliament and the President of the commission, adding Employment and 'Flexibility' clauses, and providing for greater transparency. This treaty, also, is summarised in Appendix 8.

7 The Treaty of Nice, agreed in December 2000 and signed in February 2001, which will only come into force when ratified by all the contracting parties. It was rejected by a referendum in Ireland in June 2001, and will effectively be void if it is not approved by a further referendum expected late in 2002. The treaty, which is summarised in Appendix 8, is mainly concerned with revising the membership and voting powers of the EU institutions following the expected large increase in the number of member states during the first decade of the 21st century.

2

THE INSTITUTIONS

Under the Treaty of Rome, four main institutions were established to give effect to the provisions of the treaty. The following is a simple definition of their functions.

- The European Commission initiates policies and implements those already decided upon.
- The Council of Ministers decides, or legislates, on the basis of proposals brought forward by the commission.
- The European Parliament had a largely advisory role, but its powers have subsequently been increased.
- The European Court of Justice interprets the Community's decisions and the provisions of the treaty in the event of dispute.

The Community institutions continue their function under the Treaty on European Union (the Maastricht treaty) and the Amsterdam treaty. In addition, powers have been acquired by the European Union that are not subject to the institutions of the EC, but are dealt with on an inter-governmental basis. These include a common foreign and security policy (see Chapter 36) and co-operation over judicial, police and immigration issues (see Chapter 29). Strictly speaking the EU is now a hybrid organisation consisting of the EC, with its carefully defined division of powers between its constituent institutions, and an additional inter-governmental component. Part II of this book describes in some detail the principal EC institutions.

4 The Commission

The European Commission is the executive organ of the Community. It is often seen as the embodiment of the European idea as its members, although appointed by national governments, are under no obligation to them, and their total loyalty is pledged to the interests of the Community as a whole. Each commissioner, on assuming office, makes the following solemn declaration.

> I solemnly undertake:
>
> To perform my duties in complete independence, in the general interest of the Communities;
>
> In carrying out my duties, neither to seek nor to take instructions from any Government or body;
>
> To refrain from any action incompatible with my duties.
>
> I formally note the undertaking of each Member State to respect this principle and not to seek to influence Members of the commission in the performance of their task.
>
> I further undertake to respect, both during and after my term of office, the obligations arising therefrom, and in particular the duty to behave with integrity and discretion as regards the acceptance, after I have ceased to hold office, of certain appointments or benefits.

To the extent that the reality falls short of these aspirations, the commissioners will be failing in their allotted role, and the purposes of the Community will be imperfectly realised.

The commissioners

The commission currently consists of 20 members, two each from the five larger states (France, Germany, Italy, Spain and the UK) and one each from the ten smaller members (Austria, Belgium, Denmark, Finland, Greece, Ireland, Luxembourg, the Netherlands, Portugal and Sweden). They were appointed for a five-year term by the Council of Ministers, on the nomination of their own national governments. Before 1995 the term was only four years. The term of office is renewable, and in the past at the end of each four- or five-year period typically about half of the commissioners have been reappointed, the remainder being replaced by new nominees. Most of the commissioners are politicians, usually from the governing party (or parties) in the member states, but the UK practice has invariably been for one of its nominees to come from the main opposition party, even though the choice is made by the prime minister of the day. A minority of commissioners have been senior administrators, trade union leaders or businessmen.

The presidency

The president of the commission was originally appointed for a two-year term, although in practice this was normally extended to four years, virtually automatically. Each commission term is referred to colloquially under the name of its president; for example, the Jenkins commission, the Thorn commission, the Delors commission. Under the Maastricht treaty the arrangements for appointing the commission were changed. From January 1st 1995 the term of office of both the commission and the president was increased to five years. The governments of the member states are now required to consult the European Parliament before nominating the president of the commission. They must also consult the president-elect before nominating the other commissioners. The president and other members of the commission are then subject to approval, as a body, by a vote of the European Parliament. Only if this vote is positive will the president and the commission be formally appointed by the governments of the member states.

When Jacques Santer was nominated by the EU heads of government in July 1994 he narrowly survived an attempt in the European Parliament to reject his nomination. The Parliament went on to vet each of the prospective commissioners and approved the appointment of the whole commission by a substantial majority in January 1995. Following the resignation of the Santer Commission, in March 1999 (see pages 34–5), the EU heads of government nominated Romano Prodi as his successor and subsequently, after consultation with Prodi, 19 other commissioners. They, also, were vetted by the Parliament, which, in September 1999, voted by a three-to-one majority to appoint them to serve out the remaining four months of the term of the Santer Commission, as well as for a full five-year term from January 2000 to January 2005.

The Maastricht treaty also changed the provisions regarding vice-presidents of the commission. Hitherto six commissioners were designated by the Council of Ministers as vice-presidents, a distinction which had little practical significance, except that they drew somewhat larger salaries than their colleagues. Now, according to the treaty, the commission itself "may appoint a vice-president or two vice-presidents from among its members". The commissioner (or commissioners) thus chosen should be seen much more clearly as deputising for the president when occasion demands. In September 1999 the commission elected two of its members as vice-presidents, Neil Kinnock and Loyola De Palacio.

The president of the commission is often misleadingly compared with a prime minister of a member state in relation to his or her cabinet. In fact the president's dominance over his colleagues is normally much less. He neither selects nor dismisses them, and does not determine what portfolios they should hold. His influence on this point is considerable, as he makes a proposal for the distribution of responsibilities at the outset of each term of office, but the actual decision is taken by the commissioners themselves, if necessary by majority vote. In future the president will undoubtedly have more clout, partly because of his increased powers under the Amsterdam treaty (see page 41), but mostly because of the circumstances of Romano Prodi's nomination. The crisis following the resignation of the Santer Commission enabled him to acquire more authority than any of his predecessors. He was able to insist on the right to allocate portfolios and to change them round, if he chose, at a later stage. He also asked for, and obtained, assurances from each of the nominees that they would resign, at his request, if he felt that this would be in the intererests of the EU.

Under the Treaty of Nice, the larger member states will lose their right to a second commissioner when the next commission assumes office in January 2005. When the membership of the EU reaches 27 or more, member states will no longer have a right to appoint commissioners, who will be allocated on a rotation system in which all states, large or small, will be treated equally. The president will continue to be nominated by the European Council, but in future by qualified majority vote rather than by unanimity.

Responsibilities of commissioners

Commissioners are each allocated an area of responsibility under the treaty, and parts of the administrative machine will report directly to them (see Appendix 3 for the current distribution of responsibilities). They also have the assistance of a small cabinet of half a dozen personal appointees who not only act as advisers but also customarily intervene on the commissioners' behalf at all levels of the commission's bureaucracy.

47

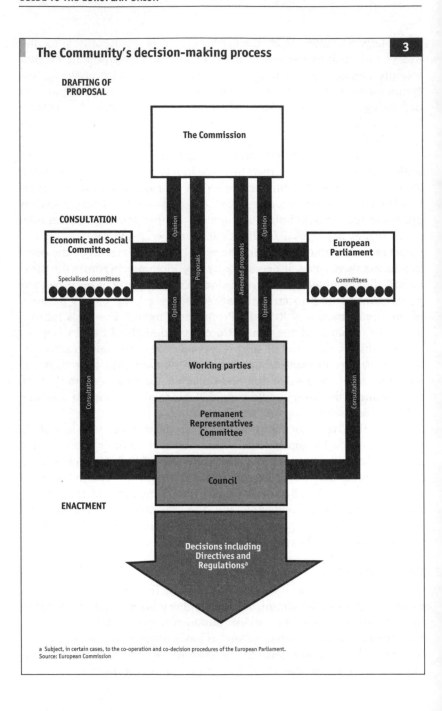

The Community's decision-making process

3

DRAFTING OF
PROPOSAL

The Commission

CONSULTATION

Economic and Social
Committee

Specialised committees

Opinion

Proposals

Amended proposals

Opinion

European
Parliament

Committees

Opinion

Opinion

Consultation

Consultation

Working parties

Permanent
Representatives
Committee

Council

ENACTMENT

Decisions including
Directives and
Regulations[a]

a Subject, in certain cases, to the co-operation and co-decision procedures of the European Parliament.
Source: European Commission

Decision-making in the Community

There are five ways in which the institutions of the Community are able to change or influence the law in the member states. The Council of Ministers and/or the commission is able to issue:

- regulations
- directives
- decisions
- recommendations
- opinions.

Legislation, as normally understood, is undertaken through regulations and directives. Both are initiated by the commission and adopted by the Council of Ministers, in most cases after having received an opinion from the European Parliament and, when appropriate, the Economic and Social Committee and the Committee of the Regions. Regulations are of general applicability: they are binding in their entirety and directly applicable in all member states. Directives are binding on the member states to which they are addressed as regards the result to be achieved, but leave the form and methods of achieving it to the discretion of the national authorities (most often this is achieved by passing national legislation, based on the directive).

Decisions by the council or the commission, derived from the authority bestowed by the Rome treaty or through regulations or directives already approved, may be addressed to a government, an enterprise or an individual. They are binding in their entirety on those to whom they are addressed. Recommendations and opinions are not binding. (See also Figure 3.)

A sixth way in which national laws are affected is by case law resulting from decisions taken by the Court of Justice, whose role is to interpret the Rome treaties affecting the European Community, and to adjudicate in disputes between the other institutions or between any of them and one or more member states (see Chapter 9).

Responsibilities of the commission

The responsibilities of the commission are listed in Article 155 of the Rome treaty. They have been summarised as being those of initiative, implementation and supervision.

Initiative. The treaty gives a general responsibility to the commission to ensure that its provisions are carried out, but it also gives it the specific right to put proposals before the Council of Ministers, which in most circumstances is unable to make decisions in the absence of such a proposal.

Implementation. The commission is entrusted with the implementation of the decisions taken by the council. In respect of the coal and steel industries, the commission itself has a wide range of decision-making powers, inherited from the former High Authority of the ECSC, which it may exercise without reference to the Council of Ministers. It also has substantial autonomous powers relating to competition policy and the running of the common agricultural policy. The commission administers the various funds established by the Community (the Agricultural Guidance and Guarantee Fund (EAGGF), Social Fund, Regional Fund, Cohesion Fund, and so on). It prepares a draft budget which must be approved by the council and the European Parliament. It also negotiates international agreements on behalf of the Community, though these can only be concluded by the council.

Supervision. The commission supervises the implementation of Community law by the member states. Whenever it concludes that a member state has infringed its treaty obligations it is required to deliver an "opinion" to this effect, and may afterwards bring an action in the Court of Justice against the state concerned.

Location

The commission is based in Brussels, and normally occupies the Berlaymont building, a purpose-built glass-fronted building constructed in 1969. In early 1992 the Berlaymont was closed down, and will be comprehensively reconstructed over a period of at least 7-8 years, owing to the risk of infection from the large amounts of asbestos contained in the original structure. In the meantime the commission and its immediate staff have been housed in the nearby Breydel building, and the remainder of the personnel are based in a score of other locations. When the

Prodi Commission took over in September 1999 the individual commissioners' offices were transferred to the buildings where their respective directorates-general were housed, leaving only the president and the general secretariat in the Breydel building.

Staff

The commission employs about 17,000 people, one-third of whom are concerned with interpreting or translating between the 11 official languages of the Community (English, French, German, Italian, Dutch, Danish, Greek, Spanish, Portuguese, Swedish and Finnish). A further 4,000 or so commission employees are engaged in scientific research work at Ispra in Italy, Culham in the UK, Geel in Belgium and various other centres, or are working for other EU agencies.

The staff, part of which is based in Luxembourg, is organised in 36 departments and directorates-general, each of which is subject to one or more commissioners (see Appendix 4).

Working practices

The commission meets as a body every Wednesday morning, and if there is a heavy agenda the meeting may be resumed after lunch. Additional meetings are frequently scheduled, occasionally in more relaxed surroundings, to discuss particular topics or long-term perspectives. Decisions within the commission are normally adopted on the basis of a simple majority vote, and subsequently the principle of collective responsibility applies.

Although all official documents are translated and meetings involving national officials are simultaneously interpreted into all 11 languages, most day-to-day business within the commission is conducted in French or English.

5 The Council of Ministers

If the commission is the institution representing the general European interest, the Council of Ministers is certainly that in which the particular interests of each member state are brought to bear. It is unquestionably the most powerful of the Community's organs and, in the words of the Directorate-General for Research of the European Parliament, "It has now evolved into the actual centre of political control in the European Community".[1]

Structure

The council consists of representatives from each of the member states, and its meetings are also attended by at least one commissioner as well as by officials of its own secretariat. The membership, however, is constantly changing. If agriculture is on the agenda agricultural ministers will attend; industry ministers will come for industrial matters; and finance ministers will attend when the budget is being discussed.

The foreign ministers' meeting, held at least once a month except in August, is known as the General Affairs Council. As well as discussing foreign policy matters, foreign ministers are supposed to exercise general co-ordination over the work of the other ministerial councils and to tackle particularly complicated and/or urgent matters which do not readily fall within the scope of their more specialist colleagues. It is also their task to prepare the now twice-yearly meetings of the heads of government, known as the European Council (see Chapter 6).

The presidency

The council has a rotating chairmanship or presidency, with ministers from each member state taking turns for a six-month period in the chair. The foreign minister of the state concerned assumes the title of president of the Council of Ministers, and the foreign ministry of his or her country undertakes, with the help of the council secretariat, the organisation of the council's business during the six months. A period will thus be characterised as that of the French presidency, the Dutch presidency, and so on, according to which nationality is in the chair.

It is accepted that it is part of the presidency's duty to oil the wheels of the Community and to strive to get agreement on as many issues as possible. The presidency is therefore expected to exert itself to produce compromise proposals whenever there is a deadlock and to cajole its own national representatives as well as those of other member states to modify their demands.

During the course of each presidency there will be a summit meeting (or European Council) of heads of government in the country concerned, while most of the specialist councils will hold informal meetings, usually in a secluded country house, for an exchange of views on long-term issues, uncomplicated by the mass of more ephemeral items which normally clutter their agenda. Such informal gatherings are known in Eurocircles as Gymnich-type meetings, after Schloss Gymnich in western Germany where the first of them was held.

The rota of the presidency was previously determined alphabetically, but from 1996 onwards a new order was determined, primarily to ensure that the larger states were reasonably well spaced out, rather than being bunched together as they had been.

Table 1 **Countries holding the presidency, 1996–2007**

	January–June	*July–December*
1996	Italy	Ireland
1997	Netherlands	Luxembourg
1998	United Kingdom	Austria
1999	Germany	Finland
2000	Portugal	France
2001	Sweden	Belgium
2002	Spain	Denmark
2003	Greece	Italy
2004	Ireland	Netherlands
2005	Luxembourg	United Kingdom
2006	Austria	Finland
2007	Germany	Portugal

Permanent Representatives

Few items reach the agenda of council meetings without having been previously discussed, usually exhaustively, at a lower level. Each member state maintains a large delegation in Brussels, known as its Permanent Representation. These are staffed not only by diplomats but also by officials from each of the domestic ministries that is liable to be affected by decisions taken by the EC. They are backed up by further officials in their home capitals who are deputed to liaise with them.

Coreper.   The heads of delegations, the Permanent Representatives, who have the rank of senior ambassadors, meet at least once a week in the Committee of Permanent Representatives, known by its French language initials as Coreper. Coreper will work methodically through all the issues which are awaiting ministerial decision. If, on the basis of instructions which they have received from their national governments, the Permanent Representatives find themselves in complete agreement on a draft proposal it is normally placed on the council agenda as an "A" point. This would then, except in the unusual event of a government having a last minute change of mind, be adopted without discussion at a subsequent council meeting. More often the Permanent Representatives find that their viewpoints are still fairly wide apart, and the proposals are referred to expert groups, at a lower level, for more detailed discussion. In most cases it is only when no more than one or two governments are in disagreement with the rest that an issue is passed on to the Council of Ministers in the hope of getting a decision.

Other working groups.   Even though the Permanent Representatives are highly versatile, they cannot possibly maintain a uniform level of expertise on all the highly detailed topics which may appear on their agenda. A substantial range of subjects is entrusted to their deputies who have a parallel weekly meeting, known as Coreper II, while agricultural issues are by tradition invariably dealt with by the Special Committee for Agriculture (SCA), consisting of senior officials of national ministries or of the agricultural councillors at the Permanent Representations. A large number of working groups staffed by less senior officials meet regularly to haggle over the details of virtually every proposal for Community legislation.

Legislative role

Unlike in a nation state, where the parliament is responsible for enacting legislation, the legislative role in the EC is performed by the Council of Ministers. Community legislation, known as directives or regulations (see page 49), can only be initiated by the commission. The opinion of the European Parliament and frequently of the Economic and Social Committee must in most cases be sought, but the proposals are adopted (or not, as the case may be) by the council. Again, contrary to the practice of national parliaments, the legislative function takes place behind closed doors, although hardly in secret as the large Brussels press corps is normally extensively briefed after each meeting of the council by spokesmen for each of the national governments concerned.

Meetings
In its various forms, the council meets around 80–90 times a year, usually for one day, sometimes for two and occasionally for longer. Often two or three meetings take place simultaneously, with, for example, foreign ministers in one chamber and finance ministers in another.

Making decisions
When a proposal actually reaches a council meeting, except as an "A" point, it is by no means assured of being adopted. The Treaty of Rome lays down precise rules on decision-making within the council, but these have not been applied in the manner originally intended. Under Article 148 of the treaty, decisions may be taken by a simple majority, by a qualified majority (now 62 votes out of 87), or unanimously.

Simple majority decisions are restricted to minor matters, often of a purely procedural nature. Under the Rome treaty it was envisaged that most decisions would be reached by a qualified majority, leaving the unanimity rule for a limited number of issues of major importance. During a transitional period, which was intended to end in 1965, unanimity was prescribed for a much wider range of issues, but at the moment that the Community was scheduled to change over to qualified majority voting a major crisis broke out between the French Gaullist government and the other five original members of the EEC (see page 11).

The Luxembourg compromise
As a result of this crisis, the five members reluctantly acquiesced in the so-called "Luxembourg compromise" to ensure continued French membership of the Community. The operative sentence of this was:

> *Where, in the case of decisions which may be taken by a majority vote on a proposal from the commission, very important interests of one or more partners are at stake, the Members of the Council will endeavour, within a reasonable time, to reach solutions which can be adopted by all the Members of the Council while respecting their mutual interests and those of the Community, in accordance with Article 2 of the Treaty.*

If subsequent practice had accorded with the wording of the "compromise", which referred specifically to "very important interests", it might not have affected the decision-making process very often. In practice, however, the council showed extreme reluctance to bring any issue at all to a vote, and the unanimity rule was effectively extended to a vast range of decisions which could not conceivably be regarded as affecting the "very important interests" of member states. Accordingly, the Luxembourg compromise has seldom been formally invoked. One occasion was in May 1982 when the UK government attempted to block a farm price settlement for purely tactical reasons related to a quite different issue (the UK budget dispute). The other members refused to accept the validity of the UK claim and proceeded to approve each of the 20-odd draft regulations involved in the settlement by qualified majority voting.

Amendments under the Single European Act

After that there was a growing feeling, shared by the French government, that qualified majority voting should be used more often. Although the Luxembourg compromise, which had no legal force, still stands, the Single European Act, which came into force in July 1987, amended the Treaty of Rome to reduce the number of issues on which unanimity was required. In particular, qualified majority voting was authorised for most of the 300 or so measures which had to be adopted if the 1992 programme to complete the EC's internal market was to be ratified. The Maastricht treaty, which came into force in January 1993, also extended the range of issues to which qualified majority voting would apply, including transport and the environment, and the list was further extended by the Amsterdam treaty which took effect in May 1999. Consequently, in the areas concerned it is no longer possible for proposals to be held up for years because one or two member states object to them.

Decisions are taken

In view of the above it is hard to see how any decisions are made at all, given the difficulty of persuading 15 separate nation states to sink their differences. In fact many decisions are taken on a "log-rolling" basis, with governments giving way on particular points on which they are not convinced in exchange for concessions on often unrelated issues.

Allocation of votes

Under the system of qualified majority voting the member states are allocated votes roughly in proportion to their size. Germany, France, Italy and the UK have ten votes each, Spain eight votes, Belgium, Greece, the Netherlands and Portugal five votes each, Austria and Sweden four votes each, Denmark, Finland and Ireland three votes each and Luxembourg two votes. As 62 votes (out of 87) are needed for a proposal to be adopted, it follows that a "blocking minority" must muster 26 votes. Thus three large states acting together, or two large states plus two small ones (except for Luxembourg), can block a proposal, but it would require at least six of the smaller states (with five votes each or fewer) to do so. The arithmetic changed in January 1995, when three new member states joined the Union. Previously there had been a total of 76 votes, with 54 needed for a qualified majority and a blocking minority of 23. In the face of objections from the UK and Spanish governments, which wanted to make it more difficult for majority decisions to be taken, it was agreed by the Council of Ministers in March 1994 that if between 23 and 25 votes were cast against a proposal a decision should be delayed "for a reasonable period of time" while a compromise was sought.

At the Nice summit in December 2000, a major reweighting of votes was agreed in order to increase the relative weight of the larger states, and also to make provision for the 12 candidate countries currently negotiating membership. The new system, which will take effect only if the Nice treaty is ratified by all member states, is illustrated in Table 2 on the next page.

Other council responsibilities

As well as adopting EC legislation, the council has joint responsibility with the European Parliament (whose role, however, is a subordinate one) to adopt the Community budget. It also has the power of appointment to the other institutions, such as the Economic and Social Committee and the Court of Auditors. The multifarious nature of its activities has been well summarised by a former British Permanent Representative, Sir Michael Butler, who wrote:

> In one sense, Coreper and the council together are a forum for a permanent negotiation between member governments on a wide range of issues simultaneously. In another, they are the legislature of the Community. In a third, they are the senior board of directors taking many of the day-to-day decisions on its policies.[2]

Table 2 **The weighting of votes under the Nice treaty**

Members of the Council	Weighted votes	Members of the Council	Weighted votes
Germany	29	Sweden	10
United Kingdom	29	Bulgaria	10
France	29	Austria	10
Italy	29	Slovakia	7
Spain	27	Denmark	7
Poland	27	Finland	7
Romania	14	Ireland	7
Netherlands	13	Lithuania	7
Greece	12	Latvia	4
Czech Republic	12	Slovenia	4
Belgium	12	Estonia	4
Hungary	12	Cyprus	4
Portugal	12	Luxembourg	4
		Malta	3
Total EU-27	**345**		

Acts of the council shall require for their adoption at least 258 votes in favour, cast by a majority of members, where this treaty requires them to be adopted on a proposal from the commission. In other cases, for their adoption acts of the council shall require at least 258 votes in favour cast by at least two-thirds of the members. When a decision is to be adopted by the council by a qualified majority, a member of the council may request verification that the member states constituting the qualified majority represent at least 62% of the total population of the Union. If that condition is shown not to have been met, the decision in question shall not be adopted.

Location

The council and its secretariat are based in the Justus Lipsius building in Brussels, a vast, tasteless mausoleum facing the Berlaymont across the road. This was opened in 1995, the Council previously occupying the Charlemagne Building, next door to the Berlaymont. During three months of the year (April, June and October), however, its meetings are held in Luxembourg, a legacy from the merger of the three Communities which took place in 1965, the former ECSC having been based in Luxembourg.

Notes

1   Fact Sheet 1/B/2, European Parliament, Directorate-General for Research, 1987.
2   Michael Butler, *Europe: More than a Continent*, Heinemann, London, 1986, page 30.

6 The European Council

The Treaty of Rome makes no provision for meetings of the heads of government of the member states, and during the first ten years of the EEC they met on only three occasions. Yet it gradually became clear that a more regular exchange of views was necessary to give a sense of strategic direction to the Community and to resolve problems to which the Council of Ministers and the European Commission had not been able to find solutions through the EC's normal processes.

Inauguration

In December 1974 it was formally decided at a summit meeting in Paris that the heads of government should meet three times each year under the title of the European Council. Starting in Dublin in March 1975, the European Council duly met on this basis until December 1985, when it was agreed that only two meetings a year would henceforward be held. However, since 1990, when two additional "emergency" summits were held, it has been accepted that there may, in fact, be three or four meetings of the European Council each year. These meetings take place in the member state currently holding the presidency of the Council of Ministers, and its prime minister (or, in the case of France, its president) takes the chair and is responsible for the organisation of the meetings. Under the Treaty of Nice, all meetings of the European Council will be held in Brussels, once the membership of the Union reaches 18 or more, which is likely to be in 2004.

Status

The Single European Act, adopted in December 1985, gave legal recognition to the European Council without, however, defining its powers. In fact it has had the same status as an ordinary meeting of the Council of Ministers, although it has usually avoided giving formal effect to the decisions it has taken, leaving it to a subsequent meeting of foreign ministers to adopt them on a "rubber stamp" basis. Indeed, a major purpose of the European Council is that its deliberations are informal. They take place without the presence of national officials, the heads of government sitting round the table, accompanied only by their foreign ministers, while the president of the commission is supported only by one vice-president. The more sensitive discussions normally take place in the intervals between the actual sessions (which are spread over two days), particularly during and after dinner on the evening of the first day when most if not all of the heads of government speak in English and simultaneous interpretation is dispensed with.

Its increasing influence ...

The European Council has, to a large extent, replaced the commission as the motor of the Community. This was especially notable during the period 1974–81, when President Valéry Giscard d'Estaing and Chancellor Helmut Schmidt co-operated closely to play a leadership role. Their joint departure within a few months heralded the beginning of a period of 2–3 years in which few significant decisions were taken by the European Council. The deadlock was broken at Fontainebleau in June 1984 when, largely owing to the initiative of President François Mitterrand, a solution was finally found to the UK budget problem (see pages 18–20) which had plagued the Community for several years, and the way was cleared for the admission to membership of Spain and Portugal.

Since then the go-ahead for other major new Community initiatives, like the launch of the 1992 programme, the acceptance of a united Germany within the EC, the convening of inter-governmental conferences on economic and monetary union and on political union, the offer of economic aid to the former Soviet Republics and the decision in principle to negotiate membership with the countries of Central and Eastern Europe, has been given at meetings of the European Council. The European Council also agreed the Single European Act at Luxembourg in December 1985, the Treaty on European Union at Maastricht in December 1991 and the Treaty of Amsterdam in June 1997.

Such major and difficult issues can only be resolved at a summit, as only the heads of government have the authority and political clout not only to impose unwelcome decisions but also to reconcile them with political forces and pressure groups in their home countries.

... holds up decision-making on minor issues

On the debit side, however, is the undoubted fact that the existence of regular summit meetings actually retards decision-making on many less far-reaching issues which would otherwise be resolved at a lower level. Time and again the heads of government have been called upon to discuss technical matters on which their subordinates have failed to agree because they were unwilling to take the responsibility. The European Council ought not to have to act as a final court of appeal, except on issues of the first importance, but it seems condemned to do so.

7 The European Parliament

The European Parliament is intended to bring a measure of democratic control and accountability to the other institutions of the EC.
Its powers, however, are severely restricted; it is not the legislative
authority of the Community, and its status compares badly with that of
the national parliaments in the different member states. The European
Parliament is the successor to the Assembly of the ECSC, which was
established in Strasbourg as a purely advisory body in September 1952.
It had 78 members, all of them members of national parliaments who
had been deputed to attend the Assembly as an ancillary duty to their
main functions. The Assembly was expanded to 142 members in 1958,
when its competences were extended to the EEC and Euratom, which
merged with the ECSC seven years later. Its membership was increased
to 198 in 1973, with the accession of Denmark, Ireland and the UK, and
its powers (particularly in the budgetary field) were modestly increased
under treaties signed in Luxembourg in April 1970 and in Brussels in July
1975.

Direct elections instituted in 1979

Much more significant was the institution of direct elections to the Parliament in June 1979 when 410 members were elected, during a four-day
period from nine member states, to a greatly enlarged Parliament. In the
second direct elections in June 1984, 434 members (or Euro-MPs) were
elected from ten member states, comprising 81 each from France, West
Germany, Italy and the UK, 25 from the Netherlands, 24 from Belgium
and Greece, 16 from Denmark, 15 from Ireland and 6 from Luxembourg.
They were later joined by 60 Spanish and 24 Portuguese members,
making a total of 518. Yet this much larger Parliament of 518 full-time
members directly elected by over 100m voters was given no greater
formal power than had been enjoyed by the previous appointed Assembly of part-timers. (Later still the total membership was increased to 626,
including 59 members from Austria, Finland and Sweden.) The pre-
dictable result was constant conflict between the parliamentarians and
the Council of Ministers, and a high degree of frustration among Euro-
MPs.

Euro-MPs

Euro-MPs are elected for fixed five-year terms, and the next election is due in June 2004. Under Article 138 of the Rome treaty there should be a common electoral system in all member states, and the Parliament itself proposed such a system in 1982 and again in 1993. However, the Council of Ministers was unable to agree to this, largely because of the reluctance of the then UK government to abandon its first-past-the-post system in favour of proportional representation (PR). Thus the first four direct elections were held with different systems operating in all the member states, although all except the UK have used variations of PR. The Labour government elected in the UK in May 1997 agreed that the UK, too, would adopt PR for the next Euro-elections in June 1999. Thus, although these elections were held under 15 different systems, all the Euro-MPs for the first time were chosen by proportional representation.

Salaries.   Euro-MPs are paid the same salary as MPs in their own countries which means that there is a wide variation, with the Portuguese being paid the least and the French and Germans the most. In addition there are generous travel, attendance, research and secretarial allowances which are paid on the same basis to all members. In mid-2002 it was expected that an agreement would soon be reached under which all MEPs would in future be paid the same salary.

Political groups.   Euro-MPs do not sit in national delegations but in cross-national political groups. After the 1999 election there were seven of these, with 27 members choosing to remain non-affiliated. The membership was made up as follows.

European People's Party (Christian Democrats) (EPP)	233
Party of European Socialists (PES)	180
European Liberal, Democratic and Reformist Group (ELDR)	50
Greens/ European Free Alliance (EFA)	48
European United Left/Nordic Green Left Group (EUL/NGL)	42
Union for a Europe of Nations (UEN)	30
Europe of Democracies and Diversities	16
Independents (non-affiliated)	27
Total	**626**

The two largest groups combined can command almost two-thirds of the membership of the Parliament, and when they work together can dominate its proceedings. The European People's Party comprises Christian Democrat and Centre Right parties from all member states, including Fine Gael from Ireland and the Ulster Unionist Party. The British Conservatives belong to the group, but are not attached to the party itself. The Party of European Socialists comprises Labour, Socialist or Social Democratic parties in all 15 member states, including the former Italian Communist Party, renamed the Party of Democratic Socialism. The European Liberal, Democratic and Reformist Group, where the largest contingent is now from the British Liberal Democrats, includes one Irish Independent, who is the group's leader.

The Greens/EFA group comprises 38 MEPs from Green parties in 11 member states, who are joined by ten others from home rule or separatist parties in Scotland, Wales, the Basque country, Galicia and Andalusia. The Confederal Group of the European United Left/Nordic Green Left Group comprises representatives of Left/Green parties from Denmark, Finland, Germany, Greece, Italy, the Netherlands, Spain and Sweden as well as members of Communist parties from France, Greece and Portugal. The Union for a Europe of Nations Group comprises MEPs from France, Italy, Ireland, Denmark and Portugal who are opposed to further European integration. The Europe of Democracies and Diversities Group comprises six members from the French pro-hunting/defence of rural traditions group, the three MEPs from the UK Independence Party, four anti-EU Danish members and three Dutch Calvinists. The non-affiliated members are largely made up of extreme right-wing groups, including Ian Paisley from the Democratic Unionist Party, together with the Italian Radicals and one Basque separatist. (See also Appendix 6, which reflects small numerical changes in the strengths of the party groups up to April 2002.)

Voting in the European Parliament is less disciplined than in most national parliaments and ad hoc coalitions are often formed on issues that cross normal ideological and national barriers. There is, accordingly, often some uncertainty about how the Parliament may vote.

Elections to the European Parliament

Since 1979 the European Parliament has been elected simultaneously in all the member states. The term of office is five years, with no provision for early dissolution. There should be a common electoral system but, as mentioned above, agreement on this has not yet been reached. Consequently each member state has used its own system, which, in most cases, resembles that used for the election of its own national Parliament.

Table 3 **European Parliament election, 1999**

Country	Seats	Voting method
Austria	21	PR, national lists
Belgium	25	PR, regional lists
Denmark	16	PR, national lists
Finland	16	PR, national lists
France	87	PR, national lists
Germany	99	PR, regional lists
Greece	25	PR, national lists
Ireland	15	PR, single transferable vote
Italy	87	PR, regional lists
Luxembourg	6	PR, national lists
Netherlands	31	PR, national lists
Portugal	25	PR, national lists
Spain	64	PR, regional lists
Sweden	22	PR, national lists
UK	87	PR, regional lists
of which:		
Northern Ireland	3	PR, single transferable vote

The following elections have been held.

- ◪ The 1979 election was held in nine member states on June 7th–10th 1979. Greece, which joined the Community on January 1st 1981, subsequently elected 24 members on October 18th 1981.
- ◪ The 1981 election was held in ten member states, on June 14th–17th 1984. Spain and Portugal, both of which joined the EC on January 1st 1986, subsequently elected 60 and 24 members respectively, on June 10th and July 19th 1987.
- ◪ The third election, when all the states polled simultaneously, was held on June 15th–18th 1989.
- ◪ The fourth election, for an enlarged house comprising 567 members, took place on June 9th–12th 1994.
- ◪ Separate elections were held during 1995 and 1996 to elect a further 59 members from the new member states of Austria, Finland and Sweden, making a total membership of 626.
- ◪ The fifth election, for a house of 626 members, was held in all member states on June 10th–13th 1999.

Table 4 **European Parliament: revised allocation of seats**

Member state	No. of seats	Member state	No. of seats
Germany	99	Sweden	18
France	72	Austria	17
Italy	72	Bulgaria	17
United Kingdom	72	Denmark	13
Poland	50	Finland	13
Spain	50	Slovakia	13
Romania	33	Ireland	12
Netherlands	25	Lithuania	12
Belgium	22	Latvia	8
Greece	22	Slovenia	7
Portugal	22	Cyprus	6
Czech Republic	20	Estonia	6
Hungary	20	Luxembourg	6
		Malta	5
Total	**732**		

The electoral systems used in 1999, and the number of members for each country, are shown in Table 3.

The size of the European Parliament will increase to a maximum of 732 members if the membership negotiations of the 12 candidate countries currently negotiating prove successful. Under the Treaty of Nice, the future distribution of seats will be as set out as in Table 4.

Powers of the European Parliament

The European Parliament has supervisory powers over the commission and the council, the right of participation in the legislative process and budgetary powers.

Supervisory powers. These are defined by the Treaty of Rome as including the right to put questions, written or oral, to the commission, to discuss its Annual General Report, to discharge the annual budget and to adopt a motion of censure which would lead to the resignation of the commission as a body. Thus in 2001 some 3,302 written and 673 oral questions were put to the commission, and a further 413 written and 421 oral questions to the Council of Ministers. These were answered by ministers from the country currently holding the presidency, who attend each plenary session of the Parliament for this purpose. Since December 1981 the practice has grown up that the prime minister of this country makes a personal report to the Parliament after each meeting of the European Council. The Parliament is able to exercise more intensive supervision over the commission than the treaty envisages, as members and senior officials of the commission attend meetings of its committees and the commission submits its annual programme of work in advance to the Parliament, as well as its annual report, which can only be used as the basis for retrospective checks.

The power of the Parliament to dismiss the commission remained for many years largely a theoretical threat. The motion of censure may be carried only by a two-thirds majority of the votes cast, representing a majority of the Euro-MPs. It is not possible to censure a particular commissioner, which might prove a more effective sanction. In practice Euro-MPs had regarded the power as analogous to possession of a nuclear weapon, the consequences of actually using it being regarded as too horrible to contemplate. Yet in March 1999 it became clear that, as the Parliament was frustrated by its inability to secure the dismissal of Edith Cresson, a French commissioner accused of nepotism and other shortcomings, a large majority of its members were prepared to vote to dismiss the whole commission. In anticipation of this, the entire Santer Commission submitted its resignation, prompting a major crisis in EU affairs (see pages 34–5). One effect of this was undoubtedly to raise the profile of the Parliament and make the Council of Ministers and the commission more wary of coming into conflict with it.

Under the Maastricht Treaty, the Parliament was authorised to appoint a European ombudsman to consider complaints of maladministration by the EC institutions (other than the Court of Justice). The first ombudsman, Jacob Söderman, was appointed in July 1995. He is empowered to receive complaints from any citizen of the Union or any natural person residing in a member state or legal person (that is, a company or organisation) having its registered office there. By the end of 1997 the ombudsman had received 2,257 complaints, but only about one-quarter of these were admissible as the others did not fall within the jurisdiction of EC institutions. The ombudsman is now attempting to circulate information about his institutional role more widely so as not to raise false expectations about the possibilities for redress.

Legislative role. The legislative role of the Parliament is essentially an advisory one. The treaties designate a large number of areas in which the Council of Ministers cannot enact legislation without first consulting the European Parliament. In practice, in addition to this mandatory consultation the Parliament is normally invited to submit an opinion on any other draft directives or regulations tabled by the commission. Amendments proposed by the Parliament may be incorporated by the commission when it presents a revised draft to the council, and it has undertaken to explain to the Parliament the reasons why an amendment has not been adopted.

The legislative role of the Parliament has been significantly strengthened by the Single European Act, which came into effect in July 1987, and by the Maastricht treaty, which took effect in November 1993. This provides for processes of consultation and co-decision by the Parliament which strengthen its ability to amend legislation and, through a "negative assent" procedure, gives it the right to veto certain legislation by a vote of a majority of its members. The Maastricht treaty gives the Parliament a new right of initiative, whereby it may by a majority vote require the commission to propose action in any area. The treaty also gives the right to any EU citizen to petition the Parliament if the matter is of direct and individual concern, and it authorises the Parliament to appoint an ombudsman to receive complaints about deficiencies in the administration of EC institutions. The Parliament may, at the request of a quarter of its members, set up a temporary committee to examine allegations of infringement or bad administration of Community law, unless the matter is *sub judice*. Under the Amsterdam treaty, which came into force in May 1999, the co-decision procedure, enabling the Parliament to veto proposed legislation, was extended to a majority of the policy areas where the EU has competence. Despite these changes the Parliament still falls short of being an equal partner of the Council of Ministers in the legislative process.

Budgetary powers.   The budgetary powers of the Parliament are more substantial. It is officially designated as jointly forming the budgetary authority with the Council of Ministers, and no budget may be adopted without its agreement. Even so, its influence, although considerable, is clearly less than that of the council, as a brief description of the process will make clear.

There are five stages in the budgetary process.

1   The tabling of the preliminary draft budget, which is the responsibility of the commission. This is laid before the Council of Ministers by September 1st of the previous year.

2 The council amends the preliminary draft, invariably reducing the expenditure proposed, and establishes the draft budget, which is submitted to the Parliament by October 5th.

3 The Parliament has 45 days to state its position; it may propose modifications to the compulsory part of the budget and amendments to the non-compulsory part. The compulsory part (currently 66% of the whole) consists of expenditure on policies directly arising out of the treaties, mainly agriculture. The non-compulsory part covers other policies adopted by the EC, and this expenditure the Parliament is free to amend, although it may not increase it beyond a so-called "maximum rate" set by the council each year.

4 The council takes a final decision on the Parliament's proposed modifications to the compulsory expenditure, which it may reject. If the modifications involve no increase in expenditure they require only a qualified majority for acceptance by the council; if any increase is involved a positive majority is required to reject them. The council may also reject the Parliament's amendments on the non-compulsory side. In that case a compromise has to be reached between the two institutions by means of a "conciliation procedure".

5 The Parliament may amend these modifications and it then adopts the budget. It may decline to do so by a two-thirds majority of the votes cast, representing a majority of all members.

The Parliament has refused to adopt the budget on three occasions, which resulted in the Community entering a new calendar year without a budget being approved. When this happens, total expenditure is restricted during each month to one-twelfth of the total budgeted for the previous year. On each of these occasions the Parliament subsequently adopted a revised draft which differed only marginally from the budget it had originally rejected. On the whole, it has enjoyed more success when it has used the established conciliation procedures and has played off one member state against another in the Council of Ministers than when it has gone for outright rejection. Every year, however, there is a struggle of wills between the council and Parliament, with the latter invariably wanting a larger budget and one less heavily committed to agriculture. Euro-MPs are intensely dissatisfied with their inability to amend compulsory expenditure and with the council's power to determine the "maximum rate".

Location

The member states have not yet fulfilled their obligation under the treaties to establish a single seat for the Parliament, and its effectiveness is undermined by the geographical fragmentation of its work. The monthly plenary sessions are held in Strasbourg (with additional meetings in Brussels), most committees meet in Brussels and the bulk of the secretariat is based in Luxembourg. This, plus the fact that it needs to conduct its business in 11 different languages with simultaneous interpretation, and the requirement that all documents shall be translated into each of the 11 languages, greatly increases the cost of running the institution, which in 1997 amounted to some 884m ecus ($1,020m or £630m).

Most Euro-MPs would undoubtedly prefer that the Parliament's activities should be concentrated in Brussels, but the Luxembourg and French governments are vehemently opposed to this and they have prevented a decision on a permanent seat from being taken. Under the treaties this would need to be unanimous. A protocol to the Amsterdam treaty, adopted in June 1997, confirmed that 12 plenary sessions per year, including the budget session, will continue to be held in Strasbourg, that additional plenary sessions and committee meetings will be in Brussels and the secretariat will remain in Luxembourg.

Sessions

The Parliament normally meets in plenary session for one week in each calendar month except August, with additional part sessions in March and October to consider its opinions on agricultural prices and the annual budget. Much of its work, however, takes place in committees or subcommittees, of which there are currently 45. These usually meet during two other weeks each month, leaving at least one week free for party or constituency activities.

8 The Economic and Social Committee and the Committee of the Regions

A purely advisory body, the Economic and Social Committee (ESC) must nevertheless be consulted by the European Commission and the Council of Ministers over a wide range of issues. The Treaty of Rome specifies a number of areas where consultation is mandatory before directives and regulations may be approved, but the council and the commission customarily consult with the ESC over many other issues. In general, there is little hindrance to the ESC offering opinions on any subject on which its members may wish to pronounce.

Membership

The membership of the ESC is made up of interest groups throughout the Community, and it provides a useful sounding board for their representatives whenever legislation that concerns them is envisaged. The members are divided into three groups:

- Group I representing employers;
- Group II representing workers;
- Group III representing various interests such as consumers, farmers, the self-employed, academics, and so on.

Members are appointed by the Council of Ministers on the nomination of their governments, which normally consult with the interest groups most concerned (particularly the trade unions and employers' organisations) before choosing their nominees.

The current membership is 222, consisting of 24 each from France, Germany, Italy and the UK, 21 from Spain, 12 each from Austria, Belgium, Greece, the Netherlands, Portugal and Sweden, 9 each from Denmark, Finland and Ireland and 6 from Luxembourg. The members are appointed for a renewable term of four years; the current term of office ends in September 2002. The ESC elects its own chairman, who serves for two years, and it is customary to rotate the chairmanship between the three groups. ESC members are part-timers, who are allowed time off from their normal jobs.

Location and working practices

The headquarters of the ESC is in Brussels and it meets there every month. Its detailed work is, however, undertaken in specialist sections (currently nine), which draft opinions for approval by the ESC meeting in plenary session. The sections are as follows.

- Agriculture
- Transport and Communications
- Energy and Nuclear Questions
- Economic and Financial Questions
- Industry, Commerce, Crafts and Services
- Social Questions
- External Relations
- Regional Development
- Protection of the Environment, Public Health and Consumer Affairs

On issues such as workers' rights to be consulted or to participate in management, the ESC normally splits on left-right lines, with the members of Groups I and II on opposing sides. In these circumstances the members of Group III are left with the casting votes, and more often than not they have come down predominantly on the trade union rather than the employers' side. On most questions considered by the ESC, however, divisions occur within each group rather than between them. The influence of the ESC, which by 1998 had given well over 2,500 opinions, is in any event seldom significant on controversial political matters. Where it can, and does, influence the content of Community legislation is on more technical issues, where the expertise of its members is often brought to bear.

Committee of the Regions

A similar body, known as the Committee of the Regions, was appointed under the Maastricht treaty provisions, and met for the first time in March 1994. This committee is asked to give its opinion on proposed EC legislation likely to have an impact on the various regions of the member states. In particular, it must be consulted on five policy areas:

- education, vocational training and youth;
- culture;
- public health;

- ◪ trans-European networks for transport, telecommunications and energy;
- ◪ economic and social cohesion.

Like the ESC, it has 222 members appointed for a four-year renewable term. The national membership quotas are the same as for the ESC. The committee is based in Brussels and at the beginning shared premises and secretariat with the ESC. Since 1997, however, it has had its own establishment.

9 The Court of Justice

The task of ensuring that the law is applied throughout the Community in accordance with the provisions of the treaties is devolved upon the European Court of Justice,[1] based in Luxembourg.

Composition

The court currently comprises 15 judges (one from each member state) and nine advocates-general.

The judges are chosen by the Council of Ministers, on the nomination of member states, "from persons whose independence is beyond doubt and who possess the qualifications required for appointment to the highest judicial offices in their respective countries or who are juriconsultants of recognised competence" (Article 167 of the Treaty of Rome). They are appointed for a renewable term of six years, half the court being renewed every three years. The advocates-general are appointed on the same basis.

The judges select one of their number to be president of the court for a renewable term of three years. For more important cases, and invariably in cases brought by a member state or a Community institution, the court sits as a single body. Other cases are assigned to chambers set up within the court: there are currently four chambers composed of three judges and two chambers composed of six judges. At any stage a chamber may refer a case to the full court if it considers that it raises points of law requiring definitive rulings.

Jurisdiction

In general six types of cases come before the court or its chambers.

- Disputes between member states.
- Disputes between the EC and member states.
- Disputes between the institutions.
- Disputes between individuals, or corporate bodies, and the Community (including staff cases).
- Opinions on international agreements.
- Preliminary rulings on cases referred by national courts.

The last type of case is of crucial importance for ensuring that

Community law is uniformly applied throughout the EC. It illustrates an essential difference between the Court of Justice and the US Supreme Court, with which it is often compared. Both courts are supreme in the sense that there is no appeal against their decisions. But the US court is at the apex of a structure of federal, state and district courts, all of whose rulings may be appealed upwards to it. The Court of Justice is, by contrast, the only EC court within the Community, and has no hierarchical relationship to the lower courts, all of which form part of one of 15 different legal systems. When a case comes before a national court involving Community law, which takes precedence over national laws, if there is any question as to the effect of the Community law with regard to that case it should be referred to the Court of Justice for a preliminary ruling, which the judges in the national court must then apply in giving their own judgments. In the application and interpretation of purely national laws, which make up the great bulk of cases in other courts, the Court of Justice has no jurisdiction whatever.

Court procedure

Proceedings before the court may be initiated by a member state, a Community institution (most often the commission) or by a corporate body or individual (providing he or she has a direct personal interest in the subject of the case). The court procedure involves two separate stages, one written and one oral.

In the first stage, on receipt of a written application from a plaintiff, the court establishes that it falls within its jurisdiction and that it has been lodged within the time limitations determined by the treaties. The application is then served on the opposing party, which normally has one month in which to lodge a statement of defence. The applicant has a further month to table a reply, and the defendant one more month for a rejoinder.

Each case is supervised by a judge-rapporteur, who is appointed by the president. On receipt of all the documents the judge-rapporteur presents a preliminary report to the court, which decides whether a preparatory enquiry (involving the appearance of the parties, requests for further documents, oral testimony, and so on) is necessary, and whether the case shall appear before the full court or be assigned to one of the chambers. The president then sets the date for the public hearing, at which the two sides appear before the judges, present their arguments and call evidence if they so wish. The judges and the advocate-general (whose role is somewhat similar to that of the public prosecutor in French courts) put to the parties any questions they think fit. Some weeks later the advocate-general gives his opinion, at a further hearing, analysing the facts and the legal aspects in detail and proposing a solution to the dispute.

The advocate-general's opinion often gives a clear indication of which way the judgment will go, but this is not invariably the case. The judges consider their ruling in private, on the basis of a draft prepared by the judge-rapporteur. If, during their deliberations, they require additional information they may reopen the procedure and ask the parties for further explanation, oral or written, or order further enquiries.

The judgments of the court are reached by majority vote; where the court is equally divided the vote of the most junior judge is disregarded, although in most cases it is arranged that an uneven number of judges will be sitting (the quorum for the full court is seven). The judgment is given at a public hearing, which, on average, occurs some 18 months after the receipt of an application.

Case load

The case load of the court has built up steadily since its foundation in 1953. Some 11,406 cases had been brought before the Court by December 31st 1999. Table 5 on the next page gives a detailed breakdown by subject matter of the cases heard in 1999. Given the importance and complexity of the common agricultural policy, it is not surprising that agriculture figures prominently in the list, as it has done in every year since 1953. Yet, given the rights of free movement and establishment, reinforced by the single market legislation carried through under the 1992 programme, it is in these fields – as well as increasingly in taxation and environmental cases – that the court is now most active.

Until quite recently, the largest number of cases had concerned complaints brought by employees of the different EC institutions on such matters as recruitment, salaries, promotion, disciplinary procedures, and so on, which under national administrations would go to employment tribunals. It was an anomaly that the Court of Justice, whose primary function should be to rule on significant issues of Community law, should have its timetable clogged up with a mass of petty cases, most of which could be adequately dealt with at a far lower level.

Court of First Instance

The Single European Act (see page 39), which took effect in July 1987, provided for the establishment of a Court of First Instance, which

Table 5 **Court of Justice: 1999 cases analysed by subject matter**

Subject matter of the action	Direct actions	References for a preliminary ruling	Appeal	Total	Special forms of procedure
Agriculture	49	18	13	80	–
Approximation of laws	26	16	–	42	–
Association of the Overseas countries and territories	–	–	1	1	–
Brussels Convention	–	2	–	2	–
Commercial policy	–	11	–	11	–
Community own resources	–	1	–	1	–
Company law	1	9	–	10	–
Competition	9	7	13	29	–
Energy	2	–	–	2	–
Environment and consumers	34	7	–	41	–
European citizenship	–	2	–	2	–
External relations	–	10	2	12	–
Freedom of movement for persons	11	57	1	69	–
Freedom to provide services	14	9	–	23	–
Free movement of capital	–	3	–	3	–
Free movement of goods	6	15	2	23	–
Industrial policy	4	1	–	5	–
Intellectual property	–	1	1	2	–
Law governing the institutions	7	–	4	11	1
Principles of Community law	–	4	–	4	–
Procedure	–	1	–	1	–
Regional policy	2	–	–	2	–
Social policy	11	19	3	33	–
State aid	13	1	1	15	–
Taxation	6	55	–	61	–
Transport	16	5	1	22	–
Total EC treaty	211	254	42	507	1

would hear certain classes of cases brought by individuals, including actions brought by officials of the Community. This court, which consists of 15 judges, began work in September 1989. The removal of staff cases from the work of the main court should shorten the delay in arriving at judgments in other cases. In 1999 the Court of First Instance heard 384 cases, of which 84 were staff cases.

Who brings the cases

Cases involving member states, normally alleging failure to carry out their obligations under the treaties, are often initiated by the commission. Occasionally, one member state is brought to court by another. As Table 6 on the next page shows, Italy has historically been the major culprit, although in 1998 its record was much better. The Italian Parliament is notoriously slow in passing laws, and a large number of these actions have been for failure to apply directives, adopted by the Council of Ministers, within the appointed time. The commission easily heads the lists both of complainants and defendants. It is its responsibility to take action, against individuals and companies as well as member states, to ensure that the treaties are being applied, for example in competition cases. However, it is also the commission that is the defendant in virtually all actions alleging loss or damage caused by the carrying out of EC policies.

Sometimes cases have involved one institution lodging a complaint against another. The Council of Ministers has more than once initiated action against the Parliament for allegedly exceeding its budgetary powers, while the Parliament took the council to court for failure to implement a common transport policy within the period foreseen by the Rome treaty.

Beneficial effect of judgments

The judgments of the court have helped to consolidate the Community, ensuring that its citizens as well as national governments are both protected by, and subject to, the provisions of Community law. It has been effective in many of its judgments in preventing governments from backsliding from the obligations that they (or their predecessors) assumed in signing the treaties. Also, although it has few sanctions against member states – being unable, for example, to send erring ministers to prison – its judgments have nearly always been complied with, occasionally after some delay, and sometimes following a further ruling by the court. The Maastricht treaty gave the court the power to impose fines on member states failing to comply with its judgments within a time-limit set by the commission.

One particular judgment has provided a useful stimulus to the removal of non-tariff barriers to intra-Community trade. In 1979 and 1980 the court ruled in the "Cassis de Dijon" case that where a product (in this case a category of alcoholic drink, but it has subsequently been applied to particular foodstuffs) is legally retailed in one member state, its sale cannot be prohibited in another member state except on the grounds of risk to public health.

Table 6 **Actions for failure to fulfil obligations**

Brought against	1999	1953–99
Belgium	13	238
Denmark	1	22
Germany	9	131
Greece	12	172
Spain	7	67
France	35	220
Ireland	13	97
Italy	29	384
Luxembourg	14	100
Netherlands	1	60
Austria	8	13
Portugal	13	54
Finland	1	1
Sweden	1	2
UK	6	47
Total	**163**	**1,608**

Source: European Court of Justice.

Note

1 Not to be confused with the European Court of Human Rights, based in Strasbourg, which was set up by the Council of Europe, under the European Convention of Human Rights, signed in 1950. All the member states of the EU recognise the jurisdiction of this court in human rights cases.

10 The Court of Auditors

The least known of the EC's institutions is the Court of Auditors, based in Luxembourg. It was established in 1977, when it replaced an earlier Audit Board which had less sweeping authority.

Membership

There are 15 members, one from each member state, who are chosen from persons who belong or have belonged to external audit departments in their own countries, or who are otherwise specially qualified. They are appointed for a renewable six-year term by the Council of Ministers, and appoint their own chairman from among their number for a renewable term of three years.

Responsibilities

The court's task is to examine all accounts of revenue and expenditure of Community institutions, and of any other bodies set up by the EC, to ensure that all revenue has been received and all expenditure incurred in a legal manner. It also has the responsibility of ensuring that the financial management has been sound. Its function is similar to that of bodies like the Comptroller and Auditor General's department in the UK.

An influential role

The court produces an annual report, as well as periodic specific reports undertaken at the request of any of the Community's other institutions or on its own initiative. It has frequently thrown up evidence of wasteful expenditure, especially on support to agriculture, and occasionally of financial misconduct. Its role is highly influential, and its reports have led to a considerable tightening up of EC procedures.

11 The European Investment Bank

The European Investment Bank (EIB) is both a Community institution and a bank. Established in 1958, under Article 130 of the Rome treaty, it is the EC's bank for financing capital investment promoting the balanced development of the Community. It raises the bulk of its financial resources on capital markets (where it has a AAA rating), and on-lends the proceeds, on a non-profit-making basis, for capital investment meeting priority EC objectives. The major part of its lending activity is focused on the Community's less prosperous regions. It also contributes towards deploying EC development aid programmes, notably under the co-operation or association agreements which the Community has concluded with 12 countries in the Mediterranean region and with 78 African, Caribbean and Pacific countries under the fourth Lomé Convention (see Chapter 35). It also lends considerable amounts, under the EU's Phare and TACIS programmes, to countries in Central and Eastern Europe and the former Soviet Union, as well as, on a smaller scale, to a number of Asian and Latin American countries and, since 1995, to South Africa.

Members and financial resources

The members of the EIB are the 15 member states of the EC. They have collectively subscribed the bank's capital of 100 billion ecus (of which 6 billion ecus is paid up). Up to the end of 2001 the bank had raised some €340 billion in loans. During 2001 it borrowed €32.3 billion and lent €36.8 billion. It is now, by a wide margin, the largest borrower and lender on international financial markets.

Activities in the EC

Loans are made to each of the member states. Italy and the UK have long been major recipients, but both Spain and Portugal (which already benefited from EIB loans before their accession to the Community) have rapidly increased their drawings from the bank. Germany has also become a major borrower since unification, mainly to finance investments in eastern Germany, and in 1998 was the largest recipient.

EIB loans within the Community during 1998 were principally for regional development, energy, industry, advanced technology, modernisation and conversion of enterprises, transport, telecommunications and other infrastructure development, and environmental protection.

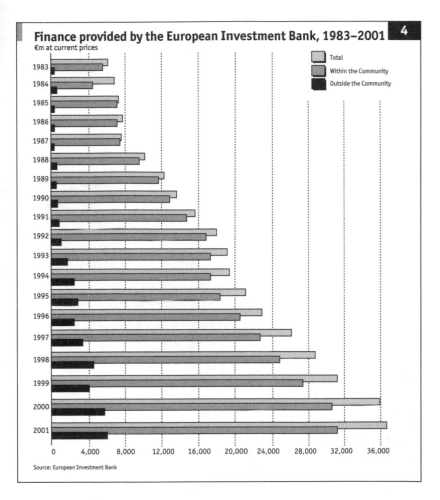

Finance provided by the European Investment Bank, 1983–2001
€m at current prices

Legend:
- Total
- Within the Community
- Outside the Community

Years: 1983, 1984, 1985, 1986, 1987, 1988, 1989, 1990, 1991, 1992, 1993, 1994, 1995, 1996, 1997, 1998, 1999, 2000, 2001

x-axis: 0, 4,000, 8,000, 12,000, 16,000, 20,000, 24,000, 28,000, 32,000, 36,000

Source: European Investment Bank

Location and structure

The EIB is based in Luxembourg. Its Board of Governors consists of the finance ministers of the member states, who meet once a year. It also has a part-time Board of Directors (24 members nominated by the member states and one member nominated by the European Commission), and a full-time Management Committee of the bank's president and seven vice-presidents. They are appointed by the Board of Governors, on the nomination of the Board of Directors, for a renewable six-year term.

Table 7 **Geographical breakdown of loans granted, 2001 and 1997–2001**

	2001		1997–2001	
	€m	%	€m	%
Within EU				
Belgium	365	1.2	3,091	2.3
Denmark	1,172	3.8	4,536	3.3
Germany	6,017	19.3	26,045	19.1
Greece	1,658	5.3	6,271	4.6
Spain	4,559	14.6	18,592	13.6
France	3,825	12.3	16,908	12.4
Ireland	525	1.7	1,454	1.1
Italy	5,488	17.6	22,901	16.8
Luxembourg	10	0.03	511	0.4
Netherlands	787	2.5	2,156	1.6
Austria	820	2.6	3,045	2.2
Portugal	1,799	5.8	8,098	5.9
Finland	695	2.2	2,668	2.0
Sweden	953	3.1	3,695	2.7
United Kingdom	2,337	7.5	15,626	11.4
Other	174	0.6	1,058	0.8
Total within EU	**31,184**	**100.0**	**136,655**	**100.0**
Outside EU				
Applicant countries	2,659	47.6	11,898	52.4
Mediterranean countries[a]	1,401	25.1	5,366	23.7
ACP & OCT countries	520	9.3	1,896	8.4
South Africa	150	2.7	776	3.4
Asia & Latin America	543	9.7	2,124	9.4
Balkans	319	5.7	625	2.8
Total outside EU	**5,592**	**100.0**	**22,685**	**100.0**
Overall total	**36,776**		**159,340**	

Note: Totals may not add up owing to rounding.
a Excluding Cyprus and Malta.
Source: European Investment Bank

European Bank for Reconstruction and Development

Since 1990 the EIB has been lending money to countries in Eastern Europe to help towards their transition to market economies. It also contributed to the establishment in April 1991 of the European Bank for Reconstruction and Development (EBRD), which has its headquarters in London, whose specific function is to lend money for this purpose. Although 40 countries participated in its establishment, more than half of the EBRD's capital of $10 billion was contributed by the European Community and its member states. The EIB's share in the bank's capital is 3%.

12 Other EU bodies

As well as the main European institutions described on the preceding pages, there are a number of specialised agencies, foundations and centres set up by a decision of the European Commission or the European Council. Most of these were established in 1994 or 1995, following decisions made at the Brussels summit in December 1993, although two of them were established 20 years earlier. In a different category was the **European Monetary Institute**, set up under the Maastricht Treaty as a forerunner to the **European Central Bank**, which replaced it in June 1998. The bank is based in Frankfurt, and its functions are described on pages 133–5.

European Agency for the Evaluation of Medicinal Products (EMEA)
With its base in London, the EMEA became operational on January 1st 1995. Its purpose is to ensure that in the EU's single market pharmaceutical products are marketed with identical conditions of usage and should benefit from an independent, scientifically based evaluation to protect both the consumer and the industry.

European Environment Agency (EEA)
The EEA and its wider network, EIONET, were set up in Copenhagen in 1994 to deliver high-quality environmental information to the member states of the EU, as well as to the general public. The main aims of the agency are to describe the present and foreseeable state of the environment and to provide relevant information for the implementation of the Community's environment policy.

European Training Foundation
The European Training Foundation was inaugurated in Turin in January 1995. It was set up to co-ordinate and support all EU activities in the field of post-compulsory education. This was part of the overall Phare and TACIS programmes (see page 254) for economic restructuring in the partner states of Central and Eastern Europe and Central Asia.

European Centre for the Development of Vocational Training (CEDEFOP)

CEDEFOP was established in Berlin in 1975, but recently moved to Salonica. The centre is contributing to the development of vocational training in Europe through its academic and technical activities.

European Centre for Drugs and Drug Addiction (EMCDDA)

EMCDDA was established in 1994 and located in Lisbon. The centre's aim is to provide "objective, reliable and comparable information at European level concerning drugs, drug addiction and their consequences". As the drugs phenomenon comprises many complex and closely interwoven aspects, the centre has the task of providing an overall statistical, documentary and technical picture of the drugs problem to the member states and the Community institutions as they embark on combat measures.

European Foundation for the Improvement of Living and Working Conditions

Established in Dublin in 1975, the foundation's aim is "to contribute to the planning and establishment of better working and living conditions through action designed to increase and disseminate knowledge likely to assist this development". Effectively an advisory body, its main task is to supply the commission and other EU institutions with scientific information and technical data.

Office for Harmonisation in the Internal Market (OHIM)

OHIM (Trade Marks and Designs) began its work on September 1st 1994 in Alicante. The office is responsible for the registration and subsequent administration of Community trade marks, and in the future Community designs, which have effect throughout the EU. The aim of the OHIM is to contribute to harmonisation in the internal market in the domain of intellectual property, in particular trademarks and designs.

Community Plant Variety Rights Office

This office became operational on April 27th 1995, and is temporarily located in Brussels. It is independent of the EU's institutions and is exclusively responsible for the implementation of the new regime of Community plant variety rights, like patents and copyrights. Plant breeders may ask for protection throughout the EU by a single application to the Community Plant Variety Rights Office.

European Agency for Safety and Health at Work

Located in Bilbao, the agency began work on October 27th 1995. Its first priority is to create a network linking up national information networks and to facilitate the provision of information in the field of safety and health at work.

Translation Centre for Bodies in the European Union

The Translation Centre for Bodies in the European Union was set up in 1994 in Luxembourg. It carries out translations for most of the bodies and agencies mentioned above.

The establishment of some 12 other new EU agencies has been approved in principle, but their creation has been delayed because of the inability of the European Council, at successive summit meetings, to agree on their location. The latest such failure was at Laeken in December 2001, when, however, it was agreed that, as a temporary measure, two of the bodies for which there was the most pressing need should start work in "provisional" locations. The Food Safety Agency will begin its operations in Brussels, and Eurojust (the European judicial co-operation unit) will join Europol in the Hague.

13 The bureaucracy: facts, figures and costs

Number of employees

Despite frequent suggestions that the EU has a vast bureaucracy, its payroll is modest compared with that of the national civil services of the member states. The European Commission has fewer than 17,000 permanent employees, excluding some 4,500 working in scientific research institutes and other units; the remaining institutions together employ about half that number. The total number of employees at the end of 2001 is shown in Table 8.

Table 8 **EU employees, end-2001**

	Permanent	Temporary
Commission	16,999	588
Research institutions etc	4,556	127
Council of Ministers	2,497	63
Parliament	3,550	635
Court of Justice	785	290
Court of Auditors	457	95
ESC and Committee of the Regions	830	48
Total	**29,647**	**1,846**

Recruitment

Recruitment to the commission's staff, apart from a limited number of senior posts to which national governments make nominations, are filled by open competition, the competitions being advertised periodically in the *Official Journal* of the Community, and in leading newspapers in the member states. Normally there is an upper age limit for new recruits, which effectively means that most Eurocrats join early in their careers, in their 20s or early 30s. Appointments are made without regard to race, creed or sex and, in principle, no posts are reserved for nationals of any specific state. In practice, there are unofficial national quotas designed to ensure that each member state gets a reasonable share of posts at each level of the administration. Otherwise the general qualifications are as set out in Article 28 of the Community's Staff Regulations. An official may be appointed only on condition that:

> *(a) he is a national of one of the Member States of the Communities, unless an exception is authorised by the appointing authority, and enjoys his full rights as a citizen;*
> *(b) he has fulfilled any obligations imposed on him by the laws concerning military service;*
> *(c) he produces the appropriate character references as to his suitability for the performance of his duties;*
> *(d) he has ... passed a competition based on either qualifications or tests, or both qualifications and tests;*
> *(e) he is physically fit to perform his duties; and*
> *(f) he produces evidence of a thorough knowledge of one of the languages of the Communities and of a satisfactory knowledge of another language of the Communities to the extent necessary for the performance of his duties.*

Candidates for posts as interpreters or translators must have a good knowledge of two Community languages other than their own.

Training

In addition to its permanent staff, the commission makes provision for the in-service training of about 200 stagiaires each year. The training lasts for 3–5 months, and the posts are open, also on a competition basis, primarily to recently graduated students. There is no guarantee of future employment, but the "stages" provide excellent experience for those interested in future careers at a European level, either with the Community or otherwise.

Salaries

The remuneration of members of the commission is linked to the maximum of the A1 scale. The president of the commission receives 138% of this (€250,250), vice-presidents 125% (€226,683) and commissioners 112.5% (€204,000). They all also qualify for the various allowances paid to employees, notably the expatriation allowance, which adds 14% to the above figures for all except the Belgian commissioner.

EU employees pay income tax to the Community (currently at a standard rate of 25%) rather than to the country in which they are

Table 9 **Basic monthly salaries in each category, 2001 (€)**

Category A

A1	Director-general	11,940.71–15,112.21
A2	Director	10,596.40–13,622.75
A3	Head of Division	8,775.74–12,481.82
A4 }	Principal Administrator	7,372.55–10,265.23
A5		6,078.30–8,599.00
A6 }	Administrator	5,252.79–7,258.99
A7		4,521.59–5,646.54
A8	Assistant Administrator	3,998.94–4,160.21

Category B

B1 {	Principal Administrative Assistant Senior Administrative Assistant	5,259.79–7,258.99
B2	Senior Technical Assistant	4,551.14–6,044.73
B3 {	Senior Secretarial Assistant Administrative Assistant	3,817.46–5,059.40
B4	Technical Assistant	3,301.76–4,378.78
B5	Secretarial Assistant	2,951.34–3,324.87

Category C

C1 {	Executive Secretary Principal Secretary Principal Clerical Officer	3,367.66–4,318.26
C2	Secretary/Shorthand-typist	2,929.16–3,800.31
C3	Clerical Officer	2,732.35–3,478.69
C4	Typist	2,468.89–3,168.96
C5	Clerical Assistant	2,276.47–2,556.31

Category D

D1	Head of Unit	2,572.75–3,360.18
D2	Skilled Employee	2,345.85–3,045.22
D3	Skilled Worker Unskilled Employee	2,183.37–2,837.52
D4	Unskilled Worker	2,058.62–2,311.88

Note: On May 1st 2002 the euro was worth £0.62 and $0.92.

employed, and the rates of pay are set rather higher than for national civil servants in order to compensate for living and working in a different country. In addition to basic salaries, there are family allowances and expatriation allowances, and a number of other "perks", such as free education for children at one of the European schools maintained by the commission. The salary scales are published from time to time in the *Official Journal*, where they are expressed monthly in euros (€). The most recent scales, which came into force on July 1st 2001, are shown in Table 9 on the previous page.

3

THE COMPETENCES

The European Union is still a long way from becoming the political union to which its founders aspired, and which has several times been re-affirmed, most recently at Amsterdam in June 1997, by the EC's heads of government as their eventual aim. It is far from being a European government, and its progress has been markedly lopsided. The removal of customs duties between member states and the development of a common agricultural policy long remained the most concrete achievements of the Community, but there are many other areas of economic activity where it has a competence, which is often shared, to a varying extent, with that of the member states. The Maastricht treaty enshrined the principle of "subsidiarity" by asserting that decisions should be "taken as closely as possible to the citizens", but nevertheless extended the competences of the EC institutions in several directions, as did the Amsterdam treaty five years later. Part III surveys the principal fields of action of the Community without, however, purporting to provide a comprehensive account of all of its activities.

14 Financing the Union

The EU's budget is modest compared with that of the member states, no more than around 2.5% of the sum of the national budgets. In 1997, according to the European Commission, each EU citizen would have paid an average of 220 ecus to the Union, and perhaps 50 times that amount to their own country. Despite this disparity, the EU's budget has been a source of periodic dispute between the member states and between them, the commission and the Parliament.

Revenue

Sources

The EC's sources of revenue have changed over the years. The ECSC, which had its own operational budget (196m ecus in 1999), was always financed by a levy on the production of coal and steel firms. The general Community budget was originally financed by a system of national contributions based mainly on the GDP of the member states. In 1970 it was decided progressively to replace these contributions by the Community's "own resources". These consist of sources of revenue which, although collected mainly in the member states, belong to the Community as a right. At present they consist of four separate elements.

1 Customs duties, levied on products imported from outside the Community.
2 Agricultural levies, charged on imports of various foodstuffs to bring the price up to Community level plus levies on products in surplus supply.
3 A proportion of value-added tax. By far the largest element, this was originally set at a maximum of 1% of the final selling price of a common base of goods and services (this was necessary, as both the rates and the incidence of VAT vary widely from one country to another). The limit was raised to 1.4% in 1986, but had gradually dropped back to 1% by 1999.
4 Contributions from member states. Based on the member state's share of the total GNP of the Community, the size of this contribution is to be limited to that which would bring the total revenue of the EC

to a maximum of 1.2% of the Community's GNP in 1993 and 1994, gradually rising to a maximum of 1.27% in 1999.

Table 10 **Budget revenue, 2001–02 (€m)**

	2001	2002
Agricultural duties	1,132.9	1,121.7
Sugar and isoglucose levies	839.8	770.9
Customs duties	14,237.3	15,765.9
Own resources collection costs	−1,621.0	−1,765.8
VAT own resources	30,625.1	36,603.9
GNP-based own resources	34,460.2	42,318.7
Balance of VAT and GNP-based own resources from previous years	1,044.0	a
Budget balance from previous year	11,612.7	a
Other revenue	1,284.0	783.2
Total	**93,615.0**	**95,598.5**
% GNP		
Maximum own resources which may be assigned to the budget	1.27	1.27
Own resources actually assigned to the budget	1.07	1.05

a Token entry.
Source: European Commission

Budgetary reform

The fourth resource was added in 1989, following the agreement on budgetary reform reached at the Brussels summit of February 1988. For the first time for several years the Community was thus able to have a budget based on an amount of available own resources sufficient to finance all its political, economic and social operations. For several years previously a growing shortfall had had to be met by non-refundable advances from the member states. Table 10 shows the estimated revenue for 2001 and 2002.

The previous methods of financing the budget had become increasingly unsatisfactory, and the 1986 and 1987 budgets were balanced only by various forms of creative accountancy. The yield from customs duties had slowly declined as the Community's external tariffs were adjusted downwards, and agricultural levies fell as the EC became self-sufficient in an increasing number of products. This put pressure on the VAT contributions, which were already up to the maximum level of 1.4% of the value of purchases in the Community within a year of the ceiling being raised from 1%. The addition of the fourth resource enabled the long-term planning of budgetary commitments until 1992, later extended to 1999, by which time it had become the largest single source of revenue.

Expenditure

Figure 5 on the next page shows the expenditure provided for in the EU's general budget of 1999, and compares it with 1973, the first year in which the UK was a member. The principal elements in the budget are as follows.

Agriculture and fisheries.   45.5% of estimated expenditure in 2001, a sharp reduction on previous years. The main reason agriculture absorbs such a high proportion of the budget is that it is the one area of major expenditure where a substantial amount of publicly financed support passes through the EU's budget. It threatens to crowd out programmes in other areas, for example, technological research, where the Union ought to be making a far larger contribution. Efforts have been made in recent years to curtail agricultural spending, and at least to ensure that it rises at a slower rate than EU expenditure as a whole (see pages 152–5).

Regional policy.   Some 16.3% of estimated expenditure in 2001. In 1973 there was no regional spending in the budget. The European Regional Development Fund was established in 1975, following the accession in 1973 of the UK, Denmark and Ireland. It helps to finance development programmes, infrastructural investment and industrial and service projects in poorer regions and areas particularly hit by recession. The fund normally operates on the basis of matching contributions from the member state concerned. Under the Maastricht treaty, a new Cohesion Fund (3.3% of estimated expenditure in 2001) was established to provide assistance for infrastructure investment in the four poorest member states: Greece, Portugal, Spain and Ireland.

Social policy.   Approximately 6.9% of estimated expenditure in 2001, a small percentage increase compared with 1973 despite the massive increase in unemployment in the intervening years. Most of this

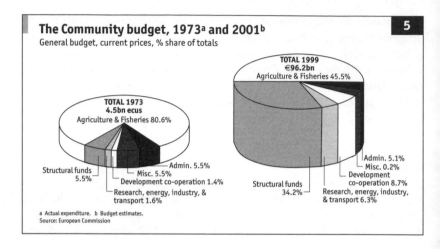

The Community budget, 1973ª and 2001ᵇ
General budget, current prices, % share of totals

5

TOTAL 1999
€96.2bn
Agriculture & Fisheries 45.5%

TOTAL 1973
4.5bn ecus
Agriculture & Fisheries 80.6%

Structural funds
5.5%
Admin. 5.5%
Misc. 5.5%
Development co-operation 1.4%
Research, energy, industry, &
transport 1.6%

Admin. 5.1%
Misc. 0.2%
Development
co-operation 8.7%
Structural funds
34.2%
Research, energy, industry,
& transport 6.3%

a Actual expenditure. b Budget estimates.
Source: European Commission

expenditure is through the European Social Fund, which co-finances training and retraining schemes and aid for recruitment. In 1988 it was agreed that total expenditure on the "structural funds", that is the regional fund, the social fund and the agricultural guidance fund, would double by 1993. By 2001 they amounted together with the Cohesion Fund to 34.2% of the total budget.

Energy, research, industry, transport and the environment. These accounted for only 6.3% of Union spending in 2001, which is evidently only a tiny fraction of the amount spent by member states in these fields. The largest proportion went on research, which was widely seen as being a totally inadequate response to the research efforts of the United States and Japan. Attempts by the commission to persuade the member states sharply to increase the appropriations for research have so far met with only partial success.

Development co-operation. 8.7% of estimated expenditure in 2001, mainly on co-operation programmes with the countries of Central and Eastern Europe, the former Soviet Union and former Yugoslavia, and with Mediterranean countries. It also includes emergency food aid and assistance to Asian and Latin American countries. Additionally, the Lomé Convention provides for financial and technical aid to 78 African, Caribbean and Pacific countries, which is in practice financed separately from the EU budget through national contributions and loans from the European Investment Bank (see Chapter 35).

Appropriations and expenditure

The procedure for approving the annual budget is described on pages 67–8. Total appropriations for 2001 were for €96,238m, but the estimated expenditure is €76,863m, as each year the actual spending falls short as not all the commitments are taken up. The main appropriations for 2001 are shown in Table 11.

Table 11 **General EU budget, 2001 appropriations (2001 prices)**

Sector	€m
Common agricultural policy	44,530
Structural operations (incl Cohesion Fund)	32,270
Internal policies (other than structural operations)	6,272
External action	4,735
Administrative expenditure	4,776
Reserves	916
Total	**96,238**
Payment appropriations required as % of GNP	1.09
Own resources ceiling as % of GNP	1.27

Source: European Commission

Expenditure proposals for 2000–06

By 1999 a new long-term financial perspective, covering a five- or seven-year period from 2000 onwards, was due to be approved by the Council of Ministers. In July 1997 the commission produced its "Agenda 2000" report, which concluded that it would be unnecessary to raise the current expenditure ceiling of 1.27% of GNP. On the basis of an average expected growth rate of 2.5% in the EU, and of 4% in the applicant countries, it expected additional resources by 2006 of around 20 billion ecus. Projected total spending would rise by 17%, which would leave a cushion of reserves because it is less than the 24% anticipated rise in GNP. It proposed that for the seven-year period 2000–06 total EU expenditure should amount to some €684 billion, of which €21.84 billion should be provided as pre-accession aid to the candidate members in Central and Eastern Europe. At the Berlin summit in March 1999 the heads of government cut the figure by some 6.6% to €640 billion, but left the sum for pre-accession aid intact. Table 12

Table 12 Financial perspective, 2000–06 (€m, 2000 prices)

	2000	2003	2006
Appropriations for commitments			
1 Agriculture	41,738	44,646	42,493
CAP (not including rural development)	37,352	40,219	38,036
Rural development & accompanying measures	4,386	4,427	4,457
2 Structural operations	32,678	30,882	29,746
Structural funds	30,019	28,223	27,193
Cohesion fund	2,659	2,659	2,553
3 Internal policies	6,031	6,366	6,712
4 External action			
(not including Phare from 1999 onwards)	4,627	4,658	4,688
5 Administration	4,638	4,882	5,187
6 Reserves	906	406	406
Monetary reserve	500		
Emergency aid reserve	203	203	203
Guarantee reserve	203	203	203
7 Pre-accession aid	3,174	3,174	3,174
Agriculture	529	529	529
Pre-accession structural instrument	1,058	1,058	1,058
Phare (applicant countries)	1,587	1,587	1,587
Total appropriations for commitments	93,792	95,014	92,406
Total appropriations for payments	91,322	96,714	91,347
Appropriations for payments as % of GNP	1.13%	1.11%	0.98%
Available for accession			
(appropriations for payments)		6,842	14,501
Agriculture		2,071	3,468
Other expenditure		4,771	11,033
Ceiling, appropriations for payments	91,322	103,556	105,848
Ceiling, payments as % of GNP	1.13%	1.19%	1.13%
Margin for unforeseen expenditure	0.14%	0.08%	0.14%
Own resources ceiling	1.27%	1.27%	1.27%

Source: European Commission

gives the detailed financial perspective, as approved by the Berlin summit, for 2000, 2003 and 2006.

Who gains, who loses?

For many years there was no precise information about the net contributors and net beneficiaries of the EU budget. Everybody knew that Germany was, by far, the biggest contributor, that the UK's contribution was substantially reduced by the annual rebates it had received since 1984 and that Ireland – in relation to its size – was the biggest beneficiary. The debate over the "Agenda 2000" report provoked a demand for more precise details, as German public opinion agitated for a lessening of Germany's burden and other member states called for the ending of the UK's rebate. The commission accordingly published its own best estimate of national contributions (see Table 13) in November 1998, which showed that the Netherlands, Sweden and Austria also contributed more than their "fair share" of the budget. The settlement reached at Berlin gave some marginal relief to these four countries, which were let off three quarters of the amount that they would normally be required to pay towards the UK's rebate. The balance was to be made up by the remaining ten members. As for the UK, its rebate – currently worth around €3 billion – remained intact, but in exchange the UK government agreed to forgo some €240m which it would have gained from other budgetary changes.

Table 13 **EU budget balances of member states, 1998 estimates (Ecu bn; after UK rebate)**

Net contributors		Net beneficiaries	
Germany	11.46	Spain	5.54
France	1.76	Greece	4.31
Netherlands	1.22	Ireland	2.80
Sweden	1.20	Portugal	2.68
Austria	0.87	Belgium	1.71
UK	0.66	Luxembourg	0.72
Italy	0.56	Denmark	0.09
		Finland	0.001

Source: European Commission

15 Trade

Removal of tariff barriers

The Treaty of Rome provided for the removal of all tariff barriers inside the Community within 12 years, and in fact the original six member states completed the process 18 months early, in 1968. The consequence was an enormous and sustained growth in intra-EU trade (see Figure 6). Later entrants proceeded in stages: the UK, Ireland and Denmark by 1977; and Greece by 1986. Spain and Portugal, which joined the Community in 1986, removed all their tariffs against other EC members by the end of 1992. Austria, Finland and Sweden had already removed theirs long before joining the EU in 1995. As internal tariffs were removed, a common external tariff was introduced against the goods of other countries. Originally set at an average of around 10%, this was gradually reduced, following successive rounds of negotiations in the General Agreement on Tariffs and Trade (GATT), and the weighted average of EU customs duties fell to just under 5%, a little lower than in the United States but higher than in Japan. Under the GATT Uruguay round agreement reached in December 1993, this weighted average has fallen to around 3%, and it should be further reduced under continuing negotiations in the World Trade Organisation (WTO), which replaced the GATT in 1995.

Soon after the Uruguay round, the EU announced plans for another set of global trade talks and tried to rustle up support from the rest of the WTO. But negotiating fatigue, lingering suspicion about who was benefiting from the WTO, weak public support and organisational incompetence all led to the fiasco of the WTO's Seattle meeting in late 1999. Besieged by rioting activists, the Seattle talks broke down in mutual recrimination between rich and poor nations about how to take the agenda forward.

The EU was better prepared in November 2001, at the WTO ministerial meeting in Doha, Qatar. After spending much of the previous two years alliance building with poorer nations, Pascal Lamy, the EU trade commissioner, helped usher in the so-called Doha Development Agenda, a wide-ranging negotiating plan which is scheduled to end in 2005. One of the main sticking points in Doha was, unsurprisingly, agriculture. The delegates eventually accepted a text with the commitment to phasing out agriculture subsidies, but it was preceded by the words

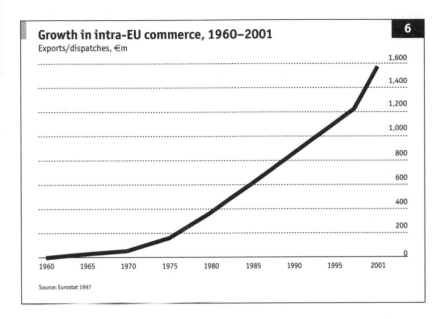

Growth in intra-EU commerce, 1960–2001
Exports/dispatches, €m

Source: Eurostat 1997

"without prejudging the outcome of the negotiations", meaning that there was no need actually to achieve that aim. Everything then seemed to fit into place: the environmental plans pushed by the EU were cleared, as were new issues of investment, competition and procurement.

Member states represented by EU

The treaty stipulated that the EC should represent its members in matters of external trade, and the member states formally transferred some of their sovereign powers to the Community. As a result some 165 countries established diplomatic relations with the EC. Most of these have embassies or missions in Brussels which often double up with embassies accredited to Belgium, although the EU role is in most cases by far the more important. The EU, normally represented by the commission, speaks for the member states in the WTO and the North Atlantic Fisheries Organisation.

The EC signed agreements with over 120 countries as well as some 30 multilateral agreements. Most of them concerned EC trade, and their effect was profoundly to modify its pattern. The trading arrangements fall into four main categories: EEA; other developed countries; former communist countries; developing countries.

EFTA

EU's largest trading partner

In 1973 the EC formed an industrial free-trade area with the then seven countries of the European Free Trade Association (EFTA): Austria, Finland, Iceland, Liechtenstein, Norway, Sweden and Switzerland. Customs duties and restrictions on trade in manufactured goods were abolished, and some reciprocal concessions were made for agricultural produce. This effectively extended the size of the common market for manufactures to 370m people. EFTA was the EU's largest trading partner.

European Economic Area

Following the launch of the EC's single market programme, the EFTA countries expressed a desire for closer association with the Community. Negotiations began in December 1989 to establish a European Economic Area (EEA) in which the EFTA states would assume many of the obligations and disciplines of EC membership, including the acceptance of the free movement of capital, persons and services, in return for sharing in most of the expected benefits of the single market programme. The negotiations ended in autumn 1991 and the EEA should have started on January 1st 1993. However, the agreement was turned down in a referendum in Switzerland in December 1992. Following further negotiations with the remaining countries it only came into effect in January 1994, with Switzerland left out and Liechtenstein's membership deferred to a later date (1995). For three of the countries concerned, however, the EEA acted as no more than a staging post on the way to full EU membership. Austria, Finland and Sweden became members of the EU in January 1995. Norway also negotiated full membership, but its voters rejected the move in a referendum in December 1994, so it remains in the EEA, along with Iceland and Liechtenstein. The Swiss government negotiated a series of bilateral agreements with the EU, its membership application being indefinitely suspended. (See also pages 274–5.) Switzerland is now the EU's second largest trading partner, after the United States.

Other developed countries

North America

Trade relations with the United States are largely governed by agreements in the GATT and the WTO. Both sides profess free-trade principles, but each often accuses the other of protectionist tendencies and/or of giving unfair advantages to its own exporters through state subsidies. Disputes concerning agriculture and steel, in particular, became increasingly frequent during the 1980s, leading on occasion to the introduction of counter-measures which were usually withdrawn when the other side belatedly offered concessions. Similar disputes concerning such topics as EU restrictions on the importation of hormone-treated meat and discrimination against banana imports by US companies in Latin America have more recently been resolved by the disputes procedure of the WTO, whose judgments on both these issues favoured the US position. A full-scale trade war, which would be as deeply damaging to both sides as to world trade as a whole, has several times seemed a distinct possibility, but so far at least cooler counsels have prevailed when tension has mounted.

But other arguments were brewing. The United States won dispute panels at the WTO against the EU's banana import regime and its ban on hormone-treated beef, leading to US sanctions worth respectively €191m and €117m. By 2001, the EU had reformed its banana regime and the United States had lifted its sanctions, but the hormone measures remained in place. In January 2002, the WTO confirmed its ruling that the US export credits known as Foreign Sales Corporations (FSCs) were illegal subsidies, paving the way to billions of euros in EU sanctions. And in March 2002, the Bush administration imposed duties on a wide range of steel imports, prompting the European Commission to impose its own quotas on steel and threaten €2.5 billion of retaliatory sanctions against the United States.

Canada is in a similar position to the United States, although in 1976 a framework agreement was concluded which established mechanisms for commercial and economic co-operation. In November 1990 a transatlantic declaration was signed between the EC, the United States and Canada, providing for closer co-operation in areas of common interest and a more permanent dialogue to resolve or contain the trade disputes that would inevitably continue to occur. This was followed up by the New Transatlantic Agenda signed by President Clinton and EU leaders in Brussels in December 1995, which should have led to an even closer relationship. Yet the passing by the US Congress of the Helms-Burton Act, with its extra-territorial effects, led to a sharp dispute with the EU (which regards it as illegal in international law) concerning trade with Cuba, Iran and Libya. In May 1998, however, at an EU-US summit, President Clinton agreed to ask the US Congress to amend the act in such a way that the EU member states would not be affected. Meanwhile, a dispute with Canada over fishing rights was settled in June 1996, leading to the conclusion of a joint action plan for closer trade and other relations, agreed in Ottawa in December 1996.

Japan

The EU's trading relations with Japan have been difficult, largely owing to the substantial trade deficit. Japan imports less than half as much from the Union than it exports to it. This imbalance is particularly painful because Japanese exports are focused on a fairly small number of sectors – cars, electronics, audio-visual equipment, computers and telecommunications – where European firms have been struggling to maintain or achieve a viable share in the world market. Although Japanese tariffs are, on average, lower than the EU's, the Union has repeatedly called for the removal of non-tariff barriers and for more decisive action by the Japanese authorities to open up their domestic market to foreign imports.

Meanwhile, Japanese exports to Europe have been curbed by a variety of measures, some taken by individual member states rather than by the EU itself, such as "voluntary" limitation agreements on the number of Japanese cars that may be imported in any one year. The commission has increasingly resorted to anti-dumping measures to restrict the importation of goods such as photocopiers, computer printers and electronic typewriters; and imports of colour TV sets, numerically controlled machine tools, CD players, video recorders and microwave ovens have been formally or informally restricted in recent years.

High-level meetings with Japanese ministers and officials take place regularly, as well as quadrilateral meetings that include the United States and Canada. The pressure applied at these meetings resulted in Japanese initiatives to encourage importers and to ease or remove impediments in their domestic markets. The Japanese trade surplus with the EC more than halved in the five years to 1990, but it rose steeply again during 1991 and succeeding years. The EC pressed for further market-opening measures to be taken by Japan, which blamed lack of enterprise by EC exporters for their failure to increase their penetration of the market. In July 1991 the EC and Japan signed a joint declaration providing for close economic and political co-operation in the future. This was revamped with a more ambitious ten-year action plan, signed in December 2001. A Trade Assessment Mechanism (TAM) was established in 1993 to find out why EU businesses which perform well internationally fare less well in Japan, and to propose action to remove internal obstacles to trade. Meanwhile, negotiations were proceeding to phase out EU restrictions on Japanese car exports, which were not, however, expected to gain completely free access to the EU market before January 1st 2000.

Australasia

Australia and New Zealand have no trade agreements with the EU. They are, however, important trading partners, supplying food and raw materials and taking mainly manufactured goods from the Union. Australian and New Zealand food exports to the UK were adversely affected when the UK joined the EC. New Zealand was partially compensated by the award of temporary export quotas for cheese and butter. The cheese quota expired after five years, but the arrangements for importing a limited amount of butter have been extended, despite the EU's own excess production.

In 1997, the EU and Australia signed a four-page joint declaration, covering trade and co-operation in a wide range of areas. But it could only be negotiated when Canberra balked at signing a more committal framework agreement, which contains a standard human-rights clause committing both parties to the broad principles of the UN Declaration on Human Rights. At the time Australia complained, saying it left the country open to trade-related sanctions if it was seen to be in breach of any human rights. The declaration includes a number of areas of co-operation, such as trade in goods and services, investment and market access, and regular contacts in sectors such as agriculture, fishing and industry, technology and information, mining, transport and energy, as well as competition policies and consumer protection. New Zealand signed a declaration with the EU in 1998 committing the two sides to co-operation on international economic and political issues. The three-page document sets out a brief series of common goals and lists the areas of future economic and political co-operation between the two sides.

Former communist countries

Trade with the countries of Central and Eastern Europe before the collapse of communist rule in 1988–90 was hampered by the lack of normal trading relations and by the inherent inefficiencies of command economies. A mutual recognition agreement was reached in June 1988 with Comecon, the economic organisation linking most of the communist countries, which was wound up in 1991. This opened the way to the establishment of diplomatic relations between the EC and individual East European countries as well as Cuba. Trade and co-operation agreements were subsequently signed with Poland, Hungary, Czechoslovakia, Bulgaria, Romania and the Soviet Union. At the same time considerable economic and technical aid was made available to the first three countries, and humanitarian aid was given to Bulgaria, Romania and the Soviet Union.

Association agreements

Negotiations began in 1990–91 with a view to concluding far-reaching association agreements (known as Europe Agreements) with the new democracies of Central and Eastern Europe. These would provide tariff-free access for most of their manufacturing goods while maintaining restrictions on their free export of textiles and agricultural products. The first three agreements were concluded with Czechoslovakia, Hungary and Poland in December 1991. The agreement with Czechoslovakia was later replaced by separate agreements with the Czech Republic and Slovakia, and others were signed with Bulgaria and Romania. Less comprehensive agreements were subsequently concluded with Albania, Slovenia, the three Baltic states and the former Soviet republics of Ukraine, Belarus, Kazakhstan, Kirgizstan, Georgia, Armenia, Azerbaijan, Moldova and Uzbekistan, and exploratory talks were opened with Turkmenistan. A partnership and co-operation agreement, which may later lead to an EU-Russia Free Trade Area, was signed with the Russian president, Boris Yeltsin, at the Corfu summit in June 1994. A trade agreement with former Yugoslavia, concluded in 1970, is no longer in operation. The Union has a large deficit with the former Comecon countries, largely because of Russian energy sales to Western Europe, and has been anxious to build up its export of manufactured goods. Progress, however, has been slow. It has been further impeded by the quasi-collapse of the Russian economy.

Developing countries

The Mediterranean

The Community concluded association or co-operation agreements with 12 Mediterranean countries (excluding Albania and Libya). These give duty-free access to all, or most, of their industrial products, specific concessions for some of their agricultural produce and a certain amount of financial aid in the form of grants and loans. A similar agreement came into force in January 1990 with the countries belonging to the Gulf Co-operation Council.

Three countries have association agreements. In 1987 Turkey applied for full membership (see page 272–3), and entered into a customs union with the EU on December 31st 1995. An earlier two-stage agreement for a customs union, including agricultural produce, came fully into force during 1997. Cyprus applied for EU membership in 1990, as did the third association country, Malta (see pages 273–4).

The ACP

EU relations with the 78 African, Caribbean and Pacific countries (ACP) are governed by the 20-year Partnership Agreement, signed in Cotonou, Benin, on June 23rd 2000 (see page 253 and Appendix 7). All the ACP countries are signatories to the Cotonou Agreement: 48 African countries, covering all sub-Saharan Africa, 15 countries in the Caribbean and 14 states in the Pacific. Of the 49 least developed countries covered by the EU's "Everything But Arms" initiative, 40 are ACP. South Africa is a signatory of the Cotonou Agreement but its membership of the ACP group is qualified. In 2000, EU trade with the ACP countries totalled over €55 billion, with the EU importing some €28.6 billion and exporting some €26.4 billion. For most of the ACP countries – and for virtually all African ACP countries – the EU is the main trading partner, representing about one-third of both imports and exports. ACP countries already export about 93% of their goods, in value terms, duty free into the EU.

However, although the EU insists that various market-opening initiatives help developing countries, figures show that their share of world trade is falling. ACP world exports fell from 3.4% of the global market in 1976 to 1.1% in 2000 and their share in developing countries exports from 13.3% in 1976 to 3.6% in 2000. Trade with the EU followed similar pattern: while doubling in real terms over the past decade, the share of EU imports from the ACP in total EU imports fell from 6.7% in 1976 to 2.8% in 2000.

Asia

Countries such as India, Bangladesh, Pakistan and Sri Lanka benefit from the EU's generalised system of preferences, which gives developing countries duty-free access for finished and semi-finished goods. The

EU also has separate economic and development agreements with India and Pakistan, and a co-operation agreement with the Association of South-East Asian Nations (ASEAN): Brunei, Indonesia, Malaysia, the Philippines, Singapore, Vietnam and Thailand. The first Asia-Europe (ASEM) summit meeting, in Bangkok in March 1996, which included Japan, China and South Korea as well as the seven ASEAN countries, did little to improve economic and political links in the short term, but it established a framework for continuing consultation at heads of government level every two years. The second ASEM summit in London, in April 1998, launched several new initiatives, including the creation of an ASEM trust fund at the World Bank, a European network of financial experts to facilitate financial reform in Asia, action plans to promote trade and investment and a "Vision Group", charged with examining the long-term prospects for relations between Asia and Europe. An Asia-Europe Environmental Technology Centre has been established in Bangkok and an Asia-Europe Foundation in Singapore.

Latin America

There are economic and trade co-operation agreements with most of the principal countries, including the Mercosur association, the five members of the Andean Pact and the six countries of the Central American isthmus. All Latin American countries benefit from generalised preferences.

Trade policy

Industrial products

The external trading policy of the EU is based on free trade, or the aspiration to achieve it, so far as industrial products are concerned, although this attitude has been greatly modified in relation to Japan. Notable exceptions are shipbuilding, steel and textiles. Textile imports into the EU have been regulated by the Multi-Fibre Arrangement (MFA). The MFA was a deal between the United States, the EC and low-cost suppliers, conceived in 1973, to open up markets to developing country suppliers while the ailing textile industries of the industrialised world were slowly run down. It soon became apparent, however, that it was being used as a protectionist device to keep imports from developing countries at modest levels. Under the Uruguay round agreement the MFA will be gradually dismantled over a period of ten years and the EU market will be progressively opened up to textile imports.

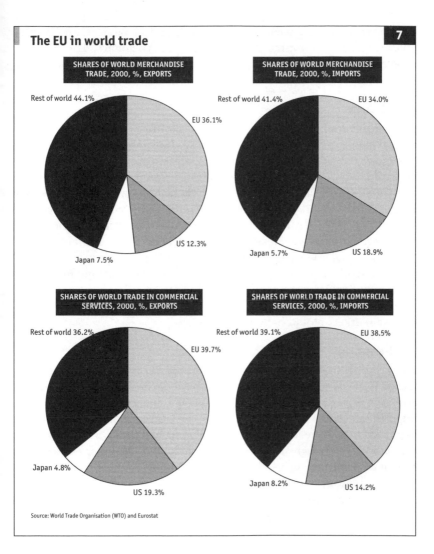

The EU in world trade

7

SHARES OF WORLD MERCHANDISE TRADE, 2000, %, EXPORTS

Rest of world 44.1%
EU 36.1%
US 12.3%
Japan 7.5%

SHARES OF WORLD MERCHANDISE TRADE, 2000, %, IMPORTS

Rest of world 41.4%
EU 34.0%
US 18.9%
Japan 5.7%

SHARES OF WORLD TRADE IN COMMERCIAL SERVICES, 2000, %, EXPORTS

Rest of world 36.2%
EU 39.7%
US 19.3%
Japan 4.8%

SHARES OF WORLD TRADE IN COMMERCIAL SERVICES, 2000, %, IMPORTS

Rest of world 39.1%
EU 38.5%
US 14.2%
Japan 8.2%

Source: World Trade Organisation (WTO) and Eurostat

In the mid-1990s, the EU also began negotiating Mutual Recognition Agreements (MRAs) with its main trading partners. These were designed to cut red tape in safety and testing standards by setting single certification procedures for various products. For example, with the United States, it meant companies were able to test their products in the EU according to American rules of certification to gain access to the American market, and vice versa. The EU has MRAs with the United States in a number of sectors such as chemicals, medical devices, foodstuffs, pharmaceuticals, automobiles and tyres, and cosmetics. The EU also entered into similar agreements with Australia, Canada, Japan and New Zealand.

Agriculture

Agricultural trade is governed by protectionism. Apart from special arrangements to buy quotas of sugar from India and the ACP countries at guaranteed prices, virtually no temperate agricultural products are imported into the EU since the agricultural levies (see Chapter 20) effectively make them uncompetitive. This will be less true in the future as a result of the Uruguay round. The EU remains, however, the world's largest food importer. It still has a substantial deficit in its agricultural trade because of its purchases of tropical products and animal feed.

In 2001, plans were unveiled to open up the EU market to exports from the world's poorest 48 countries under the "Everything But Arms" (EBA) initiative. However, the EU somewhat spoiled its good intentions by adding that its sugar and rice market would open only in 2008, while banana markets would have until 2006.

EU the world's leading trader

The result of these arrangements is that the EU is the world's leading trader. It needs to trade to this extent because of its paucity of energy and raw materials. Nearly 45% of the EU's energy needs are met by imports, as well as three-quarters of other vital raw materials. In order to pay for these it needs to export mainly finished products to the rest of the world. Although internal trade between member states has expanded enormously since the establishment of the Community in 1958, its share of world trade has somewhat declined in the face of much stronger competition from Japan and from newly industrialised countries such as South Korea, Brazil and Singapore.

16 The single market

"Common market" proved to be elusive

In the early 1980s concern was expressed with growing urgency that 15 years or so after the six founding members of the EC had abolished all quota restrictions and duties on their internal trade, the Community was still far from being the "common market" that it was usually called.

- Frontier formalities delayed and added to the cost of transporting goods from one member state to another.
- It was still impossible for many EC citizens to pursue their professional duties in another member state, despite the provisions of the Rome treaty concerning free movement.
- Service industries such as insurance were prevented from operating on a Community-wide basis.
- Differential indirect tax rates distorted intra-Community trade.
- Public procurement contracts in each member state were effectively reserved for national suppliers rather than being put out to open tender.

An influential report to the European Parliament by two leading economists, one French and the other British,[1] estimated that such restrictions cost every worker in the Community the equivalent of a week's wages every year. It was evident that the Community was largely failing to reap the benefits which a unified market of 321m people (following Spanish and Portuguese accession in 1986) should provide in relation to the smaller population base of both of its main industrial rivals, the United States and Japan.

The European Council takes action

The problem was discussed at successive meetings of the European Council between 1982 and 1985. At several of these the heads of government pledged themselves to the completion of the internal market as a high priority, but this had little noticeable effect. An enormous backlog of draft directives and regulations, tabled by the European Commission, had built up in the Council of Ministers, which was often prevented from taking a decision through the resistance or hesitancy of only one member state.

Finally, in 1985, more decisive action was taken at two consecutive European Council meetings (at Brussels in March and at Milan in June). In Brussels it was decided to instruct the commission to draw up a detailed programme with a specific timetable for completing the single market by 1992. In Milan it was resolved to summon an inter-governmental conference which would consider, among other matters, the desirability of amending the Rome treaty to enable qualified major-ity voting to be applied to most of the internal market issues which had previously required unanimity. This eventually led to the Single Euro-pean Act, which came into force on July 1st 1987 (see page 56).

White paper on single market drawn up
The call from the Brussels summit was soon answered by the commis-sion, which produced a white paper drawn up by Lord Cockfield, the commissioner responsible for the internal market, in time for it to be approved at Milan. This document listed some 300 actions which would need to be taken if the single market was to be achieved. These were divided into three categories:

- the removal of physical barriers;
- the removal of technical barriers;
- the removal of fiscal barriers.

Physical barriers.   The white paper set as its target the total abolition, not simply the alleviation, of frontier controls by 1992. Measures which would relax and simplify existing controls – beginning with the intro-duction in 1988 of the so-called Single Administrative Document (SAD) which replaced up to 70 forms previously required by truck drivers crossing internal EC frontiers – were set out, paving the way for the com-plete removal at the end of the period of all restrictions on goods and individual travellers.

Technical barriers.   The second part of the white paper was intended to remove the barriers created by different national regulations and standards. The commission proposed that its laborious programme to harmonise national standards for thousands of different manufacturing processes should be replaced by a system of mutual recognition of national standards, pending the adoption of European standards. The EC should instead confine itself to laying down minimum health and safety requirements which would be obligatory in all member states.

Other proposals included:

- the liberalisation of public procurement;
- the establishment of a common market for services such as transport, banking, insurance and information marketing;
- the free movement of capital throughout the Community;
- the removal of legal restraints on the formation of EC-wide companies; and
- the adoption of a Community trademark system.

Fiscal barriers.   The third part of the white paper was mainly concerned with the approximation of VAT and excise-duty rates throughout the Community. The commission did not consider that total harmonisation was necessary for the completion of the internal market. It would be content to see rates varying by +/-2.5% of whatever target rate or norm was chosen.

Target dates set in timetable for completion

The timetable for completing the internal market set target dates for each of the 300 proposals, both for the commission to table draft directives or regulations and for their adoption by the Council of Ministers. Despite the enthusiasm of the heads of government, there was a great deal of scepticism as to whether the programme would be carried out. Yet it soon gathered momentum, partly because of the dedication that Jacques Delors and Lord Cockfield brought to the task of following up the white paper proposals. The 1992 target aroused intense interest, both within the member states and in other countries, whose governments and traders feared the consequences of a more integrated European market from which they might be excluded. Lord Cockfield was not reappointed in January 1989 to serve in the second Delors Commission, but by then his programme was progressing without interruption, helped by the new voting procedures under the Single European Act which speeded up progress in the Council of Ministers. The 300 measures were later consolidated into 282 proposed directives or regulations. By the target date of December 31st 1992 no fewer than 258 of these (over 90%) had been adopted by the Council of Ministers, and 79% were already being implemented by the member states. In some cases, notably concerning the harmonisation of indirect taxes (see Chapter 19), there had been a certain watering down of the original proposal, but it was undeniable that the great bulk of the programme was legislated as planned.

The Schengen Agreement

The biggest failure was that, although all customs controls on goods were abolished at internal EU frontiers on January 1st 1993, systematic passport checks continued to be made at many frontier crossings, particularly at seaports and airports. Already several years earlier some governments, notably that of the UK, had argued that to abolish border checks would cause problems relating to the control of terrorism, illegal immigrants and drug-trafficking, and the containment of animal-borne diseases. It was in order to bypass this opposition that, in June 1990, five member states decided to go ahead on their own with an agreement to do away with all their internal EC frontiers, while strengthening controls at external borders. Thus the Schengen Agreement, named after the Luxembourg village where it was signed, was concluded by Belgium, France, Germany, Luxembourg and the Netherlands. Two important areas covered by the agreement are as follows.

External borders.   The objective is to harmonise visa requirements and to issue visas which would be valid for all the Schengen countries. It is envisaged that a common list will be drawn up of about 100 countries whose citizens would require entry visas. A joint list of suspect individuals would also be compiled, and a watch kept out for them at external frontiers. Political asylum procedures would also be aligned.

Judicial matters.   Provision is made for close co-operation in cases involving irregularities in taxation, excise duties and customs payments, while sentences delivered in courts in one member state may be served in the country where the offender resides. Police forces will co-operate more closely, and will have the right of hot pursuit over borders, although France will not allow actual arrests to be made on its territory by foreign police forces. The Schengen Information Service, established in Strasbourg, will collate files on people and goods sought by the police in each member state. Safeguards were agreed concerning the confidentiality of these files. The Schengen countries will harmonise their laws on the ownership and use of weapons and will co-operate closely to combat drug-trafficking.

The agreement was due to come into force early in 1992, but there were repeated delays and it only got under way towards the end of 1994. By 1997, 13 of the 15 member states had agreed to join, together with Norway and Iceland from outside the EU. The only member state that was adamant not to give up its border controls was the UK, but Ireland also stayed out of the Schengen Agreement because it wished to maintain existing arrangements whereby Irish citizens do not face passport checks when entering the UK and vice versa. Under the Amsterdam treaty, concluded in June 1997, the Schengen Agreement has been incorporated in the EU, with the UK and Ireland opting out.

Cecchini report and its aftermath

The 1992 programme was launched in the belief that it would bring substantial economic benefits to the countries and people of the Community. In an attempt to quantify the benefits the commission appointed an expert committee presided over by Paolo Cecchini, a recently retired senior EC official. Its report, published in 1988 and based on a survey of 11,000 industrialists and econometric modelling, estimated that over 5–6 years the cumulative impact of the measures would add 4.5% to the GDP of the member states, reduce price levels by around 6%, create an extra 2m jobs and "put Europe on an upward trajectory of economic growth lasting into the next century". In October 1996 the commission issued a progress report, which showed that in the first three and a half years, GDP had risen by between 1.1% and 1.5%, investment was 2.7% higher and up to 900,000 extra jobs had been created. Inflation had also markedly been reduced, but there were several black spots largely owing to the failure of some member states adequately to enforce the single market legislation. This was especially true with regard to public procurement. The failure to agree on a common collection system for VAT meant that suppliers still had to face a mass of burdensome paperwork, and the lack of progress on tax harmonisation has undoubtedly acted as a restriction on trade.

In March 1997 Mario Monti, the commissioner responsible for the internal market, called for a big push to complete it by the planned beginning of economic and monetary union on January 1st 1999. Monti's objectives were not fully achieved, but a great deal of progress was made, notably in the fields of taxation, where harmful tax competition was successfully combatted, intellectual property and the prevention of piracy and counterfeiting, and financial services, with the adoption of an overall framework of legislative measures. All in all, the single market is substantially in place, with few gaps remaining.

The Lisbon summit

By 2000, it was clear there was much unfinished business left from the supposed completion of the single market in 1992, with the European Commission launching a staggering 1,500 lawsuits against EU governments for failing to respect single-market rules. The commission itself was focusing on practical measures to improve the functioning of the single market; it elicited a sympathetic reception from an alliance of member states. Tony Blair, the British prime minister, allied with the Portuguese and Belgian prime ministers, helped pushed through an agenda that aimed to tackle financial barriers, streamline labour markets and transform the EU into the most competitive region in the world.

The Lisbon "dotcom summit" of March 2000 set the target of making the EU the most competitive economic area in the world by 2010. The leaders agreed to create at least 20m jobs in a decade, matching the American job-creation and technology-harnessing record with practical steps. Chief among these is dismantling local telephone monopolies – opening the "local loop" to competition, to use the jargon – so that rival phone and cable operators can provide high-speed services directly to homes and install their equipment in the incumbent's local exchanges. The summit also called for EU-wide legislation establishing a legal framework for e-commerce, copyright, e-money and the distance selling of financial services. However, Lionel Jospin, the French prime minister, blocked plans to tackle transport and energy, saying that the liberalisation of transport and energy is irrelevant to the "new economy".

The leaders also agreed to flank the measures with the European Social Policy Agenda, which aims both to liberalise labour markets and to provide crucial guarantees for workers (see page 181). They agreed that the employment rate should be raised from 61% to 70% by 2010, and at the same time the number of women in employment should be increased from 51% to 60%. The legislation pushed through afterwards contained a consultation directive that gives unions a say in management decisions, including layoffs and company restructuring, full rights to temporary workers, and gender and race laws. Lisbon also launched the idea of a regular spring summit on economic and social affairs to establish a strategy for the year's economic and social policy, give a mandate to EU ministers in the various council formations and ensure that decisions are effectively implemented.

One of the principal decisions at Lisbon was to endorse the Financial Services Action Plan (FSAP), launched by the commission in 1999. This included some 42 measures, from binding regulations to voluntary codes of conduct, and covered the entire financial services field from securities and banking to insurance, and from financial institutions to retail customers. The main thrust of the grand project was to harmonise rules – eradicating differences that could hamper trade in the single market and country-of-origin control, where companies operating legally in their home market can use a financial services "passport" to ply their trade elsewhere in the EU. Lisbon set a tight timetable to ensure that the FSAP was implemented by 2005 and the Risk Capital Action Plan by 2003.

For capital markets, a specific blueprint emerged in February 2001 when Baron Alexandre Lamfalussy, a former Belgian central banker and president of the European Monetary Institute, issued a final report on regulatory reform for securities. The Lamfalussy report offered the prospect of microeconomic gains, in terms of more rational allocation of capital; greater liquidity and competition, making it easier and cheaper for companies to finance their business activities; higher net yields for consumers; and cheaper cross-border clearing and settlement. It also represented a halfway house between the desire of some EU governments to see Europe set up an American-style Securities and Exchanges Commission (SEC) and those hostile to the idea of creating a new central EU institution.

At their Stockholm summit in March 2001, EU leaders settled some of the problems when they agreed to try to legislate on securities through simpler framework laws, leaving the details to be filled in later by the new European Securities Committee (ESC) advised by a separate group of regulators. The main demand of the Lamfalussy report was the setting up of two new committees on securities – the ESC and a Committee of European Securities Regulators (CESR). The ESC is composed of high-level representatives of the EU member states and will advise the commission on issues relating to securities policy. At a later stage, when implementing powers are devolved to it through a co-decision procedure, it will also act as a regulatory committee. The CESR is an independent advisory body composed of representatives of the national public authorities competent in the field of securities. It will advise the commission on the technical details of securities legislation, and will also help enhance co-operation between supervisory authorities to ensure more consistent day-to-day implementation of EU legislation in the member states.

Progress on the FASP has been incremental on both the legislative and non-legislative fronts. The adoption of the money-laundering directive, agreement on the cross-border payments regulation, adoption of the European Company Statute, political agreement on the distance-marketing directive and the establishment of the committees for securities proposed in the Lamfalussy report are some of the breakthroughs.

The Fraud Prevention Action Plan will similarly help in increasing public confidence in cross-border payment systems and in the development of e-commerce – even if the many European stock exchanges that police their own markets fear they may lose this role to a single regulatory authority a step removed from the "crime". The EU is expected to continue to play a leading role in the Financial Action Task Force, a global organisation to counter money-laundering. Discussions are also under way on the cross-border transport of cash and the easing of bank secrecy laws so that the financial trails left by terrorists can be followed more efficiently.

One of the principal reforms, however, has emerged from outside the EU, in the Swiss financial centre of Basle. The Basle Committee of international financiers is pushing new rules – which must be incorporated in a new EU directive – to change the amounts of capital kept in reserve to cover bad debts, reflecting an evolution in the tools industry has at its disposal to measure the risk of loans. In December 2001 the committee announced a revised process for finalising its so-called Capital Accord on capital standards. This will incorporate an additional review of the overall impact of the new accord before publication of a third consultative document. For its part, the commission will reschedule publication of its own consultative package on capital standards in line with the Basle Committee's calendar.

But there are still challenges ahead. In its progress report on the FSAP in December 2001, the commission insisted there were urgent reasons to complete the project. The launch of euro notes and coins, the economic slowdown, turmoil in financial markets in the aftermath of September 11th and the fight against terrorism all require urgent measures to shield financial markets against instability, boost consumer confidence and stimulate growth. And it admitted that meeting the FSAP deadlines remained a concern. The proposals on pension funds, prospectuses, financial conglomerates and International Accounting Standards, and a new proposal on Takeover Bids following the European Parliament setback in July 2001, were measures that should be adopted by the end of 2002 if they were to be implemented by the agreed deadlines, the commission argued.

Note

1   Albert, M. and Ball, R.J., *Towards European Economic Recovery in the 1980s*, Report to the European Parliament, 1983.

17 Competition policy

There was little point in creating a customs union, the EC's founding fathers thought, if free competition between firms from different member states could be thwarted by cartels and restrictive agreements. Thus Articles 85 and 86 were inserted into the Treaty of Rome. The first outlaws deals between companies to fix prices, share out markets, limit production, technical development and investment, and other restrictive practices. The second bans "abuses of dominant position" by firms or groups of firms. Furthermore, Articles 92–94 forbid government subsidies that distort or threaten to distort competition.

The commission has wide powers

The power to prevent such abuses is in the hands of the commission, which can act without reference to the Council of Ministers, although its decisions may be, and often are, challenged before the Court of Justice by the companies concerned. The commission acts either on its own initiative or following complaints by member states, companies or individuals. Several hundred cases are dealt with each year involving firms with household names as well as more obscure ones – some in both categories having their headquarters outside the EU – and covering a range of industries and products.

In many instances cases are resolved by voluntary policy changes by the countries or companies concerned. A famous example was when IBM was accused, in 1980, of abusing a dominant position in the computer market by withholding information on new products and "bundling" its products (that is, selling several of them together in a package, so that customers must either take all of them or none). After spending a small fortune in lawyers' fees, IBM eventually backed down in 1984 and came to a voluntary agreement with the commission to modify its trading practices. In other cases the commission finds in favour of the accused or it finds the case proved, and orders policy changes or imposes fines, sometimes running to millions of ecus (there is no limit to such fines, although they may not amount to more than 10% of the actual sales affected by the abuse with which a company is charged).

The commission has wide powers of investigation. Its staff can visit companies without warning to demand access to documents and to take away photocopies as evidence. It then holds hearings with the companies concerned to discuss the case before giving its verdict. Convicted firms may appeal to the Court of Justice against both the conviction and the size of the fine, which has sometimes been reduced on appeal. The court has built up a large body of case law. EC competition law takes precedence over national law and is directly applicable in member states. Businesses and individuals believing themselves to be victims of infringements of EC competition rules can bring direct actions before national courts.

Any agreements that may fall foul of the Rome treaty provisions must be notified in advance to the commission. Companies may apply for a "negative clearance", which means that free competition is not threatened, or for an "exemption", which spares a restrictive agreement from the overall ban if substantial public benefits (as defined in the treaty) can be demonstrated. The commission is empowered to declare illegal and order the termination of an agreement or other unacceptable practices at any time.

The commission has banned the following types of agreements.

- **Market-sharing agreements.** For example, the quinine cartel (1969), which led the commission to impose its first fines; the sugar producers' cartel (1973); and the zinc and flat glass manufacturers' cartels (1984), which were fined a total of 4m ecus.
- **Price-fixing agreements.** For example, the dye-stuffs cartel (1969), which controlled 80% of the European market. It was the first case in which firms with head offices outside the Community were fined by the commission. In 1998 British Sugar and three other firms, controlling 90% of the UK market, were fined €50.2m for concluding price-fixing agreements for white granulated sugar. In July 2001, eight companies were fined a total of €218.8m for fixing the price and sharing the market for graphite electrodes. Also that year, eight firms were fined €855.2m for fixing prices and sales quotas of vitamins.
- **Exclusive purchase agreements.** These have been banned for a wide variety of products ranging from gramophone records to heating equipment.
- **Agreements on industrial and commercial property rights.** The exclusive use of patents, trademarks or works of art is not necessarily exempt from competition rules. In a 1982 case, involving maize seed, the Court of Justice ruled against the total territorial protection granted by a patent licensing contract.

◪ **Exclusive or selective distribution agreements.** For example, those, such as in the motor car trade, which seek to restrict parallel imports. Among companies which have been heavily fined, or otherwise penalised, for applying such agreements have been Ford, AEG-Telefunken and the Moët-Hennessy group. In 1998 Volkswagen, for example, was fined €102m for prohibiting its Italian dealers selling cars to foreign buyers.

Enforcement has become more rigorous

The commission was somewhat lax in applying the competition policy until 1977, since when there has been a substantial increase in its activity. This is largely because the individual commissioners holding the competition portfolio since that year have been far keener on exercising their powers than their predecessors. The commission has, however, continued to use its power to give industrial exemptions or en bloc waivers, where it judged that the threat to competition was small or non-existent and was outweighed by the likely public benefits. It has been particularly concerned not to hamper co-operation between small and medium-sized enterprises, and it has identified a number of types of agreement which it feels should escape the general ban. These are as follows.

◪ Exclusive representation contracts given to trade representatives.
◪ Small-scale agreements, based on turnover (not more than 50m ecus) and market share (not more than 5%).
◪ Subcontracting agreements.
◪ Information exchanges between companies, joint studies and joint use of plant.

The commission also takes account of the economic climate facing companies seeking individual exemptions. If there is a long-term downturn in demand for a product, it has been known to authorise firms to co-ordinate a run-down in overcapacity. This occurred, for example, in the synthetic fibre sector in 1984.

Jurisdiction over mergers ...

Until 1990 the commission had no specific power to prevent mergers, although it intervened on several occasions, using the general authority given to it under Articles 85 and 86 of the Rome treaty (now renumbered Articles 81 and 82 of the Nice treaty), when it believed that they posed a threat to effective competition in the Community. As long ago as 1973 it sought agreement on a regulation which would give it powers to vet cross-border mergers in advance, while leaving member states to police mergers within their own territories. The proposal was revived in 1987, and following detailed negotiations with the member states finally came into effect on September 21st 1990. It gave the commission jurisdiction over larger-scale company mergers and takeovers affecting more than one member state and exceeding certain thresholds. The main thresholds concerned were:

- 5 billion ecus for the worldwide turnover of the companies concerned; and
- 250m ecus for the individual turnover within the EC of at least two of the companies concerned, while no more than two-thirds of this turnover should be concentrated within a single member state.

Projected mergers which meet these criteria must be reported in advance to the commission, which will decide within one month whether there is a possibility that they would breach the competition rules of the EC. If no such possibility is discerned, the merger may go ahead; otherwise an investigation will be launched which must be completed within a further four months.

When worldwide turnover is less than 2 billion ecus the commission has no jurisdiction. It falls to a national anti-trust body, such as the Monopolies and Mergers Commission in the UK. Within the 2 billion–5 billion ecus bracket the national authorities will be responsible, unless they ask the European Commission to carry out an investigation on their behalf. The commission regarded the thresholds as being too low, and gave notice that it would propose before 1993 that the main threshold should be lowered from 5 billion ecus to 2 billion ecus.

In the event, the commission reported in July 1993 on the working of the merger control regulation and recommended that the thresholds should be reviewed by 1996. In the first two and a half years of operation it had received 164 formal notifications of proposed mergers, of which 17 cases fell outside the scope of the regulation. Of the other 147 cases, 131 (nearly 90%) were cleared within the initial one-month deadline, and enquiries were opened concerning the remaining 16. Of these, seven were later approved conditionally, two without condition and five were withdrawn. In only one case, the proposed acquisition in 1991 of the Canadian aircraft manufacturer De Havilland by a Franco-Italian consortium, Aérospatiale-Alenia, was the merger prohibited.

Subsequently, the number of notifications of mergers substantially increased. In 1996 there were 131, on which 125 final decisions were taken. In three cases mergers were prohibited, as being incompatible with the common market, and in three others the commission made the proposed concentration subject to conditions. Despite the commission's recommendations no review of the thresholds was undertaken in 1996 and they remain as originally fixed. In 1997 the number of notifications again increased, to 172, and 135 final decisions were adopted. One of these was Boeing's acquisition of the McDonnell Douglas Corporation, which came under the commission's jurisdiction because of the extensive European operations of the two aircraft companies. The merger was eventually approved, but only after Boeing had greatly modified its original proposal and had given commitments concerning several specific elements, including the cessation of existing and future exclusive supply deals, the 'ring-fencing' of McDonnell's commercial aircraft activities and the licensing of patents to other jet aircraft manufacturers.

In 1998 there was a further increase in merger activity, with 225 notifications and 238 final decisions. A merger between pharmaceuticals companies Hoffmann-La Roche and Boehringer Mannheim was approved, subject to La Roche divesting itself of its clinical chemistry diagnostics business. After an investigation, a merger between two of the Big Six accounting firms, Price Waterhouse and Coopers & Lybrand, was also given the go-ahead, but two separate mergers involving German firms, Bertelsmann and Deutsche Telekom, were prohibited because they would have created monopolies or dominant positions in the pay-television sector.

The numbers kept rising, and by 2001, the commission had received 335 notifications and adopted 322 final decisions. The most controversial decision of the year – like McDonnell Douglas/Boeing – concerned two American companies and the avionics sector: General Electric's (GE) planned takeover of Honeywell. The case also exposed a difference in cultures, with the EU's competition policy geared towards preventing dominant positions and the far more laissez-faire American antitrust rules. The €47 billion merger was cleared easily enough in the United States, and Jack Welch, GE's ebullient chairman, assumed the EU decision would be a mere formality. But the commission thought otherwise, saying the bid would create an unhealthily dominant aerospace giant, giving it the leverage to eliminate competition. It was the first time the commission had killed off a merger between two American companies that had already been approved in the United States.

Neither the Rome nor the Paris treaty makes any distinction between private and publicly owned firms, so that neither nationalisation nor privatisation proposals, in themselves, would conflict with them. State-owned concerns, however, must respect the EC's competition law in the same way as any privately owned company. In 1980 a directive was adopted providing for financial "transparency" in dealings between member states and state-owned enterprises.

... and government subsidies

Government subsidies to either publicly owned or private firms are normally banned if they distort or threaten to distort competition. Some types of aid are exempt from control, including: special help at times of natural disasters; aid to depressed regions; and aid to promote new economic activities.

Member states are supposed to notify the commission of all aid planned, and it decides whether the aid can be exempted from the treaty rules. It has the power to order the repayment of unauthorised aid and may impose fines on member states that break the rules. Two examples occurred during 1988, when Sir Leon Brittan, the competition commissioner, required both the French and the UK governments to secure repayment of illegal state aids that they had provided. The French government reluctantly agreed to reclaim FFr6 billion (about £600m) paid to Renault, which had then failed to fulfil the conditions the commission had attached to the project. The UK government was also forced to seek repayment of the secret "sweeteners", worth £44m, that it had paid to British Aerospace as an inducement to buy the Rover car company.

During the 1970s and early 1980s the commission approved guidelines for state aid to industries that were especially hard hit by the recession. It insisted that such aid must be exceptional, limited in duration and geared directly to the objective of restoring long-term viability by reducing capacity in struggling sectors. In four industries most severely affected – shipbuilding, textiles, synthetic fibres and steel (see Chapter 25) – special provisions were made. Most aid awards are made under schemes that were approved many years ago, so in 1990 the commission embarked upon a review of all systems of aid existing in the member states. This review, which was carried out under Article 93 (1) of the Rome treaty (now renumbered Article 88 (1) of the Nice treaty), should enable changes in the economic and industrial situation owing to the completion of the internal market to be taken into account. In principle, the commission believes that all categories of state aid should be kept to a minimum, and as it seeks to enforce the rules more rigorously they are increasingly coming into conflict with national governments under political pressure to maintain employment opportunities for their own citizens. In 1998 the commission opened proceedings concerning 100 cases of state aid, which it believed might be in breach of Article 93 (2) of the Rome treaty (now Article 88 (2) of the Nice treaty), and in 40 cases ruled that they should not go ahead.

In July 2001, the European Parliament split 273–273 on plans to push through a new directive establishing a cross-border code for company takeovers in Europe. Under parliamentary rules, the measure was deemed to have failed. The vote seemed to end 12 years of work on the takeover directive, designed to make it harder for European corporate bosses to ward off a hostile bid without first consulting shareholders (a mere 2% of takeovers in Europe are hostile). However, the European Commission has since set up an expert group to advise it on a new takeover law it hopes to unveil before the end of 2002.

18 Economic and financial policy

Lack of co-ordination in economic policy ...

Although Article 103 of the Rome treaty requires member states to determine their economic policies in consultation with each other, as yet little co-ordination has been achieved. In so far as most governments followed rather similar policies in the 1970s and 1980s, it was because they were reacting to worldwide economic pressures rather than a result of joint planning of their overall strategies. Thus despite regular discussions between ministers, there was no common European policy on pooling energy supplies, containing inflation or reducing unemployment. The annual economic reports produced by the commission gave advice to national governments, but were by no means binding upon them.

Broad discussions do take place between the heads of government at meetings of the European Council, when "the economic and social situation in the world and in the Community" is invariably an item on the agenda. More detailed exchanges take place between economic and finance ministers, who meet approximately every two months in Ecofin[1] councils, and sometimes more frequently in the Monetary and Economic Policy committees. The governors of the central banks of the member states also meet regularly in their own consultative committee. National leaders are thus well informed about each other's views and policies, and no doubt take them into account to some extent, but each government remains firmly in charge of its own economic policy.

... means EU element is ancillary

Nor is the EU's budget sufficiently large to have a significant macroeconomic effect on the West European economy in a manner comparable with the way in which national budgets point their economies in an expansionist or deflationary direction. In so far as there is an EU element in the economic policy of member states, it is undoubtedly an ancillary one, and seems likely to remain so for the foreseeable future.

Loans made by EC institutions

There are two areas, however, where the EC undoubtedly plays a significant part. One is in raising loans on behalf of member states, the other in regulating fluctuations in exchange rates. During 1996, for example, EC institutions made well over 23 billion ecus available, principally through the following channels.

- The European Investment Bank (see Chapter 11) lent some 21 billion ecus within the Union. Nearly three-quarters went towards developing the economy of the less prosperous regions. Other projects which received EIB assistance included energy saving, the modernisation and redevelopment of industry, new technologies and environmental protection. In addition, the EIB lent some 2.5 billion ecus to countries outside the Union, particularly in Central and Eastern Europe and the Mediterranean region.
- The European Coal and Steel Community lent approximately 280 million ecus, mainly for productive investment in the coal and steel industries. In addition, it financed projects which aim to improve the marketing and transport of coal and steel, and schemes to bring new industries to coal and steel areas. It also financed the building or modernisation of workers' homes.
- Euratom, which has a loan facility of 4 billion ecus mainly for investments in the nuclear energy and nuclear fuels sectors, has made no new loans since 1992 because of the unfavourable situation in the industry.
- The Edinburgh Growth Initiative, agreed at the December 1992 Edinburgh summit, under which a new temporary lending facility of 5 billion ecus was established within the EIB, while a European Investment Fund (EIF) was created with a capital of 2 billion ecus, which it was hoped would cover guarantees between 10 billion and 16 billion ecus. By the end of 1996 projects totalling 2.3 billion ecus had been approved. The EIF targets its activities on large infrastructure projects associated with trans-European networks (TENs) and on small and medium-sized enterprises (SMEs).

There is also a facility available for short-term loans to member states in temporary balance of payments difficulties. In 1993, 8 billion ecus was lent, all to Italy. Since then no country has used this facility, and by 1998 the EIB was responsible for no less than 98.6% of the total of €29.95 billion lent by EU institutions.

The European Monetary System

The European Monetary System (EMS) was devised primarily as a means of stabilising currency fluctuations within the EC, following the breakdown in the early 1970s of the fixed-rate exchange system established by the 1944 Bretton Woods agreement. The first attempt, in 1972, to regulate European currencies within the so-called "snake", with permitted fluctuations of +/-2.25%, was largely unsuccessful. Only West Germany, Denmark and the Benelux countries were able to remain within these limits. The EMS, which was originally proposed by Roy Jenkins in October 1977, was a more ambitious project, in which the exchange rate mechanism (ERM) was bolstered by various financial solidarity mechanisms and a common currency unit (the ecu).

Under the ERM each participating currency has a central rate against the ecu. Only eight currencies[2] participated initially, the UK "temporarily" staying out when the system was inaugurated in March 1979. The three later entrants to the EC – Greece, Spain and Portugal – felt that they were not yet ready to join. Spain eventually joined in June 1989 and the UK followed suit in October 1990, an earlier decision having consistently been blocked by Mrs Thatcher, who only agreed to the move a month or so before she left office. Portugal joined in April 1992, leaving Greece as the odd man out. The central rate for each currency can be "realigned" if necessary by mutual agreement of the participating countries. From the ecu central rate, bilateral central rates are calculated for each currency against each of the other participants. Each currency is allowed to fluctuate by +/-2.25% around these central rates, or by +/-6% in the case of the pound and the peseta.

If a currency reaches its "floor" or "ceiling" rate, the central banks are obliged to intervene in the foreign-exchange markets to maintain it within the agreed limits. In practice, this means selling the currency which has reached its ceiling rate and buying the one that is at its floor. When this occurs, various credit mechanisms have been created within the EMS to provide short-term support for countries in difficulties. If a currency stays at its floor or ceiling over a lengthy period, or appears likely to do so, it is a clear sign that it should be realigned. When this happens the finance ministers of the EU meet, normally over a weekend in Brussels, to approve a realignment. This does not normally take the form of a simple up or down revaluation for a particular currency, but the opportunity is taken to make a number of marginal adjustments, in both directions, to other currencies as well. The consequence has been that the sudden, often competitive devaluations of the past have been avoided, and the currencies within the system have fluctuated much less violently than others (including the pound) which have not been included.

The value of the EMS was diminished, to some extent, by the fact that the UK held aloof for so long from bringing the pound into the ERM, a perverse decision which most economists feel did more harm to the UK than to the EC. Nevertheless, even with the UK "quarter in, three-quarters out", as the former UK permanent representative, Sir Michael Butler, put it,[3] the EMS brought benefits beyond that of currency stabilisation. It helped to bring about a greater convergence in the economies of the member states, and the disciplines built into the system were credited with playing a part in the marked reduction in inflation in the early 1980s in all the participating states. On average, inflation fell from 12% in 1980 to 5% in 1985, and the average divergence between countries went down from 6.2% to 2.8%. Other countries outside the EC recognised the value of the ERM in providing tighter guidelines for their own economic policies. Three Nordic countries – Finland, Norway and Sweden – each tied their own currencies to the ecu in 1990 or early 1991.

In 1992 the ERM came under great strain, partly because of the recession and partly because the removal of financial controls meant that vast amounts of currency changed hands each day, opening the system to manipulation by speculators. The situation was exacerbated by the fact that the pound had been brought into the ERM at an unrealistically high exchange rate and the UK government stubbornly resisted pressure to agree to an orderly devaluation. Consequently, in September 1992 massive speculative movements led to the forced devaluation of several currencies, and the pound and the lira were withdrawn from the ERM altogether and allowed to float. A similar speculative attack in July 1993 was fended off by a decision to widen temporarily the fluctuation margin within the ERM to 15% either side of the bilateral central rates. In practice, the currencies did not fluctuate much beyond the previous more narrow limits, which suggests that, unlike the previous year, none of the currencies were seriously over- or under-valued. The mechanism remained in operation, but without the participation of the UK, Italy and Greece. Italy rejoined the ERM in November 1996, and Greece in March 1998, leaving the UK and Sweden outside. The ERM lost much of its significance on December 31st 1998, when the exchange rates of the 11 countries joining the euro were irrevocably fixed (see page 137), leaving only the Greek drachma and the Danish krona to fluctuate within agreed bands.

The ecu

The ecu (European currency unit)[4] has had several other functions besides acting as a marker for the national currencies of the EC. It took the place of the former EUA (European Unit of Account), which was a purely book-keeping measurement for establishing the relative value of payments into and out of the EC accounts. But the ecu (which had the advantage of euphony, and of having the same name as a famous pre-revolutionary French coin) had the backing of a large reserve fund, the European Monetary Co-operation Fund (EMCF), into which the member states were required to pay 20% of their gold reserves and 20% of their dollar reserves.

Consequently, there was a great deal of international confidence in the ecu, which was used for many dealings quite unrelated to the funds of the EU (by 1986 it was already the third most common currency used for international bond issues, after the dollar and the Deutschemark). More and more companies and individuals used the ecu for denominating their bank deposits and travellers' cheques, or for commercial invoices and payments. This was quite an achievement for a currency which did not exist, in so far as neither coins nor banknotes were normally issued in ecus.[5] Its utility for private and commercial financial transactions lay in the fact that its value was unlikely to fluctuate by as much as any individual national currency.

Economic and monetary union

Although anything approaching total convergence (or "cohesion" as it is now known in Eurojargon) between the national economies is unlikely to come about for many years – in the absence of massive financial transfers from north to south within the Union – the institution of the EMS has proved to be at least a step on the way. It was undoubtedly the most significant move towards the long-term objective of an economic and monetary union (EMU) that the EC had made until June 1988, when the Hanover summit determined that the time had arrived to give a new impetus in this direction. It commissioned a report by a committee of European central bankers and some independent monetary experts, under the chairmanship of Jacques Delors, the commission's president, into how EMU might be obtained. The Delors committee reported in April 1989, proposing a three-stage process towards union, but without attaching any timetable.

Stage one.   Co-operation and co-ordination in the economic and monetary fields were to be improved. This would lead, among other things, to a strengthening of the EMS, the role of the ecu and the terms of reference of the Committee of Central Bank Governors. The introduction of a multilateral surveillance procedure would pave the way for more effective co-ordination and for closer convergence of national economic policies and performances.

Stage two. This could not begin until a new treaty (or amendments to the Rome treaty) had been agreed, laying down the basic institutional and operational rules necessary for the realisation of EMU. It would consist of consolidating and assessing the measures taken under the 1992 programme (see Chapter 16) and would be a sort of running-in period for the new procedures. During this transitional period a start could be made on gradually transferring decision-making powers from national to Community level. The most important feature of stage two could be the creation of a federal-type European System of Central Banks (ESCB or EuroFed) which, in the light of experience, would become increasingly independent as regards monetary policies and policies on exchange-market intervention. However, the national central banks would still retain ultimate responsibility for decision-making.

Stage three. Commencing with the move to irrevocably locked exchange rates and the transfer of responsibilities provided for in the new treaty, this stage would eventually lead to the adoption of a single currency.

The general approach of the Delors committee was acceptable to 11 of the then 12 member states, but the UK government, under Mrs Thatcher's leadership, reacted coolly and was particularly hostile to the concept of a single currency, even though authoritative studies showed that this would bring major economic benefits, estimated at 15 billion ecus per year, or 0.4% of GDP.[6] Although it was agreeable to stage one of the process beginning on July 1st 1990, it emphatically reserved its position regarding stages two and three.

Despite Mrs Thatcher's objections, the EC heads of government decided at the Strasbourg summit in December 1989 that the requisite majority existed to convene an inter-governmental conference (IGC) to decide on the treaty changes which stages two and three would necessitate. It was subsequently agreed that two IGCs, one on EMU and one on political union, should be held, both convening in Rome in December

1990 and completing their work in time to report to the Maastricht summit, scheduled for December 1991.

Before then, the first Rome summit of October 1990 agreed – against Mrs Thatcher's strong objections – that stage two of EMU, with the creation of the EuroFed, would begin on January 1st 1994. It was her intemperate reaction to this decision which set off the chain of events leading to her resignation a month later. The UK government agreed to take part in the two IGCs, and its attitude became a great deal more conciliatory following Mrs Thatcher's departure. Within the IGC on EMU, it put forward a plan for a 13th currency, or "hard ecu", which would take the place of the single currency advocated by the Delors report. Although aspects of this proposal were sympathetically received by some other member states the prevailing view was that a single currency was necessary if the main benefits of EMU were to be obtained. It was anticipated that John Major, who had launched the "hard ecu" proposal when he was still chancellor of the exchequer, would eventually withdraw it and would agree to a compromise under which treaty changes permitting a single currency would be accepted, but that the UK parliament would retain the right to decide if and when this currency would replace the pound.

Treaty on European Union

This is effectively what was decided at the Maastricht summit in December 1991, when the Treaty on European Union was agreed. The treaty included four chapters relevant to the creation of EMU: those on economic policy, monetary policy, institutions and trans-national provisions. The chapter on economic policy requires member states to conduct their economic policy in such a way as to achieve the objectives of EMU and "in accordance with the principle of an open market economy with free competition". Member states are to regard their economic policies as a matter of common concern and are to co-ordinate them through the Ecofin Council. The broad guidelines of economic policy are to be defined by the European Council (that is, by EU summit meetings) and are then to be adopted within the Ecofin Council by qualified majority vote.

A multilateral surveillance procedure had already been instituted under which, to ensure closer co-ordination and sustained convergence in the economic performance of member states, the Ecofin Council, on the basis of reports submitted by the commission, monitors economic developments in each member state. Where it considers that economic policies are not consistent with the broad guidelines agreed, the council is entitled, by qualified majority vote, to make policy recommendations to a member state which it may choose to make public. If, in the future, a member state persists in applying policies inconsistent with the guidelines, and in particular if it persists in incurring excessive budget deficits, it may lay itself open to a range of sanctions culminating in a freeze on lending from EC institutions, a requirement to make non-interest bearing deposits and, ultimately, the imposition of "fines of an appropriate size". The treaty makes clear that there is no question of the EC "bailing out" a member state that gets into financial difficulties, although financial assistance may be available in the event of "natural disasters" or other problems not caused by the improvidence of the member state concerned.

On monetary policy, it is laid down that the primary objective "shall be to maintain price stability", that is, a minimal level of inflation. For this purpose a European System of Central Banks (ECSB) was to be created, made up of the national central banks (NCBs) of the member states, all of which should become independent of their national governments, and a new European Central Bank (ECB), to be established at the beginning of the third stage of EMU.

The treaty confirmed that the second stage of EMU would commence on January 1st 1994, by which date all member states were expected to have implemented measures to provide for the free movement of capital, and to have adopted multi-annual programmes to ensure lasting convergence necessary for EMU, in particular with regard to price stability and sound public finances. At the beginning of stage two, the European Monetary Institute (EMI) was set up as the forerunner of the ECB. Its members were the various national banks, and it replaced the Committee of Governors and the European Monetary Co-operation Fund, which ceased to exist. Its task was to prepare the way for stage three and to strengthen co-operation between the NCBs, on whose behalf it may hold monetary and foreign exchange reserves.

The EMI, together with the commission, was to report to the Ecofin Council on the progress of member states in making their national legislation compatible with EMU, and provide information on their record concerning price stability, budget deficits, exchange rates, convergence indicators and long-term interest rates. The council was then to assess which member states fulfilled the four conditions for adoption of a single currency, which were defined in a protocol to the treaty:

◪ Its inflation should, over the previous year, not have exceeded by more than 1.5% that achieved by an average of the three best performing states.

◪ Its currency had been within the narrow band of the ERM for at least the preceding two years and had not been devalued during that period.

◪ Its long-term interest rates had not exceeded by more than 2% over the preceding year the average of the three best-performing states so far as price stability is concerned.

◪ It was not subject to a decision of the council that it was running an excessive budget deficit.

An excessive deficit was defined in the protocol as one exceeding 3% of GDP in the annual budget, or an accumulated government debt exceeding 60% of GDP. Yet these criteria were hedged with qualifications in the Maastricht treaty itself, which provided for exceptions for countries which had "reached a level that comes close" to the 3% annual deficit level or if the excess was a result of "only exceptional and temporary" factors. Similarly, with regard to the accumulated deficit, which for several member states, notably Belgium and Italy, was far above the 60% level, the treaty referred only to the necessity for the deficit to be "sufficiently diminishing and approaching the reference value at a satisfactory pace". The inference was that countries whose economies were generally in a good shape and were over-performing on the other criteria would not be excluded from EMU if they failed to meet the deficit targets exactly.

The Maastricht treaty provided that if by 1996 the European Council decided that a majority of member states met the four conditions, the third stage should begin in 1997; if not it would definitely commence on January 1st 1999. It soon became clear that the 1997 starting date was unrealistic, and in 1995 the member states agreed that 1999 would be the beginning of the final stage.

Before July 1st 1998 the Ecofin Council would decide which member states fulfil the conditions for adoption of a single currency. A special protocol to the treaty gave the UK the right to opt out, even if it fulfilled these conditions. It stipulated that the UK should not be obliged to enter the third stage without a separate decision to do so by its government and Parliament. A similar dispensation was subsequently granted to Denmark.

At the beginning of the third stage the EMI was replaced by the ECB, whose executive board was appointed by the member states that were ready to participate in a single currency. The Ecofin Council, acting by unanimity of the participating states, was to adopt the conversion rates at which their currencies would be irrevocably fixed, at which rate the ecu was to be substituted for their currencies and become a currency in its own right.

The ECB, in conjunction with the NCBs with which it would make up the ESCB, was to be responsible for managing the new currency, but the Maastricht treaty stipulates that:

> Member states may issue coins subject to ECB approval of the volume of the issue. The council may, acting by a qualified majority on a proposal from the commission and after consulting the ECB and in co-operation with the European Parliament, adopt measures to harmonise the denominations and technical specifications of all circulation coins to the extent necessary to permit a smooth circulation of coins within the Community.

The Madrid summit in December 1995 decided that the new monetary unit should be called the euro, and that it should be exchangeable on a one-to-one basis with the ecu. It would be subdivided into 100 cents. A competition was launched in February 1996 for the design of banknotes denominated in euros, and the winning entries were displayed at the Dublin summit in December 1996. There will be notes for 5, 10, 20, 50, 100, 200 and 500 euros, and coins for 1, 2, 5, 10 and 50 cents and for 1 and 2 euros. Although many banking transactions were to be conducted in euros from 1999 onwards, the coins and notes will not go into circulation until the end of 2001 or the beginning of 2002. This is because the printing and minting of the currency is an enormous operation: replacements will be needed for some 12 billion banknotes and 70 billion coins currently circulating in the Union. There will be a period of no more than two months during which both the old and new currencies are circulating before the old currency ceases to be legal tender.

The final launch of EMU

In the spring of 1998 the commission and the EMI examined the record of the 15 member states, and reported that 11 of them had succeeded in meeting the criteria set out in the Maastricht treaty and were thus eligible to join stage three of EMU on the opening date of January 1st 1999. They were Austria, Belgium, Finland, France, Germany, Ireland, Italy, Luxembourg, the Netherlands, Portugal and Spain. Two other states – the UK and Denmark – had also met the criteria, but were exercising their right to opt out, at least at the outset of stage three. Sweden had met the economic criteria but had not taken steps to ensure the independence of its central bank, which was also a requirement for EMU membership. Greece had failed to meet the criteria, although it had made progress in this direction.

These recommendations were accepted at a special meeting of the European Council held in Brussels on May 1st–2nd 1998. So 11 countries adopted a common currency on January 1st 1999. Greece was able to join two years later, on January 1st 2001. The UK government took a more cautious stance, reiterating that it was in principle in favour of joining, but that it was unlikely to hold the referendum to which it was committed until after the next general election, due by June 2002 at the latest. Meanwhile, the Conservative opposition, under its leader, William Hague, reaffirmed its hostility and vowed not to consider membership for another ten years, if at all. The probability is that the Labour government, re-elected in 2001, will seek to join, but only if it can succeed in winning a popular referendum, which now seems likely to be held in the first half of 2003. Most observers believe that both Denmark and Sweden would follow the UK into the single currency, unless they had already decided to do so beforehand.

The May 1998 summit also proceeded to appoint the first president, and five vice-presidents, of the ECB. The president was Wim Duisenberg, a former Dutch finance minister and central bank governor, who had been head of the EMI since 1996. Fourteen of the 15 heads of government had wanted to appoint him for the full eight-year term specified by the Maastricht treaty, but this was stubbornly resisted by Jacques Chirac, the French president, who argued in vain for the appointment of Jean-Claude Trichet, head of the French central bank. Eventually, a compromise was reached, under which Duisenberg, although nominally appointed for a term of eight years, agreed to stand down during the term and make way for Trichet, who would then serve for a full eight years. This was widely regarded as an unfortunate decision, and Duisenberg made it clear that he had only reluctantly agreed to it, and that he himself would determine the timing of his departure, rather than accept the French interpretation that he would bow out after four years. On December 31st 1998 the Ecofin Council met and agreed the irrevocably fixed rates of the participating currencies against the euro (see Table 14).

Table 14 **Conversion rates for the euro**

€1 =	13.7603	Austrian schillings
	40.3399	Belgian francs
	40.3399	Luxembourg francs
	1.95583	German marks
	166.386	Spanish pesetas
	5.94573	Finnish markkaa
	6.55957	French francs
	0.787564	Irish pounds
	1,936.27	Italian lire
	2.20371	Dutch guilders
	200.482	Portuguese escudos
	340.750	Greek drachma

Euro launch

The three years between EMU and the launch of the physical currency were remarkably uneventful. The value of the new currency fell steadily against the dollar in the initial weeks, but then stabilised at around 85 cents. The euro was used in company accounts and traded in financial markets and on foreign exchanges, although many firms, retailers and consumers continued to do business in national currencies. There were regular calls on Duisenberg to cut interest rates to revive the EU's economy, but he usually ignored them. The finance ministers of the euro-zone met regularly as the Eurogroup, one day before the Ecofin Council.

The run-up to the euro's launch – an unprecedented logistical and administrative task – was meticulously planned. On December 15th, banks and post offices in the euro-zone were given "starter packs" of euro coins of every denomination to sell to the curious public. On December 31st, most banks had replaced national notes with euros in their cash machines. Around 56 billion coins and 13 billion notes had been produced by then. By January 4th, 99% of cash machines had been switched over to euros. Doomsday scenarios of robberies, a flood of counterfeit notes and chaos as shops and customers struggled to adapt

137

to the new currency failed to materialise, as a range of information campaigns stirred retailers and the general public into awareness. By January 15th, more than 90% of cash payments were being made in euros. All euro-zone countries had a transitional period where both the euro and the national currencies were legal tender, with dual pricing, although change was always given in euros. This period varied in length, with the Netherlands, Ireland and France having earlier cut-off points, but by March 1st 2002 all national currencies were no longer legal tender in the euro-zone.

The notes were the same throughout the euro-zone, but the eight different coins had national faces on one side. As well as the 12 euro-zone countries, Monaco, San Marino and the Vatican had "national" coins. Many non-EU countries, such as Macedonia, announced that they would adopt the euro, although they were, naturally, not part of the decision-making process for the new currency.

After much speculation, Duisenberg announced he would not complete his eight years as ECB president, and would step down in July 2003. His initial heir apparent, Trichet, had since become embroiled in a scandal concerning his role in the failure of Crédit Lyonnais a decade earlier, but even if he is passed over, Duisenberg's successor will almost certainly be a Frenchman.

Notes

1 The accepted abbreviation for Economic and Financial Affairs Council.
2 Including the Luxembourg franc, which is at parity with the Belgian franc.
3 Michael Butler, *op. cit.*, page 69.
4 The value of the ecu was determined by a weighted "basket" of currencies of the member states. The basket ceased to exist in 1999, when the ecu was replaced – on a one-to-one basis – by the new single currency, the euro.
5 But Belgium issued 5 ecu and 50 ecu coins in 1987, in silver and gold, to commemorate the 30th anniversary of the Rome treaty. They are legal tender in Belgium.
6 See Michael Emerson and Christopher Huhne, *The ECU Report*, Pan Books, London, 1991.

19 Taxation

Taxation has been regarded from the outset as a subject reserved to the sovereignty of the member states, except in so far as its incidence may distort competition within the Union or discriminate against nationals of other EU countries. Accordingly, except on such matters as the avoidance of double taxation, EC decisions on tax matters have been concerned almost exclusively with indirect taxation: customs duties on the one hand, and VAT and excise duties on the other. Virtually every decision relating to taxation requires unanimous agreement in the Council of Ministers, and this requirement was not relaxed in the Single European Act, which substantially widened the range of decisions subject to qualified majority vote. The incidence and range of taxation varies enormously within the Union, with Sweden and Denmark being the highest taxed countries and Greece and Ireland the lowest (see Figure 8 on the next page).

General application of VAT

The main taxation change which has occurred has been the general application of value-added tax (VAT), replacing a variety of different indirect taxes in the member states. Two directives adopted in 1967 provided for those countries not already applying VAT to introduce it within a specific timetable, and new applicant countries have also been required to change their tax systems accordingly. Spain agreed to apply VAT from its entry in 1986, Greece applied it in 1987 and Portugal brought its system into line by 1989. Austria, Finland and Sweden all introduced VAT before joining the EU in 1995. VAT commended itself to the Community because of its economic neutrality. At each stage in the making or marketing of a product, the tax paid at the preceding stage is deducted from that paid by the vendor. In this way the tax remains proportionate to the value of the goods and services, no matter how many transactions they have been through.

The member states reached agreement in 1977 on a common basis for assessing VAT, although it was subject to many exceptions. It was, however, enough to enable the EC to collect on this basis part of its "own resources", subject to a maximum rate of 1%, raised from 1986 to 1.4%. The member states continued to differ in the level at which VAT was charged, the number of different rates and the goods and services that were excluded or subject to a zero rate.

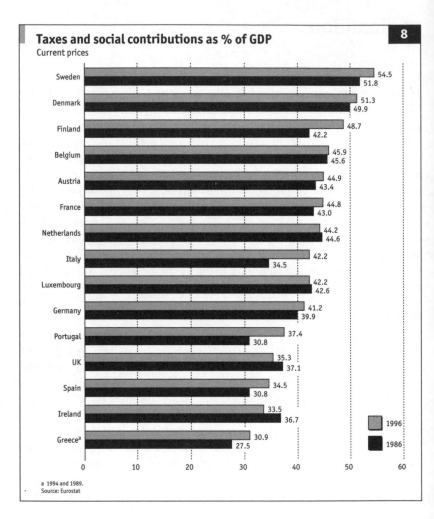

Taxes and social contributions as % of GDP
Current prices

Country	1996	1986
Sweden	54.5	51.8
Denmark	51.3	49.9
Finland	48.7	42.2
Belgium	45.9	45.6
Austria	44.9	43.4
France	44.8	43.0
Netherlands	44.2	44.6
Italy	42.2	34.5
Luxembourg	42.2	42.6
Germany	41.2	39.9
Portugal	37.4	30.8
UK	35.3	37.1
Spain	34.5	30.8
Ireland	33.5	36.7
Greece[a]	30.9	27.5

a 1994 and 1989.
Source: Eurostat

Excise duty

The other form of indirect taxation which member states have continued to levy is excise duty on certain specific products, such as alcoholic drinks, manufactured tobacco and fuels. Despite numerous proposals by the commission, the only common regulations adopted before July 1991 related to the structure of duty on cigarettes. Acting on complaints from the commission, however, the Court of Justice has delivered judgments aimed at preventing member states favouring home-produced beers, wines or spirits to the detriment of imported products, and which have led to several of them modifying their range of duties.

The commission also established a common basis for duty-free allowances for travellers between member states. In principle, duty-free allowances should have been abolished from January 1st 1993 when the EU's internal market was completed. It was decided, however, that until June 30th 1999 duty-free sales could continue at airports, on planes and on ferries travelling from one member state to another. Despite intense lobbying by the duty-free industry, largely financed by tobacco and alcoholic drinks manufacturers, the Council of Ministers refused to reverse this decision in June 1999, and duty-free sales for travellers within the EU came to an end on the due date.

Harmonisation of indirect tax rates

A strong impetus to harmonising indirect tax rates was given by the adoption in 1985 of a specific target for completing the Community's internal market. Lord Cockfield argued strongly when presenting his white paper in June 1985 (see pages 112–3) that these rates would have to be "approximated" if the objective of removing all internal frontier controls was to be achieved. By approximation he meant bringing them so closely together that no significant distortion of trade was likely to be produced. He took as his model the United States, where the different states levy varying rates of sales tax, but the difference between them is seldom great enough to attract much cross-border trade merely for the benefit of paying a lower rate of tax. In July 1987 the commission produced its proposals, which it said should be implemented by member states no later than December 31st 1992.

VAT. Two rate bands were proposed: a standard rate of 14–20%, and a reduced rate "for items of basic necessity" of 4–9%. The items suggested for this reduced rate were foodstuffs, energy for heating and lighting, water, pharmaceuticals, books, newspapers and periodicals, and passenger transport. Member states would be free to fix their national rates at any point between these 5–6 percentage point margins. "However," said Lord Cockfield in introducing the proposals, "in view of the inclusion of certain sensitive sectors, such as the cultural sector, the commission recommends that member states fix the applicable rate in the lower half of the band for the reduced rate."

Excise duty. The commission proposed a complete harmonisation, arguing that since VAT was applied in addition to excise duties, it would widen the effective range of the VAT bands even further if a similar degree of flexibility was allowed. It therefore specified a precise amount of duty for all products attracting excise duty.

Commission's proposals intended to cause least disruption ...

The commission's proposals, which needed the unanimous agreement of the Council of Ministers after it received the opinion of the European Parliament, were drawn up with the intention of causing the minimum possible disturbance to member states. Although all countries would need to make some adjustments, the commission considered that three member states (Belgium, Italy and the Netherlands) would be able to continue to obtain the same level of total tax revenue from the VAT and excise-duty rates proposed as they currently received. One member state (France) would suffer a slight budgetary loss, while three member states (Germany, Greece and the UK) would obtain small or moderate increases in budgetary receipts. Two member states (Denmark and Ireland) would suffer pronounced budgetary losses, while the other member states (Luxembourg, Spain and Portugal) would obtain substantial increases in budgetary receipts.[1]

Apart from Denmark and Ireland, which would have to compensate for "pronounced budgetary losses", the country which would have had the greatest difficulty as a result of these proposals is undoubtedly the UK, which currently levies a zero rate on many items including food, children's clothing and books (as does Ireland). In the 1987 election campaign Margaret Thatcher said that she would "veto" any attempt to prevent zero-rating being applied in the UK in the future.

... but agreement took time

Although the Cockfield proposals contained no provision for the continuation of zero-rating, they did recognise that several member states were likely to be faced with considerable "political, social or budgetary" difficulties in implementing the proposals in full. The commission therefore invited the member states, after having studied the difficulties involved, to make proposals for "derogations" (exceptions to directives or regulations which may, in principle, be only temporary, but which in practice may continue indefinitely) to allow them not to apply certain parts of the proposals.

It took four years, and a great deal of horse-trading, for the member states to reach any sort of agreement on the Cockfield proposals. In June 1991 a political agreement was reached in the Council of Ministers that they should be adopted, although in a greatly amended and watered-down form.

Table 15 **Convergence of VAT rates, 1987 and 1997**

	1987		1997	
	Maximum	*Standard*	*Maximum*	*Standard*
Austria	–	–	20	20
Belgium	33	19	21	21
Denmark	22	22	25	25
Finland	–	–	22	22
France	33.3	18.6	20.6	20.6
Germany	14	14	15	15
Greece	36	18	18	18
Ireland	25	21	21	21
Italy	38	19	19	19
Luxembourg	12	12	15	15
Netherlands	20	18.5	17.5	17.5
Portugal	30	17	17	17
Spain	33	12	16	16
Sweden	–	–	25	25
UK	15	15	17.5	17.5

VAT proposals amended

The amended proposals stipulated that, from January 1st 1993, the standard rate of VAT should be set at a minimum of 15% in all member states; no maximum was suggested. In addition, for a list of 20 or so goods and services, regarded as essential and not extensively traded across national borders (including food, domestic heating and lighting, passenger transport, and books and newspapers), one or more reduced rates of at least 5% could be applied. In a major concession to the UK it was agreed that zero and other rates less than 5% could continue if they were already in effect on January 1st 1991. Special derogations were allowed for Luxembourg, Portugal and Spain, which would have had to make especially large changes in order to comply. In the case of the UK, no changes would have to be made as a result of this agreement. The amended proposals were finally approved in July 1992, in a directive which stipulated a minimum standard VAT rate of 15% for a four-year

Table 16 **Minimum excise duties[a]**

Mineral oils	ecus/'000 litres
Leaded petrol	337
Unleaded petrol	287
Diesel fuel	245
Heating oil	0
Heavy fuel ('000kg)	13
LPG & methane	
fuel	100
industrial use	36
heating	0

Alcoholic beverages	ecus/'000 litres
Beer[b]	0.748 per Plato degree
	1.87 per degree of alcohol
Still wine	0
Sparkling wine	0
Intermediate products	450

Manufactured tobaccos	Duty
Cigarettes (100), global excise duty (specific & ad valorem without VAT)	57% of retail sale price (all taxes included) of most popular type of cigarette
Other manufactured tobacco	20%

Note: Greece and Luxembourg were granted a transitional period of two years until the end of 1994 during which the minimum rate of excise duty on diesel fuel will be 195 ecus/'000 litres. Luxembourg was also allowed minimum rates on leaded petrol (292 ecus/'000 litres) and unleaded petrol (242 ecus/'000 litres).
a As agreed in a directive adopted in 1992.
b For small independent breweries (producing under 200,000hl per year) these minimum rates are reduced by 50%.
Sources: Council of Ministers; European Commission

period. All the arrangements were linked to a transitional period, due to end no later than January 1st 1997, during which VAT on goods exported within the Community would be taxed in the country of destination rather than of origin. After that date all goods should be taxed on the same basis, irrespective of where they were sold. The commission was told to come up with proposals for a permanent system, which would make this possible by the end of 1994. Although the commission met this deadline, the member states were unable to agree on a permanent system of collection, and the transitional arrangements continue, with little prospect of an early changeover, despite the desire of both business and consumer groups for a unified system. As Table 15 on page 143 shows, there was a considerable convergence of VAT rates between 1987 and 1997, partly owing to market forces but also as a consequence of the adoption of the 1992 directive. The range of maximum rates between member states was reduced from 26% to 10% and all rates above the standard rate were eliminated.

Excise duty proposals virtually abandoned

If the approximation proposals on VAT were severely modified, those on excise duties were virtually abandoned. In place of the complete harmonisation proposed by Lord Cockfield, the Council of Ministers agreed in June 1991 that minimum duties, for the most part well below those actually paid in most member states, should be agreed for after January 1st 1993. It had been impossible to reach agreement between the northern member states, which applied high duties on both revenue and health grounds for alcohol and tobacco, and the Mediterranean countries, large producers of wine and tobacco, which traditionally applied nil or low duties. Table 16 sets out the minimum rates that were agreed.

Other forms of taxation

The commission had been concerned that certain other taxes have a bearing on the competitive position of companies based in different member states, and it seems likely that it will at some stage produce proposals for harmonising company taxation, although probably not income tax, at least for the foreseeable future. In 1989, at the behest of the French government, it attempted to secure the introduction of a common "withholding tax" on investment income, but the proposal was withdrawn when it became evident that most other member states would not agree. In 1990, however, it succeeded, after a lengthy delay, in persuading the Council of Ministers to adopt three directives which would provide for a common system of taxation applicable to mergers, and to subsidiary or associated companies when these were based in different member states. By 1997 the majority of member states were in favour of introducing a harmonised withholding tax and in May 1998 the commission approved a draft directive proposing a minimum rate of 20%. This was held up in the Council of Ministers where, despite 14 member states being in favour, the UK government had severe reservations. It feared that the directive, as it stood, would have adverse effects on the Eurobond market, which is largely based in the City of London. For over a year intense efforts followed to seek a compromise draft acceptable to the UK, but by October 1999 no agreement had been reached.

Also in May 1998 the 15 member states agreed a voluntary code of conduct to limit excessive tax competition. A study group of officials from member states and the commission was established under the chairmanship of Dawn Primarolo, the British Treasury minister, with a mandate to report during 1999 on the effects of a wide range of special tax schemes within the EU. Under the code all such schemes found to be harmful must be withdrawn by January 1st 2003.

In November 2000, the EU reached a political agreement on a draft directive on taxing savings. Under the terms of the agreement, each member state would automatically provide the others with information on the savings income of their residents. However, Belgium, Luxembourg and Austria would be exempt for a seven-year transitional period. Instead they would apply a withholding tax on the interest on savings of non-residents. This would be applied at a 15% rate for the first three years. It would then rise to 20%, and the percentage of revenue transferred to the saver's member state of residence from the member state of the paying agent would be 75%. By the time of the December European Council in Nice, EU leaders asked the commission to start talks with the United States and other countries on seeking broadly equivalent international measures. Depending on the outcome of the talks, the Council of Ministers should be able to take a decision on the directive before the end of 2002.

There has, however, been little movement on any EU energy taxes. Harmonised energy taxes were first suggested in 1993 by Mario Monti, then internal market commissioner, and have been debated since 1997, mainly as an environmental measure that would help meet the EU's obligations under the Kyoto Protocols.

Note

1   *Abolition of Fiscal Frontiers: Summary of the Commission's Proposals*, July 1987.

20 Agriculture

CAP was first common policy implemented

The common agricultural policy (CAP) of the EC was, together with the customs union, the objective spelled out in the greatest detail in the Treaty of Rome. It was, indeed, for a long time virtually the only common policy that the Community was able to implement. From the point of view of European farmers it has been a spectacular success, but that success has caused enormous problems to the Community. On the one hand the CAP has absorbed such a high proportion of the budget that the development of other policies has been aborted. On the other hand the subsidised export of a number of products in which substantial surpluses have built up has distorted world trade, bringing the EU into conflict with the United States and other traditional food exporters, as well as with developing countries whose agricultural economies risk being undermined by those exports.

Effect on EU agriculture

The aims of the CAP, as set out in Article 39 of the treaty, are as follows.

1 To increase agricultural productivity.
2 To ensure a fair standard of living for the agricultural population.
3 To stabilise markets.
4 To guarantee regular supplies.
5 To ensure reasonable prices in supplies to consumers.

The CAP has greatly contributed to the transformation of the structure of the Union's agriculture. Generous price support has combined with technological innovation to generate massive increases in production and productivity. The EU is virtually self-sufficient in all but tropical foods and a number of vegetable proteins and starches for animal feed. Owing to a two-thirds reduction since 1958 in the number of people living off the land, the average standard of living of those remaining has risen sharply. Although the policy has helped to realise the first four objectives listed above, this has generally been at the expense of the fifth. EU farm support prices are almost invariably higher than world prices, often substantially so. The EU consumer has therefore had to pay for the success of the farming sector not only through higher prices but also through taxes, which have contributed to an EU budget predominantly devoted to farm support.

The CAP has three main elements.

- A single market for farm goods (free movement throughout the Community and common prices).
- Community preference (a common tariff barrier against imports from outside the EU).
- Common financial responsibility (costs are paid from a common fund to which all members contribute).

Monetary Compensation Amounts

Common prices were introduced for the principal farm products between 1962 and 1967, but exchange rate modifications since then obliged the Community to employ so-called "green currencies" in order to maintain this common price structure. For the main product groups the difference in value between "green" and real currencies was covered by Monetary Compensation Amounts (MCAs) applied on intra-Community and third-country trade. In countries with a negative MCA prices paid to farmers were lower; in those with a positive MCA prices paid were higher than they would otherwise be. As most EC exchange rates have been more stable in recent years (in part owing to the introduction of the European Monetary System, see pages 128–9) the importance of MCAs declined, and farm prices have consequently varied less from country to country than during the 1970s. They finally disappeared in 1999 with the introduction of the single currency, but already by 1996 they represented only a tiny part of the CAP budget.

European Agricultural Guidance and Guarantee Fund

The common fund, known as the European Agricultural Guidance and Guarantee Fund (EAGGF, generally known as FEOGA, from its French acronym) is the most controversial aspect of the CAP. Its guidance section, which pays for modernisation and improvement, now accounts for less than 10% of the total, and its activities excite little opposition. It is the guarantee section which has absorbed the lion's share of the expenditure and whose activities have led to severe strains on the Union's finances.

The guarantee section's main purpose is to support, wherever necessary, the prices of the main European agricultural products to ensure the

Table 17 EU agriculture: basic data, 1999

	1	2	3	4ᵃ	5ᵃ	6	7	8ᵇ	9ᵇ	10ᵇ	11ᶜ
EU 15	135,825	6,898	4.5	6,989	18.4	273,658	1.8	6.9	6.7	-2,425	...
Austria	3,410	229	6.2	210	16.3	5,246	1.2	6.8	5.4	-1,162	15.5
Belgium	1,394	95	2.4	67	20.6	6,921	1.2	10.0	10.4	2,060	17.8
Denmark	2,684	90	3.3	63	42.6	7,722	2.0	10.2	18.8	4,490	18.1
Finland	2,201	148	6.4	91	23.7	3,533	0.9	6.9	2.4	-1,108	18.9
France	29,937	968	4.3	680	41.7	62,929	2.4	8.3	11.9	11,962	...
Germany	17,152	1,034	2.9	534	32.1	41,612	0.9	8.8	5.0	-13,636	16.0
Greece	5,109	669	17.0	821	4.3	11,285	7.1	13.2	28.8	-633	...
Ireland	4,418	136	8.6	148	29.4	5,469	2.9	7.7	12.1	4,666	19.1
Italy	15,401	1,118	5.4	2,315	6.4	42,049	2.6	10.3	7.1	-5,778	18.0
Luxembourg	127	3	1.7	3	42.5	251	0.7	10.2	6.4	-582	...
Netherlands	1,962	231	3.2	108	18.6	18,457	2.4	11.5	18.8	16,406	15.3
Portugal	3,908	611	12.7	417	9.2	6,309	3.3	10.9	6.0	-2,693	...
Spain	28,882	1,020	7.4	1,208	21.2	33,344	4.1	9.0	13.6	1,950	...
Sweden	3,071	121	3.0	90	34.7	4,385	0.7	6.5	2.3	-2,314	0.0
UK	16,169	424	1.6	233	69.3	24,147	0.9	9.0	6.0	-12,161	...

1 Utilised agricultural area ('000ha)   2 & 3 Employment 2 ('000) 3 (% working population)   4 No. holdings ('000)
5 Utilised agricultural area per holding (ha)   6 Final production (€m)   7 % agriculture in GDP   8 % agriculture in food & agricultural products
9 % food & agricultural products in all exports   10 External trade balance in food & agricultural products (€m)
11 % household expenditure on food, beverages & tobacco as proportion of total consumer expenditure
a 1997.   b For member states internal and external trade; for EU 15 external trade.   c 1998.
Source: European Commission

149

maintenance of farmers' incomes. This is done through four different mechanisms, depending on the product involved. Together these mechanisms cover 94% of all European farm produce, the remainder being left to free-market operations.

1 About 70% of products (including wheat, barley, rye, maize, rice, sugar, dairy products, beef and sheepmeat) enjoy support prices which carry either a permanent or conditional guarantee of price and sale. When market prices fall below a certain level and other conditions are fulfilled, the intervention authorities buy up any produce offered to them, stock it and eventually resell it according to Union rules. The market can also be supported by more flexible means, such as storage aids for pigmeat, subsidies for distillation of table wine and aids to the buying-in of surplus fruit and vegetables by producer organisations.

2 About 21% of produce (minor cereals, quality wines, certain fruits and vegetables, as well as pigmeat, eggs and poultry) are protected only by measures to prevent low price imports from outside the Union.

3 Direct subsidies of one kind or another apply to most other products (durum wheat, olive oil, oil seeds and tobacco). In the case of products predominantly imported by the Union, prices are kept down for the consumer while guaranteeing a minimum income for the producer. In the case of oil seeds, which are subject to variable import duties, a deficiency payment bridges the difference between the world market price and the price guaranteed to the producer.

4 Flat-rate aid according to hectares planted or quantity produced covers less than 1% of production (cotton seed, flax, hemp, hops, silkworms, seeds and dehydrated fodder).

The CAP's controversial elements

Guaranteed price system. This forms the core of the CAP. The prices are set each year by the EU farm ministers, all of whom are under pressure from their own farming communities to set the price at the highest possible level. The result has been a constant stimulus to over-production, together with from time to time enormous stocks of one product or another ("butter mountains", "wine lakes") building up, the cost of storing and disposing of which has placed an added burden on the fund. The worst offenders were the dairy farmers, whose surpluses in 1980 absorbed 43% of the guarantee fund even though milk products amounted to less than 20% of total agricultural production. Cereals

(15.8%) and sugar (10.2%) also absorbed disproportionate amounts of the fund. Since then these products have been treated more stringently in the annual price fixing exercises, and by 2002 the share of milk products was down to 4.3% and sugar to 3.2% (see Table 18). The apparent sharp rise in expenditure on cereals (to 40.5%) was due to short-term compensatory payments to farmers leaving the industry or setting aside productive land. Normal guarantee payments to cereal farmers are on a downward trend and this will be reflected in the statistics for future years.

Table 18 **EAGGF guarantee appropriation by product group, 2002 (% of total)**

Arable crops	40.5
Beef, sheepmeat, goatmeat & pigmeat	20.2
Fruit & vegetables, wine, tobacco	9.1
Milk & milk products	4.3
Sugar	3.2
Olive oil	5.3
Other sectors	8.2
Other expenditure	9.2

Source: European Commission

Export subsidies. The other expensive and controversial element in the CAP is the payment of export subsidies (known as "restitutions" or so-called refunds) to enable European produce to compete in world markets. Exporters are refunded the difference between the internal prices at which they purchase their produce and the lower price at which they must sell it on the world market. In 1986 the cost of export restitutions amounted to 8,600m ecus, nearly 40% of the total expenditure from the guarantee fund, though by 1994 the proportion had fallen to less than one-quarter.

This form of dumping has led to much protest from the United States and other competing exporters such as Argentina, Australia and New Zealand. There is also a widespread feeling that subsidised sales, and even EU gifts of food aid to poorer developing countries, inhibit those countries from developing their agricultural economies.

Table 19 **EAGGF guarantee expenditure, 1973–2002 (€m)**

1973	3,928
1977	6,830
1980	11,315
1985	19,744
1989	25,873
1990	26,522
1994	32,970
1995	34,502
1996	39,108
1997	40,423
1998	38,748
1999	39,541
2000	40,994
2001	39,529[a]
2002	39,660[a]

a Appropriation.
Source: European Commission

Budgetary pressures …

The commission has been acutely aware for several years of the need to cut back on agricultural expenditure which was rising at a much faster annual rate than the total resources of the Community. Its favoured tactic has been to attempt to make the farmers pay for their own unwanted surpluses by means of levies on surplus production (particularly on milk). Initially their attempts to secure economies were largely frustrated by the farm ministers, but the EC's budgetary crisis and the determination of several member states, particularly the UK, to curb the overall level of expenditure led to the decision at the Fontainebleau summit of June 1984 that farm spending should henceforward increase at a slower pace than the budget as a whole. This intention proved impossible to adhere to in the face of the rapidly declining value of the dollar during 1986–87, which automatically increased the cost of export restitutions (it was estimated that each 1% fall in the value of the dollar cost the Community budget 150m ecus).

... led to a few modifications ...

Quite apart from the budgetary pressures, there is now a growing realisation that the CAP is in urgent need of modification. It has engendered structural surpluses of a large number of products, and drastic changes are now necessary if production is to be aligned more closely with market demand. Ideally, these changes should concentrate on eliminating marginal production by concentrating more resources into the guidance section of FEOGA, and taking large areas of relatively infertile land out of production. Unfortunately the economic crisis since 1973 has meant that few alternative sources of employment have been available for people leaving the land and this process has been deliberately slowed down, although the agricultural labour force is still declining by about 2.5% a year.

The open-ended production subsidies provided by the system of guaranteed prices have been attenuated to some extent by the introduction of guarantee thresholds and co-responsibility levies for some products; in particular, by the application of milk quotas since 1986. In August 1987 the commission published proposals to apply a system of "stabilisers" to every product. That would involve the automatic cutting of price support whenever any crop exceeded a fixed ceiling. The imposition of such stabilisers for cereals and a long list of other products was endorsed at the Brussels summit of February 1988, as part of the overall budgetary reform settlement. New rules were also approved for restricting agricultural expenditure, so that its annual growth rate should not exceed 74% of the growth in GDP. The objective was to ensure a progressive reduction in the proportion of EC expenditure going to the CAP.

... but more major reform followed during the 1990s

In 1990–91 the EC's agricultural budget came under fresh pressure, partly because of the cost of incorporating East German farmers into the common agricultural policy. This was compounded by the demands of other farm-exporting countries for the EC to agree on sharp cuts in all its subsidy programmes. These demands came to a head in December 1990 at what was supposed to be the final phase of the Uruguay round of GATT trade talks, which were held in Brussels. Led by the United States, the other farm-exporting states proposed that the EC should make cuts of 75% in all three areas of farm support: domestic subsidies, market access and export competition. The best that the EC could offer, after prolonged wrangling between the farm ministers of the member states, was a 30% cut over ten years, back-dated to 1986. This deadlock was the principal reason for the collapse of the GATT talks, which were only restarted with great difficulty in the summer of 1991.

Meanwhile, the European Commission came forward with farmprice proposals for 1991/92 which just succeeded in remaining within the budget guidelines, through a mixture of quota cuts and price freezes. The farm commissioner, who was Ray MacSharry, subsequently produced firm proposals for a major reform of the CAP, which would replace price guarantees by direct income support for less prosperous farmers. This, it was hoped, would not only curb EC expenditure in the future, but would help to reduce the gap between EC and world prices, while making it easier to secure agreement in the agricultural sector of the resumed Uruguay round GATT negotiations.

The MacSharry proposals were amended, partly to satisfy UK objections that they discriminated against larger, more efficient farmers, and were ultimately adopted in May 1992. The centrepiece of the package was a 29% cut in cereal prices spread over the following three years. This led to cheaper feeds for livestock, enabling price cuts of 15% for beef, 20% for pork and poultry, 7–8% for butter and around 3% for bread.

Farmers are compensated for their loss of income by direct income payments. These are, however, dependent on their "setting aside" 15% of their productive land in order to ensure a sharp fall in Europe's overcapacity. The original MacSharry plan restricted these payments to small farmers, but now they are available to all farms irrespective of their acreage. The effect of these price cuts was to reduce substantially the differential between internal EU prices and those charged on the world market. This meant that by 1997 the export subsidies the EU uses to dump its surplus production had been sharply cut. This should remove the grievance of other major farm exporters, such as the United States and the Cairns group of 14 countries (including Argentina, Australia and Canada), that the EU has been stealing their markets. The new reform programme enabled the EU to agree with the US government, under the Blair House agreement of November 1992, on a joint approach to the difficult agricultural sector of the Uruguay round of GATT world trade negotiations. Despite some backsliding by the new French government elected in March 1993, the agreement held and enabled the round to be successfully concluded in December 1993.

Further modifications to the CAP resulted from the enlargement talks with Austria, Finland and Sweden, which concluded in March 1994. All three countries provided more financial support to their farmers than the CAP would have allowed, justifying this by the harsh climatic conditions

(Arctic or Alpine) under which much of their agriculture was produced. The EU insisted that prices in all three countries should immediately be aligned with those within the Union, but agreed that direct compensation could be paid to the farmers provided that it was at the expense of the national government concerned.

A more radical overhaul of the CAP is envisaged by the commission in anticipation of the enlargement of the EU into Central and Eastern Europe. In its policy statement, "Agenda 2000", published in July 1997, it noted that the potential impact would be a 50% increase in agricultural land and a doubling of the farm labour force. Nevertheless, it was determined to keep inside the current annual limit on expenditure growth of 74% of GNP growth. This would be assisted by renewed efforts to narrow the difference between EU and world prices. Cuts of 20% in the cereals intervention price in 2000, of nearly 30% in the price guarantee for beef between 2000 and 2002, and of 10% in support prices in the dairy sector by 2006, were all foreshadowed. Greater emphasis would also be placed on rural development and the creation of alternative job opportunities for farm workers.

Preparing for enlargement

One of the objectives of the commission's Agenda 2000 report, adopted in May 1997, was to put a ceiling on farm spending during the seven-year period 2000–06. The aim was to freeze it at the 1999 level of €40.5 billion. This proposal met fierce resistance from some member states, and the final outcome, agreed at the Berlin summit in March 1999, was to stabilise spending on the CAP at a slightly higher level, averaging €42.5 billion over the seven years (see Table 20 on the next page). The summit also agreed to the establishment of the SAPARD programme (Special Assistance Programme for Agriculture and Rural Development) to assist the applicant countries of Central and Eastern Europe to prepare their agricultural sectors for membership of the Union. It was agreed to allocate €520m per year for this purpose, the details of which are shown in Table 21 on the next page.

In concrete terms, SAPARD can provide funding for the following measures:

- ◪ investment in agricultural holdings;
- ◪ improvements to methods for processing and marketing agriculture and fishery products;

Table 20 **CAP expenditure 2000–06, €m, 1999 prices**

	Total future CAP	of which markets	of which rural development
2000	40,920	36,620	4,300
2001	42,800	38,480	4,320
2002	43,900	39,570	4,330
2003	43,770	39,430	4,340
2004	42,760	38,410	4,350
2005	41,930	37,570	4,360
2006	41,660	37,290	4,370
Total	**297,740**	**267,370**	**30,370**

Source: European Commission

Table 21 **SAPARD: annual indicative budget allocations (€m, 2000 prices)**

Bulgaria	53.026
Czech Republic	22.445
Estonia	12.347
Hungary	38.713
Lithuania	30.345
Latvia	22.226
Poland	171.603
Romania	153.243
Slovenia	6.447
Slovakia	18.606
Total	**529.000**

◪ veterinary and plant health controls, food quality and consumer protection;

◪ promotion of production methods that protect the environment and conserve rural heritage;

◪ diversifying economic activities and developing alternative sources of income;

◪ farm relief services and farm management services;

◪ setting up producer groups;

◪ village renewal and conservation of rural heritage;

◪ land improvement and reparcelling;
◪ updating land registers;
◪ vocational training;
◪ improvement of infrastructure in rural areas;
◪ management of water resources for agriculture;
◪ forestry and farm woodland projects, investment in private forest holdings, processing and marketing of forest products;
◪ technical assistance (studies, monitoring, information, publicity campaigns).

The BSE crisis

A serious dispute arose in March 1996, when the commission banned the export of any live cattle, beef, veal or products of bovine origin from the UK to other countries in the EU or elsewhere in the world. This followed the acknowledgement by the UK government of a possible link between bovine spongiform encephalopathy (BSE) and certain cases of Creutzfeld-Jakob disease affecting humans. The UK government unsuccessfully challenged the ban in the European Court of Justice, and reacted by blocking decision-making within the EU for nearly two months until, at the Florence summit in June 1996, a programme was agreed for phasing out the export ban, provided that the UK met the strict conditions laid down by EU veterinary experts, and received undertakings that the CAP would provide much of the finance for the compulsory slaughtering policy demanded. By mid-1998 the UK had succeeded in meeting most of these conditions and the export ban on beef from Northern Ireland was lifted, but it was not until more than a year later that the overall ban was raised, though in late 1999 France and Germany were still operating their own bans despite a commission ruling that they had no grounds for doing so.

It was partly so that the EU might be better prepared to meet similar crises to the BSE outbreak, and to provide better protection for consumers, that Franz Fischler, the commissioner responsible for agriculture, called in December 1996 for the creation of an EU Food and Drugs Agency, comparable to the US Food and Drug Administration. This proposal is certain to be considered seriously by the member states, but it is likely to be several years before such an agency is established, even if it is approved.

This was not the only farm crisis to affect the UK: in 2001, an outbreak of foot-and-mouth disease led to radical EU-wide precautionary measures. Exports of animals and animal products (except milk and milk products when properly treated) from the UK were temporarily suspended. The measures included an EU-wide ban on markets and assembly points and a "standstill" for all cloven-hoofed animals, and all vehicles travelling from the UK to other member states were disinfected. As further outbreaks emerged in other countries, similar measures were announced.

A general lack of confidence in food safety had already poisoned public sentiment towards genetically modified organisms (GMOs), which were being produced in the United States. By the mid-1990s, many GM crops had received regulatory approval in the United States, but by 1998 the approval process had stalled in the EU. Despite threatening to ignite a trade war with the United States, the EU stuck by its effective ban on GM crops. In July 2001, the commission unveiled two regulations calling for new rules on the traceability of GMOs throughout the food chain and the labelling of all GM food in order to inform consumers. Similar fears led to the EU's ban on imports of hormone-treated beef from the United States. Although the EU subsequently lost a WTO dispute panel on the issue and is required to pay €117m in annual sanctions, the ban is still far from being lifted.

21 Research and new industries

The industrial policy of the EU has had two main prongs: to help older, declining industries such as textiles, shipbuilding and steel (see Chapter 25) restructure themselves in such a way as to minimise the inevitable pain and disruption; and to assist in the development and spread of new technologies which provide the foundation for future economic growth.

EC's industrial research began in 1980s

Although the Community had for many years been heavily involved in fundamental and applied research in the nuclear industry, its involvement in industrial research began only in the early 1980s with the growing realisation that the EC was falling seriously behind the United States and Japan, and was also in danger of being outstripped by thrusting new economies such as those of South Korea, Singapore and Taiwan.

European co-operation had already borne fruit in a number of areas where a large capital investment and the capture of a significant slice of the world market were necessary conditions for success. Examples included Airbus and Ariane in the aerospace sector, which received loans from the EIB, and JET, in the thermo-nuclear fusion sector, a powerful experimental research institution built and operated by the EC (see pages 192–3). Yet the commission was worried about the wasteful duplication of research expenditure which, collectively in the EC, compared favourably with both the United States and Japan, but which was too fragmented to produce comparable results.

The commission's objective has been to stimulate co-operation between businesses, laboratories and universities throughout Europe in the development of new technologies and new products fulfilling existing or potential market needs. What needed to be stimulated, in its view, was not so much basic research as joint action in the pre-competitive stage of technological development. It would be up to business to take over at the production and marketing stage, taking advantage of the more competitive and dynamic commercial environment created by the planned completion of the internal market.

European strategic programme for information technology (ESPRIT)

ESPRIT was a five-year programme (1984–88) designed to help Europe respond to the challenge of foreign competition in information technology. The Community financed up to 50% of the pre-competition research and development work, undertaken jointly by enterprises from at least two member states, universities and research institutes. Areas covered included:

- advanced micro-electronics in high-integration circuits;
- software techniques;
- advanced information processing;
- the computerisation of offices;
- computer-controlled production techniques.

There was also an "infrastructure" side to the programme, which ensured its effective implementation through a system of information exchange between participants, co-ordination of work, consideration of standards problems and the dissemination of the results of the research. By the end of the ESPRIT I programme in 1988 a total of 227 projects had been implemented. These involved 536 participating companies, universities and research institutes, and some 3,000 full-time researchers. Of the 327 companies which participated, almost 45% were firms employing fewer than 500 people (and two in five of these employed fewer than 50). The total cost of the ESPRIT I programme was 1.5 billion ecus, of which 750m ecus was paid for by the EC.

The budget for ESPRIT II, covering the years 1989–93, was more than doubled to 3.2 billion ecus, once again financed on a 50:50 basis by the Community and the programme participants. The ESPRIT strategy in the second five years was concentrated on three technological areas:

- micro-electronics and peripheral technologies;
- the creation of technologies and tools for the design of information processing systems;
- enhancing the capacity for using and integrating information technology, principally with a view to extending the scope of its applications.

Subsequently, ESPRIT became part of the EU's fourth and fifth framework programmes for research (see below). Its work is now divided into eight domains, covering long-term research, software technologies, technologies for components and subsystems, multimedia systems, open microprocessor systems, high-performance computing and networking, technology for business processes and integration in manufacturing.

The Eureka programme

A large number of EC firms, universities and research institutes are also benefiting from the Eureka programme, which was proposed by President Mitterrand in 1985 partly as a European alternative to President Reagan's star wars initiative. Eureka is not an EC programme, however, and it is open to participation by other West European countries, including the members of EFTA.

Five-year framework research programmes

Despite these increased efforts, the European Commission remained dissatisfied by the degree of commitment of the member states to the co-ordination of their research programmes. In 1986 the president of the commission, Jacques Delors, proposed that the research share of the Community budget (including the amount spent on nuclear research, see pages 192–3) should be more than doubled, from 3% to 8% of the total. As a first step the commission proposed a five-year framework programme for 1987–91, with a total budget of 7.7 billion ecus, although this was eventually whittled down to 5.4 billion ecus by the member states. In 1989, the concept of rolling five-year programmes was accepted, and a simplified framework was approved for 1990–94, with the total increased to 5.7 billion ecus.

The European Council, at the Edinburgh summit in December 1992, stressed the need for the EU's R&TD activities to continue to focus on generic, pre-competitive research with a multi-sectoral impact. Ministers eventually approved a package of research measures, the fourth framework programme, with a budget of 12.3 billion ecus – later raised to 13.1 billion when Sweden, Finland and Austria joined the EU. A fifth framework programme, covering the years 1998–2002, was proposed by the commission in April 1997. It was to have a budget of 16.3 billion ecus, which in terms of the EU's GNP represented a 3% increase over the fourth programme. When it was ultimately adopted by the Council of Ministers in December 1998, however, this was reduced to 14.96 billion ecus. This programme aims at a better co-ordination between research fields and will concentrate on a smaller number of key projects, grouped under nine broad headings (see Table 22 on the next page).

Table 22 **Fifth framework research programme, 1998–2002, m ecus**

Key actions and other activities	
1 Quality of life & management of living resources	2,413
2 User-friendly information society	3,600
3 Competitive & sustainable growth	2,705
4 Energy, environment & sustainable development	2,125
5 Euratom: nuclear energy	979
6 Confirming the international role of Community research	475
7 Promotion of innovation and encouragement of participation of small and medium-sized enterprises	363
8 Improving human research potential & the socio-economic knowledge base	1,280
9 Joint Research Centre: direct actions	1,020
Total	**14,960**

In 2001, the EU made financial commitments within the fifth framework of €3.9 billion for some 4,800 signed contracts involving 23,000 participants.

The sixth framework programme (2002–06) has a budget of €17.5 billion – a 17% nominal increase compared with the previous programme – of which Euratom accounts for €1.23 billion (see Table 23).

European Research Area

The Lisbon European Council in March 2000 identified research and development as essential to make the EU "the most competitive and dynamic knowledge-based economy in the world". As part of this agenda, the leaders backed a commission plan to create a European Research Area (ERA), where think-tanks and university departments from member states work together regularly and effectively, maximising the EU's potential for innovation. The plan focused on the Internet, setting ambitious goals to bring the net into schools, public administration and people's homes.

However, by the Barcelona summit in March 2002, a study showed that the spread of the Internet into EU households may have halted; that only a tiny fraction of people use e-commerce regularly; that high-speed broadband access was barely available; and that Internet security is nothing like as advanced as in the United States. The study showed that Europe lost an average of 0.3–0.5 percentage points of annual growth

Table 23 **Sixth framework research programme, 2002–06 (€m)**

I Integrated research	*13,285*
1. Genomics and biotechnology for health	2,200
2. Information Society technologies	3,600
3. Nanotechnologies, intelligent materials, new production methods	1,300
4. Aeronautics and space	1,075
5. Food quality, safety and health risks	685
6. Energy, sustainable development, biodiversity and global change	2,120
7. Citizens, democracy, political and social institutions	225
8. SMEs, and anticipating scientific and technological needs	1,320
9. Joint Research Centre non-nuclear activities	760
II Structuring the European Research Area	*2,655*
1. Research and innovation	300
2. Human resources/international activities	1,630
3. Research infrastructures	665
4. Sciences and society	60
III Strengthening the foundations of the European Research Area	*330*
1. Support to co-ordination activities	280
2. Support to the consistent development of policies	50
Euratom framework programme	*1,230*
1. Thermonuclear fusion and other priorities	890
2. Other nuclear safety and training activities	50
3. Euratom actions of the Joint Research Centre	290

compared with the United States because of a lack of investment in information technology. This, it believes, is one of the reasons the EU's GDP per head subsided to 65% of the American level in 1999, the lowest for 30 years. But there have been successes since Lisbon. The number of business Internet users compares reasonably with the United States. Almost all schools have been linked to the net, and the percentage of EU homes with Internet access jumped from 18% in 2000 to 36% a year later, before it began to stall. Still, the leaders realised that something needed to be done. They agreed to increase spending on R&D and innovation from the current 1.9% of GDP to 3% by 2010, with two-thirds of new investment coming from the private sector. Such a rise would bring Europe in line with the United States, where R&D investment is 2.6% of

GDP and rising fast, and Japan, which already spends 2.9% of its national wealth on research.

Telecommunications

Europe could claim a remarkable success in fostering the mobile phone standard known as GSM (Groupe Spéciale Mobile or Global System for Mobile communications). GSM is without rival as a successful example of the merits of a pan-European industrial policy approach to technology research, resulting from an agreement on cellular technology within the European Conference for Post and Telecommunications (CEPT). Where the adoption of analogue cellular systems in Europe was piecemeal, restricting mobile-phone users to their national boundaries, GSM was accepted throughout Europe. It created the possibility of roaming from network to network in different countries and has enjoyed success beyond Europe. Competing head-on with America's D-AMPS and Japan's PDC, GSM all but swept the board. It also helped handset manufacturers such as Finland's Nokia and Sweden's Eriksson to emerge from almost nowhere to become two of the most important IT companies in the world.

Although the EU was only indirectly involved in setting the GSM standard, it was implicitly part of a process for speeding mobile-phone use in Europe. The 1993 telecommunications package set January 1998 as the date for opening up the EU's networks to free competition. For some countries, such as the UK, the market was already open. Luxembourg, Spain, Portugal, Greece and Ireland were granted exemptions until, at the latest, the end of 2000 to complete the liberalisation. But overall, the package helped precipitate competition, a new focus on consumers and tumbling prices, and inspired bold new operators, who leapt in to serve the sudden interest in mobile phones. Incredibly, Europe found itself on the cutting edge of technological development, streets ahead of even the United States when it came to developing mobile telephones.

The technology primed to succeed GSM, the so-called third generation (3G), was agreed in 1998 at a European Telecommunications Standards Institute conference in Paris. The Universal Mobile Telecommunications System (UMTS), introduced in the EU on January 1st 2002, offers users advanced features such as moving video images and Internet access at rates more than 200 times faster than previous mobile standards. UMTS is an EU-backed initiative described as the Holy Grail of mobile technology, designed to do anything fibre and broadband networks can do. However, the cost of acquiring 3G mobile-phone licences in national auctions amounted to around €180 billion.

Further measures designed to streamline the EU market have been pushed through. A package in December 2001 required national authorities to consult each other on issues such as 3G mobile-phone auctions, gave companies and consumers more rights to appeal against decisions, and granted the commission the right to enforce common technical standards for digital television if the industry failed to harmonise.

The Information Society and e-Europe

When new multimedia technologies started taking off in the 1990s, the European Commission quickly realised that it was essential to foster the entrepreneurial spirit needed to let them thrive in Europe. While the United States was talking about information superhighways straddling the globe, the commission came up with the concept of the "Information Society", which was more or less the same thing with a slightly more political context. Rather than just laying down fibre-optic cables or putting computers online, EU member states were expected to nurture the new information technologies in such a way that every section of society could take advantage of them. While recognising the tremendous potential of interactive applications, the commission warned that these benefits would be unevenly distributed if society were not prepared for the new generation of technology. In terms of legislation, the Information Society Action Plan covered a wide range of issues, including telecommunications deregulation, the development of trans-European networks (see page 194) in mobile communications and Integrated Services Digital Network (ISDN), standardisation, interconnection, interoperability, intellectual property, privacy and security on the web, and data protection.

As the nature of the Internet and the new technologies emerged, revealing a far more haphazard, market-driven phenomenon, the EU changed its approach. At the June 2000 European Council in Feira, EU leaders backed the e-Europe 2002 Action Plan as part of the Lisbon strategy (see page 181). Its aims are to:

- develop a cheaper, faster and more secure Internet, for example, by unbundling the so-called local loop and making wireless frequencies available;
- invest in people's skills and access (despite having millions of jobseekers, the EU suffers an acute shortage of IT professionals);
- stimulate Internet use with confidence-boosting measures such as legislation on copyright, distance-marketing of financial services, e-money.

The plan has chalked up some clear achievements: personal Internet penetration in Europe has doubled (from 18% in March 2000 to 36% in June 2001) and 90% of schools are online. Broadband access is gradually taking hold, although there are disparities between northern and southern Europe. Nevertheless, e-commerce has failed to take off, schools are connected but the web is not included in the curriculum, there are persistent and growing concerns over security, and personal Internet use has reach a plateau, rising by just 2% to 38% in the six months to December 2001. The commission's conclusion was that efforts needed to be intensified, and in February 2002, EU telecommunications ministers backed an extension of the e-Europe Action Plan from 2003 to 2005.

.EU

In March 2002, EU telecommunications ministers decided to create the new .EU website and e-mail address. The move, which is part of the e-Europe plan, should give businesses a pan-European brand for e-mail and web addresses. The .EU domain will complement the existing family of country code or national top-level domain (TLD) names such as .uk for the UK, .fr for France and .de for Germany, as well as the generic domains such as .com and .org. It can be used by firms operating throughout Europe. It is also aimed at creating more website address space as use of the Internet continues to grow.

Formerly, the websites of EU institutions used .int, which is based in Los Angeles and is reserved for inter-governmental treaty bodies such as NATO and the UN. The new suffix should allow European businesses and organisations to emphasise their European identity on the Internet and set themselves apart from the American-inspired names. An important aspect of the regulation concerns the register, the entity charged with the organisation, administration and management of the .EU TLD name. The new legislation specifies that this entity will be a non-profit-making organisation, and the commission will define the rules governing registration policy. These will include the policy of extra-judicial regulation of the contractors, speculative registration policy and abuse of domain names, the policy concerning the eventual repeal of domain names, problems of languages and geographical concepts and the handling of intellectual property rights.

Community patent

Registering a patent in the EU is slow and expensive: it costs an average

€49,900, compared with €10,330 in the United States and €16,450 in Japan. Translation accounts for some 40% of the cost in Europe. For the past 25 years, everybody – governments, industry, labour organisations – has concurred that a common, straightforward, less costly system for granting patents in Europe would boost competitiveness by reinforcing and strengthening innovation. But progress has been slow because it touches on issues of justice and language, which many countries consider a matter of sovereignty.

The idea of the community patent, central to liberalisation plans endorsed by two consecutive EU economic summits, is to grant inventors automatic legal protection in all 15 member states: EPO patents can be challenged from one country to another. Patents in the EU are awarded either on a national basis or through the European Patent Office (EPO) in Munich. The EPO awards "European patents" through a single procedure, but to be applicable throughout the EU they must be translated into the 11 official EU languages. A further complication is that national courts have jurisdiction in case of disputes, so 15 different sets of legal rules could apply. As well as lowering translation costs, the community patent would allow the European Court of Justice to rule on disputes. However, squabbling over languages has held up the plans. By early 2002, Spain, Greece, Italy and Portugal were still blocking agreement on the community patent because of objections to the procedure being implemented solely in French, English and German.

22 Regional policy

The regional policy of the EC was not originally directly based on the Rome treaty, though the preamble to that treaty refers to the need to "reduce the differences between the various regions and the backwardness of the less favoured regions". (The Single European Act incorporated regional policy into the treaty, and formally recognised it as one of the means of strengthening the Community's economic and social cohesion.) The impetus for developing a regional policy came from the first enlargement, in 1973, when Denmark, Ireland and the UK joined the Community. One of the British commissioners, George Thomson (now Lord Thomson of Monifieth), was given the specific responsibility of overseeing EC policy towards the regions.

Great disparity between regions

He found that there was a considerable disparity between the poorest and most prosperous regions, both within countries and within the Community as a whole. According to figures published some years later by the commission, the ratio varied from 1:1.4 in West Germany, 1:2.4 in France, 1:3.1 in the UK, 1:3.8 in Italy and 1:5.1 in the Community as a whole (the overall range became greater still with the admission of Greece, Spain and, especially, Portugal).

The less privileged regions, which comprise more than one-quarter of the EU population, may be divided into two principal groups.

- Underdeveloped rural areas, whose economy mostly depends on agriculture. These regions have low levels of income, high levels of unemployment and, frequently, poorly developed infrastructures. They include most of Greece and Portugal, southern Spain, the Italian Mezzogiorno, Ireland, Northern Ireland, Corsica and the French overseas departments.
- Areas whose former prosperity was founded on industries now in decline, and which are characterised by ageing plant and high unemployment. Most of these are in Belgium, France and the UK.

Aims of regional policy

The main objectives of the Community's policy for the regions are as follows.

- ◪ To ensure that regional problems are taken into consideration in other EC policies.
- ◪ To attempt to co-ordinate the regional policies of the member states.
- ◪ To provide a broad range of financial support for the development of the Community's poorer regions.

In order to facilitate the first objective, the commission regularly monitors the economic and social conditions of all the regions and studies the regional consequences of all EC policies. The common agricultural policy, for example, was found to be strongly geared towards helping the more prosperous agricultural areas, and modifications have been introduced which have reduced, but by no means completely removed, this anomaly. The Social Fund (see Chapter 23) has been sharply oriented towards the needy regions and special regional programmes have been designed to back up other Community policies.

So far as co-ordination of national efforts is concerned, an important aim has been to ensure that member states do not indulge in the ultimately self-defeating practice of outbidding each other by increasing the level of aid. Common rules allow the Community to avoid wasting scarce resources and to ensure a more coherent pattern of regional development. The commission has fixed upper limits on the state aids which can be offered to would-be investors in the underdeveloped regions. They range from 10% to 100% of the cost of investments, on a sliding scale according to the gravity of the problems in the particular regions.

ERDF is central element of regional policy

The central element in the Community's regional policy is, of course, the European Regional Development Fund (ERDF), set up in 1975. As it was already clear that the UK risked becoming a heavy net contributor to the EC budget (see page 18) unless it could find ways of attracting Community expenditure within its own borders, the UK government made exceptional efforts to avail itself of ERDF funds, as did Ireland and Italy, the then two poorest members of the EC. Yet from the outset it was accepted that there was no question of channelling the entire fund towards the neediest regions of the neediest countries. Each member state was awarded a quota, and its poorer regions were entitled to assistance even if they were far more prosperous than depressed or even average regions in other countries. Nevertheless, the poorer countries rightly got the larger quotas, and in the first decade, up to the end of 1984, more than 91% of ERDF spending went to five countries: France, Greece, Italy, Ireland and the UK.

In terms of spending per head of population, Ireland gained most, followed by Greece, despite having joined the Community only in 1981; Italy was in third place. Half of all ERDF grants were spent in priority regions: the Mezzogiorno, Greece (except Athens), Ireland, Northern Ireland, Greenland (which left the EC following a referendum in 1985, but previously absorbed the entire Danish quota) and the French overseas departments. During its first ten years the budget of the ERDF increased eightfold, reaching 2,140m ecus (7.8% of the budget) in 1984, which was, however, only about one-eighth of the Community's spending on the CAP. By 2001, the money allocated to the EDRF was €15.7 billion (or 16.3% of the budget), and equal to around 36% of agricultual spending.

Table 24 **ERDF allocation (%)**

	Lower limit	Upper limit
Belgium	0.61	0.82
Denmark	0.34	0.46
France	7.47	9.96
Germany	2.55	3.40
Greece	8.35	10.64
Ireland	3.81	4.61
Italy	21.59	28.79
Luxembourg	0.04	0.06
Netherlands	0.68	0.91
Portugal	10.65	14.20
Spain	17.95	23.93
UK	14.48	19.31

Source: European Commission

ERDF allocation rules changed

In 1985, after a prolonged negotiation between the commission and the member states, the rules governing the ERDF were changed in order to make them more flexible and more directed towards the least-favoured regions. Instead of fixed national quotas, each country was allocated a percentage range. These were revised in 1986, to take account of Spanish and Portuguese membership, and are now as shown in Table 24. Special provisions were made in 1995 for the three new member states of Austria, Finland and Sweden, but as each of these is among the wealthier states in the Union the amount of assistance given to their least-favoured regions is extremely small (see Table 26 on page 173).

The lower figure represents the minimum of each year's ERDF budget guaranteed to each member state, always assuming that a sufficient volume of eligible applications for aid are sent to the commission. The variation each year in allocations within the range depends on the extent to which projects presented by member states are considered by the commission to be significant in Union terms.

ERDF expenditure programmes

Expenditure by the fund is divided between programmes, projects and studies. In each case the ERDF meets 50% or 55% of the total cost, the balance being contributed by the member state or states involved. In exceptional cases the ERDF may now assume 75% of the total cost, and 80% in Greece, Portugal, Ireland and Spain. Programmes may consist, either jointly or separately, of infrastructure development, grants to industry, crafts or services, or measures to exploit the potential for internally generated development of the regions themselves. There are two kinds of programmes.

European Union programmes. Undertaken at the initiative of the commission, these programmes aim to help to solve serious social and economic difficulties in one or more regions. They consist of coherent groupings of projects, spread over a number of years, aimed specifically at Union objectives and the implementation of Union policies. In general, Union programmes will affect several member states with their agreement (for example, the Lorraine iron-making area, which includes parts of France, Belgium, Germany and Luxembourg).

National programmes of Union interest. These are proposed to the commission by national governments and pursue national objectives while contributing to the achievement of Union policy goals. The ERDF can finance programmes of this kind only in areas or regions designated by member states for the purpose of their regional aid schemes. One particular type of programme is intended to exploit the indigenous potential of regions by mobilising small-scale local resources, including for the development of tourism. Much the largest amount of money is expended, however, on individual projects put up by member states, often on behalf of local authorities, other public bodies or commercial firms, in their own countries.

Table 25 **Structural funds commitments, 2001 (€m)**

Objective	
1 Regions lagging behind in development	20,832
2 Economic and social conversion	3,613
3 Education, training and employment	3,575
Other structural operations (outside Objective 1)	164
Total	**28,184**

Source: European Commission

Other EU grants and loans
Apart from the ERDF funds, the regions also benefit from a range of other EU sources, including the following.

- ◪ Grants and loans to coal and steel areas from ECSC funds.
- ◪ Loans from the European Investment Bank and other EU funds.
- ◪ Soft loans under the European Monetary System for projects in Ireland and Italy.
- ◪ Grants from the European Social Fund and from the guidance section of the European Agricultural Fund (EAGGF).

The Regional Fund, the Social Fund, the Financial Instrument for Fisheries Guidance (FIFG) and the guidance section of the EAGGF are known collectively as the structural funds of the Union, and under the Single European Act it was agreed in February 1988 that they should be doubled, in real terms, by 1993. An extra amount of 3 billion ecus was committed in 1990 to provide for regional assistance in eastern Germany in the period 1991–93. By 1993 it was envisaged that the structural funds would account for a quarter of the EU budget.

Over the five years 1989–93 a total of 73 billion ecus was allocated by the structural funds. In 1994–99 this figure rose to 141 billion ecus (at 1992 prices). For the seven-year period 2000–2006, the figure was set at

Table 26 **National shares of commitments made by the structural funds, 2001 (€m)**

| | Objectives | | | | |
	1	2	3	Total	%
Austria	39.1	222.4	78.5	340.0	0.9
Belgium	22.1	159.4	250.6	432.1	1.2
Denmark	–	30.0	54.2	84.2	0.2
Finland	136.0	75.0	59.9	270.9	0.7
France	654.2	1,925.4	674.8	3,254.4	9.0
Germany	4,075.0	921.8	680.9	5,677.7	15.7
Greece	3,113.4	–	–	3,113.4	8.6
Ireland	652.0	–	–	652.0	1.8
Italy	3,363.6	412.0	556.5	4,332.1	12.0
Luxembourg	–	6.0	5.6	11.6	0.03
Netherlands	22.1	159.4	250.6	432.1	1.2
Portugal	3,124.4	–	–	3,124.4	8.6
Spain	9,553.5	804.0	505.8	10,863.3	29.9
Sweden	106.6	73.2	107.0	286.8	0.8
UK	1,107.7	1,554.0	678.9	3,340.6	9.2
Total[a]	26,203.1	6,260.2	3,762.3	36,225.6	100.00

a Totals do not add up exactly since they include small amounts not distributed to member states.
Source: European Commission

195 billion ecus (at 1999 prices) The division of this money between the various objectives of the funds during 2001, when over 28 billion ecus were committed, is shown in Table 25. The division between member states of the amount allocated in 2001 is shown in Table 26.

The bulk of spending by the structural funds is concentrated in Objective 1 regions, defined as having a standard of living of less than 75% of the EU average. As some of these regions have prospered, partly as a result of assistance from the structural funds, they have ceased to be eligible. In 1999 the commission revised the list of eligible areas, which will together receive a total of €127.5 billion from the structural funds in the seven-year period 2000–06. Areas ceasing to be eligible will receive transitional support, which will be phased out over four years.

The eligible Objective 1 regions are:

- regions where the GDP per head is at or below 75% of the Community average;

◪ the thinly populated regions of Finland and Sweden (fewer than
eight people per sq km);
◪ the outermost regions (French overseas departments, Canary
Islands, Azores and Madeira).

Some coastal areas of Sweden are also covered (in accordance with
the Act of Accession of Sweden), along with Northern Ireland and the
border counties of Ireland, where there is a special programme for
peace and reconciliation until 2004: the PEACE programme.

◪ Austria: Burgenland
◪ Finland: East Finland, Central Finland (in part), North Finland (in
part)
◪ France: Guadeloupe, Martinique, French Guiana, Réunion
◪ Germany: Brandenburg, Mecklenburg-Western Pomerania,
Saxony, Saxony-Anhalt, Thuringia
◪ Greece: East Macedonia, Thrace, Central Macedonia, West
Macedonia, Thessaly, Epirus, Ionian Islands, Western Greece,
Continental Greece, Peloponnese, Attica, North Aegean, Crete (the
whole of the Greek territory)
◪ Ireland: Border, Midlands and Western
◪ Italy: Campania, Apulia, Basilicata, Calabria, Sicily, Sardinia
◪ Portugal: North, Centre, Alentejo, Algarve, Azores, Madeira
◪ Spain: Galicia, Asturias Principality, Castile-León, Castile-La
Mancha, Extremadura, Valencia, Andalusia, region of Murcia,
Ceuta-Melilla, Canary Islands
◪ Sweden: North-Central Sweden (in part), Central Norrland (in
part), Upper Norrland (in part)
◪ United Kingdom: South Yorkshire, West Wales and The Valleys,
Cornwall and the Isles of Scilly, Merseyside

Transitional support

The new rules provide for transitional support in the regions that were
eligible for Objective 1 during the period 1994–99 but ceased to be so in
2000. This decreasing aid system can avoid sudden termination of Community support and consolidate the gains from structural aid in the previous period.

The following must be distinguished:

◪ areas meeting the basic eligibility criteria of Objective 2. These

Table 27 **Population covered by Objective 1, 2000–06 ('000 inhabitants)**

Austria	275
Finland	1,076
France	1,644
Germany	14,153
Greece	10,476
Ireland	965
Italy	19,302
Portugal	6,616
Spain	23,219
Sweden	452
UK	5,079
EUR 11	**83,258**

have the transitional support of the four Structural Funds until December 31st 2006;
◪ other areas in which ERDF aid will stop on December 31st 2005. They will have transitional support from the ESF, the EAGGF Guidance Section and the FIFG until December 31st 2006.

Areas receiving Objective 1 transitional support:
◪ Belgium: Hainaut
◪ France: Corsica and the districts of Valenciennes, Douai and Avesnes
◪ Germany: East Berlin
◪ Ireland: Southern and Eastern
◪ Italy: Molise
◪ Netherlands: Flevoland
◪ Portugal: Lisboa e Vale do Tejo
◪ Spain: Cantabria
◪ United Kingdom: Northern Ireland, Highlands and Islands

Two special programmes will also be financed with Objective 1 resources:

◪ the PEACE programme, which will support the peace process in Northern Ireland and the border regions of Ireland (period 2000–04);

Table 28 **Cohesion Fund commitments, 2001**

	€m	%
Greece	696,574	22.28
Ireland	115,000	3.68
Portugal	528,886	16.92
Spain	1,784,766	57.11
Technical assistance	7	0.01
Total	**3,125,333**	**100.00**

Source: European Commission

◪ the special assistance programme for certain NUTS II level Swedish regions which meet the criteria of low population density stipulated in Protocol No 6 to the Swedish Act of Accession (period 2000–06).

Integrated Operations

Mention should also be made of the Community's Integrated Operations, which are intended to focus assistance upon limited areas suffering from multiple deprivation. The first two integrated operations were launched in Naples and Belfast, in 1979 and 1981 respectively, and others have since been established in four other areas of the UK, as well as in Belgium, France, the Netherlands, Portugal and Spain.

Integrated Mediterranean Programmes

On a much larger scale are the Integrated Mediterranean Programmes, eventually agreed by the Council of Ministers in 1985 as a result of pressure from Greece during the closing stages of the enlargement negotiations with Spain and Portugal (see pages 21–2). Over seven years the EC was to spend 4.1 billion ecus in grants and provide 2.5 billion ecus in loans for programmes intended to improve the socio-economic structure of the southern parts of the Community to facilitate the adjustment of those regions to the enlargement. The regions selected by the commission to benefit from these programmes were Languedoc-Roussillon, Corsica, Provence-Côte d'Azur, Aquitaine and Midi-Pyrénées in France, the Mezzogiorno, Latium, Tuscany, Umbria, the Marches, Liguria and part of Emilia-Romagna in Italy, and the whole of Greece.

Cohesion Fund

In February 1992 the commission published proposals for expenditure over the five years 1993–97. It did not, as had been predicted, propose a further doubling of overall regional spending, but it did provide that expenditure should be doubled in regions in the four poorest member states: Greece, Ireland, Portugal and Spain. It also provided for the creation of a Cohesion Fund, as agreed at the Maastricht summit, from which expenditure principally on transport, energy and telecommunications in the poorest member states could be met. Table 28 shows the projected breakdown of expenditure in the Cohesion Fund for 2001.

23 Social policy

ESF is centrepiece of social policy

At the centre of the EU's social policy is the European Social Fund (ESF), established under Article 123 of the Rome treaty. The purpose of the fund was defined as:

> *To improve employment opportunities for workers in the*
> *common market and to contribute thereby to raising the*
> *standard of living ... it shall have the task of rendering the*
> *employment of workers easier and of increasing their*
> *geographical and occupational mobility within the Community.*

In its early years the ESF operated on a very small scale, providing assistance for the retraining of workers displaced through structural changes. With the sixfold increase in unemployment between 1970 and 1986, when it reached the record level of 16m people or 12% of the working population, both the finances and the scope of the fund were greatly increased. During 1986 nearly 2.5m people (85% of them under 25 years of age) benefited from the ESF, whose financial commitments for the year amounted to more than 2,500m ecus, or 7% of the total EC budget. By 1999 the amount committed had increased to 9,611m ecus, or about 10.1% of the EU budget.

Main priorities of ESF

In 1983 the Council of Ministers decided that the ESF should henceforth have two overriding priorities, and since then the greater part of its resources has been focused on these two (overlapping) priorities.

Young people. The ESF is now required to spend the bulk of its resources on the training and employment of the under-25s. The objective is to help fulfil an undertaking made by the Council of Ministers to ensure that new training opportunities will be provided for all young people who desire them, and in particular for those with reduced employment possibilities owing to the lack or inadequacy of their education or vocational training.

The most disadvantaged regions. Some 44.5% of the expenditure of the ESF is concentrated in seven "absolute priority" zones, containing altogether about one-sixth of the Union's working population (23m people). Moreover, although expenditure from the fund normally covers a maximum of 50% of the eligible costs and does not exceed the total financial contribution made by the public authorities in the member state concerned, in the case of "absolute priority" regions, ESF aid can be increased to 55% of eligible expenditure.

ESF support for youth training programmes …

Much of the aid earmarked for young people is channelled through major schemes undertaken by several of the member states. For example, in France tens of thousands of young people have benefited from employment/training contracts, enabling them, with the ESF's assistance, to work in a business while continuing their training. In Ireland significant support has been given to the Industrial Training Authority to help set up extensive youth training programmes.

On the other hand, through national governments, the commission receives thousands of applications each year to support small-scale schemes. Normally around half of these applications are approved.

… certain categories of adults …

In addition to its efforts on behalf of young people, the ESF gives priority to adults in the following categories.

- Unemployed or underemployed workers, and especially the long-term unemployed.
- Women who wish to resume work.
- Handicapped people capable of joining the labour market.
- Migrant workers from within the EU and immigrants who have settled there in order to work, together with their families.
- Workers, particularly in small and medium-sized firms, faced with the problem of retraining owing to the introduction of new technologies or the improvement of management techniques.
- People working in the field of employment promotion; experts in vocational training or recruitment, or development agents.

… and other specific operations

Lastly, specific operations under the ESF, for which 5% of the budget must be reserved, include the following.

- European Union-type operations which are part of integrated programmes involving assistance from other EU funds (see page 172).
- Operations to help vocational training and youth employment.
- Operations linked to industrial or sectoral restructuring and the introduction of new technologies, or to the development of the labour market
- The employment of women where they are under-represented in the workforce.
- Assistance to handicapped and migrant workers and the training of instructors, vocational guidance or placement advisers.
- Specific innovatory operations involving fewer than 100 people.

The Social Charter of Workers' Rights

The other principal element in the Community's social policy is the Social Charter of Workers' Rights, signed at Strasbourg in December 1989 by 11 of the then 12 heads of government. Margaret Thatcher, who was then the UK prime minister, refused to sign on the grounds that the proposals foreshadowed by the charter would reverse the measures which her government had introduced to deregulate the labour market and would lead to higher unemployment by deterring employers from creating new jobs.

The Social Charter was originally conceived by Jacques Delors, who argued that the implementation of the 1992 programme would chiefly benefit European companies whose profits would rise as barriers to their operating on a Europe-wide basis would disappear. He success-fully persuaded all the governments except that of the UK that the 1992 programme should be buttressed by parallel measures which would improve the working and social conditions of employees.

The charter itself had no more than a declaratory effect, but it was to be followed by a Social Action programme, containing 47 pieces of leg-islation which, if adopted by the Council of Ministers, would be binding on the member states including the UK.

Much of the Social Action programme could be approved by quali-fied majority voting and would therefore be adopted despite UK oppo-sition. The draft Treaty on European Union, presented to the Maastricht summit in December 1991, would have made the remaining proposals also liable to majority voting rather than unanimity. John Major refused to accept this, however, so the other 11 member states signed a Protocol on Social Policy (also known as the Social Chapter), which provided that they could decide these matters by qualified majority voting among themselves but that the UK would not take part in the deliberations nor be bound by the outcome. This extraordinary decision, whereby 11 member states could use the institutions, procedures and mechanisms of the EC for the taking of decisions that did not apply to the 12th member, was an unprecedented development and many observers doubted whether it would last long. It was effectively terminated by the victory of the Labour Party in the UK general election on May 1st 1997. The newly elected government lost no time in declaring that it would adhere to the Protocol, which in the following month was formally incorporated in the Amsterdam Treaty.

So far the main directives adopted under the Social Action programme have been concerned with protecting the employment rights of pregnant women; restricting the number of hours that employees could be required to work within a fixed period; special provisions for restricting night work; guaranteeing subcontracted workers from other countries the same rights (on health and safety, equal opportunities and dismissal) as local workers; and giving part-time workers the right to written contracts.

New agenda

At the Lisbon European Council in March 2000, EU leaders agreed a broad agenda of economic and social reforms (see pages 115-8). They set ambitious targets for raising employment rates in the EU by 2010: to 70% for the labour force as a whole, to at least 60% for women and to 50% for older workers. As part of the so-called Lisbon process, the European Social Policy Agenda was launched to build an active welfare state, invest in human resources, consolidate cohesion, and boost the quality and quantity of jobs. In June 2000, the commission unveiled details of the new agenda, a five-year plan for 2000-05 addressing new social challenges such as introducing labour market flexibility, tackling social exclusion, adopting crucial health and safety laws, addressing pension problems, and improving training and life-long learning. A scoreboard detailing progress on the agenda was set up, and plans were made to co-ordinate the social agenda with the employment package, the broad economic guidelines and the budget. However, the means of achieving the Lisbon targets remain controversial: for example, in January 2002, the commission published plans to promote "active ageing", saying that 5m older workers had to stay in jobs beyond their planned retirement date if the EU was to hit the targets.

24 Workers' rights

Under Article 117 of the Rome treaty the member states agreed on the need to promote improved living and working conditions for workers, while Article 118 gave the commission the task of promoting close co-operation between member states in the social field, particularly in matters relating to:

- employment;
- labour law and working conditions;
- basic and advanced vocational training;
- social security;
- prevention of occupational accidents and diseases;
- occupational hygiene;
- the right of association, and collective bargaining between employers and workers.

In practice, the impact of the Community has been most marked in relation to the rights of migrant workers, equal pay for men and women (see page 233), and safety factors. Despite the activities of the European Social Fund (Chapter 23) and the European Regional Development Fund (Chapter 22), little has been achieved in terms of assuring employment for the workers of the Community, unemployment having risen to 18m, or 10.7% of the labour force by the end of 1997. It subsequently fell to 15.8m (9.3%) in July 1999, and is still slowly declining. Attempts to harmonise social security systems have enjoyed only partial success, and commission initiatives to provide a wider framework for worker participation in management decisions have been blocked by the unwillingness of some member governments (notably that of the UK) to agree to legislation in this field.

Rights of migrant workers

Nearly 5m EU citizens are now living in Union countries apart from their own (together with nearly 8m migrants from non-EU countries). Under Union law, EU migrants must be treated like nationals of the host country. Their right of free movement from one member state to another is guaranteed, and all discrimination on national grounds is forbidden, whether relating to employment, social security, trade union rights, living and working conditions, housing, education or vocational training. Union migrants going to jobs in another EU country do not need a work permit and can claim a five-year residence permit which is automatically renewable, even after their retirement.

The right to work is, in theory, subject to only two restrictions:

- ◪ for "justified reasons" of public order, health or safety; and
- ◪ for certain forms of public administration work.

In practice, member states have tried to shut off all public administration jobs from foreign applicants, but a series of decisions by the Court of Justice has gradually reduced the range of posts which can be reserved to nationals of the host country.

Mutual recognition of professional qualifications

It had taken a long time for the member states to agree on the mutual recognition of professional qualifications, so that for many years it was not possible for many workers to practise their professions in EC countries other than their own. However, doctors, nurses, veterinary surgeons, dentists and midwives are now able to do so, provided that they are nationals of an EU country and have obtained their qualifications within the EU. Lawyers established in one member state are able to offer their services in another, as are architects and pharmacists, but only since 1987 as it took the best part of 20 years for agreement to be reached in the Council of Ministers.

Improvement of working conditions

Somewhat more urgency has been shown in dealing with proposals for the improvement of working conditions. In 1975 the European Foundation for the Improvement of Living and Working Conditions was established in Dublin, and since that date it has helped to formulate EC policy in this area. The major emphasis has been on safety and health in the workplace, where more than 100,000 people are killed in accidents each year and millions injured. The ECSC was involved from the outset. It established the Mines Safety and Health Commission, a body composed of government representatives, employers and workers, to help prepare proposals for coal mines and other mining industries. A similar body with a more general remit, the Advisory Committee on Safety, Hygiene and Health Protection at Work, was set up in 1974.

In its second action programme on work safety, adopted in 1984, the EC concentrated on:

- rules for the use of dangerous substances;
- ergonomic measures and principles for preventing accidents and dangerous situations;
- improvements in organisation, training and information;
- problems posed by new technologies.

Several directives have been adopted on safety signs, on electrical equipment used in mines with firedamp, and on protection against chemical, physical or biological agents such as lead, asbestos, noise and vinyl chloride monomer. Under the Single European Act, agreement on new directives or regulations on improving the working environment and on health and safety provisions no longer requires unanimity within the Council of Ministers. This has led to a speeding-up of decision-making in this area.

Workers' rights in companies

Since the mid-1970s the European Commission has made vigorous efforts to promote the protection of workers' interests in other areas, notably by safeguarding their rights in companies. Directives have been in force since 1977 establishing minimum requirements with regard to mass redundancies, since 1979 guaranteeing established rights in the event of transfer, and since 1983 ensuring payment of salary and other claims when an employer goes out of business.

Three major commission initiatives, however, ran into determined opposition, provoking expensive, provocative but ultimately successful lobbying campaigns by employers' organisations. These involved not only the main European employers' association UNICE, but also large American-controlled multinational companies and the Japanese employers' association Keidanran. The European Trade Union Confederation (ETUC) attempted to rally support for the commission's proposals, but all three have become firmly stuck in the Council of Ministers (where they need unanimous approval). There seemed no prospect of any of them being adopted in the foreseeable future, despite the fact that all three have been welcomed by a majority of member states, several of which had already adopted domestic legislation along similar lines.

The three proposals were as follows.

European company statute. This draft statute set out an industrial relations framework for European companies which might be formed, for example, as a consequence of cross-border mergers. The original draft, which was put forward in 1975, was largely based on German experience, and contained the proposal that companies should have a two-tier board structure, a board of management and a supervisory board, with direct worker representation on the supervisory body.

Fifth Directive on the structure of limited companies. Originally tabled in 1972, this directive was intended to apply to any firm in the EC employing more than 500 people. It also provided for compulsory worker representation on supervisory boards.

The Vredeling Directive. Named after the former Dutch commissioner for social affairs, Henk Vredeling, whose proposals the commission approved in 1980, this draft directive related to "complex" companies (those having more than one branch), although its evident target was multinational companies whose very nature made them difficult to control on a purely national basis. The purpose of the directive was to require managements to provide general information about the company to employees and, in particular, to consult them on any decisions which would have consequences for their jobs (closures, redundancies, plant reorganisation, and so on).

Charter of the Fundamental Social Rights of Workers

A widespread view that the benefits of the 1992 programme would accrue mainly to the business community led to demands that it should be balanced by a comparable programme designed to enhance the rights of workers. The commission consequently produced a draft Community Charter of the Fundamental Social Rights of Workers (Social Charter), which was signed by 11 heads of government with the exception of Mrs Thatcher in Strasbourg in December 1989. The charter has no legal force in itself but it foreshadowed the introduction of a series of directives designed to entrench workers' rights with regard to such matters as:

- labour mobility;
- employment;
- social protection;
- collective bargaining and freedom of association;
- vocational training;
- health and safety;

- equal opportunity;
- consultation and participation; and
- measures to protect women workers, young people, the elderly and the disabled.

Revised European company statute

In 1989 the commission also tried to refloat its earlier proposal for a European company statute. In its revised form this would be a voluntary option for companies, but sweetened with the possibility of more favourable tax treatment. The proposals for worker participation were made a great deal more flexible, with three alternative systems on offer based respectively on French, German, and UK practices. Despite this new flexibility the then UK government remained firmly opposed. Part of the statute was, however, adopted under the Protocol on Social Policy (described on pages 180–1) which meant that, initially at least, it was applicable only in the other 14 member states. The commission approved such a proposal in April 1994, under which European Works Councils were to be established in multinational firms within the EU so that employees may be informed and consulted about strategic decision-making by their companies. This proposal, which was adopted as a directive by the Council of Ministers later in 1994, did not apply to workers in the UK, but UK companies with employees in other EU countries were required to comply. The expectation was that other multinational companies would not wish to discriminate against their British employees and would therefore include them on a voluntary basis, while UK trade unions would apply direct pressure on UK companies to introduce works councils along similar lines. In practice, the directive has largely been applied in the UK, despite the "opt-out" insisted on by the government of John Major, which was given up by the newly elected Labour government in June 1998.

The European company statute was formally adopted by EU social affairs ministers in October 2001, after more than 30 years of negotiation. The European Company (known by its Latin name of "Societas Europaea" or SE) will give companies operating in more than one member state the option of setting up as a single company under EU law, operating with one set of rules and a unified management and reporting system. It obliges SE managers to provide regular reports to a body representing the companies' employees, detailing current and future business plans, production and sales levels, implications of these for the workforce, management changes, mergers, divestments, potential closures and layoffs.

Amsterdam and Luxembourg initiatives

The inclusion of a new chapter on employment in the Amsterdam treaty, which came into force in May 1999, and the convening in Luxembourg of a special EU summit on employment in November 1997 have given a fresh boost to EU action in the employment field. Following the Luxembourg summit, the Council of Ministers adopted a series of guidelines, which the member states were required to incorporate in their own national action plans. They centred on four strategic elements: improvement of people's credibility; development of entrepreneurship; encouragement of the adaptability of businesses and their employees; and strengthening of policies for equal opportunities.

25 Energy

Common energy policy slow to evolve

The coal industry has been subjected to detailed supervision under the ECSC since 1951, and the civil nuclear industry, particularly with regard to research and development, under Euratom since 1958, yet the Community has been much slower to evolve a common energy policy which would enable it to plan and implement a joint strategy to meet all its energy needs. Since the first "oil shock" of 1973, which caught the EC woefully unprepared, there has been a certain convergence in policy and common objectives have been defined without, however, a central machinery being established to ensure that they are pursued in a co-ordinated manner. The result is a "semi-common" policy, with agreement in principle on most objectives, but a patchwork division of responsibility between the different sectors.

This is undoubtedly a significant improvement on the situation in the early 1970s, but the EC remains particularly vulnerable in the energy field where, in 1991, external sources of supply still accounted for 50% of total consumption, compared with a mere 18% for the United States. Moreover, its internal energy production is likely to remain stable or even to decline, and its demand would surely grow in the event of renewed economic growth. Of the 15 member states only the Netherlands and the UK are net exporters of energy.

A programme was finally adopted in 1974

The 1973 crisis, which saw the quadrupling of oil prices virtually overnight, was followed by the fiasco of the December 1973 Copenhagen EC summit, which singularly failed to produce a joint response to the Arab oil producers, France and the UK in particular preferring to pursue bilateral deals with oil suppliers rather than to present a united front with their EC partners. It was only in September 1974 that the Council of Ministers adopted a programme drawn up by the European Commission called "Towards a New Energy Policy Strategy". This programme, adapted in 1980 and again in 1986, has formed the framework for most subsequent discussions on energy policy.

The overriding priority laid down was the importance of reducing dependence on imported oil supplies and the desirability of diversifying the sources of supply. This objective was pursued with considerable success. Over ten years the Community cut its oil imports by half. By 1983 it was estimated that the equivalent of 250m tons of oil annually was being saved due to more efficient use of energy: an economy of more than 20%. North Sea production had been built up to nearly 130m tons, and the same amount was being saved in imports by greater use of nuclear energy. The 1986 update of the 1974 report defined new energy policy aims for the period to 1995 and listed both sectoral and horizontal targets.

Sectoral targets

Efficiency.　Efforts must be intensified to ensure a further improvement of at least 20% by 1995, despite the fall in oil prices. The commission was asked to prepare programmes for all sectors of the economy – services, industry, agriculture and transport – and to disseminate the results of national and Community demonstration projects which tested the industrial and commercial viability of new equipment. The EC spent around 150m ecus in 1978–85 in support of more than 370 energy-saving demonstration projects, and the EIB lent 3.3 billion ecus for similar projects, mostly small and medium-sized, in industry and infrastructure. In June 1990 the Community adopted a five-year programme, Thermie, with an annual budget of 350m ecus, to provide financial support for projects that promote energy technology in the rational use of energy, renewable energies, solid fuels and hydrocarbons.

Oil.　Over 12 years the EC had reduced the share of imported oil in its gross energy consumption from 62% to 31%, but this had crept back up to 35% by 1991. The level of net imports must be maintained at below one-third of total consumption by continued encouragement for economy and substitution, and promotion of internal exploration and production. More assistance for the development of innovatory technologies in the hydrocarbon field is envisaged, as well as the possibility of EU assistance in prospecting.

Natural gas.　The market share of natural gas, some 19.3% in 1991, had grown by 50% since 1973. With the prospect of a possible fall in European production, there should be greater incentives for gas exploration and for diversifying supplies from third countries. EIB loans for the construction of gas pipelines should help to achieve these objectives.

Solid fuels. A determined effort has been made to increase the market share of coal, lignite and peat (22.4% in 1991). Despite a doubling of coal imports since 1973, consumption slightly declined, owing to a 16% fall in Community coal production in the mid-1980s. Since 1989 it has been rising. The transformation of power stations from oil to coal and the use of coal for district heating schemes is encouraged by EU grants and loans, and the Union is also backing efforts to standardise and perfect technologies that cause less pollution.

Electricity generation. The drive to replace oil by coal and, above all, nuclear fuel, which had already reduced the share of oil from 50% to 25%, should be continued, with the objective of bringing it down to less than 15% by 1995. The aim was to increase the nuclear share (then approaching 30%) to 40% by 1995 and 50% by the end of the century. As a longer-term objective, the commission envisaged investment in a network of fast breeder reactors (which would multiply by 50 times the energy potential of uranium) and would be economically competitive by 2005. The Chernobyl accident in 1986, and mounting public anxiety about the operation of nuclear power stations, convinced the commission that further progress could be made only if the public concern could be allayed. In June 1986 it proposed to the Council of Ministers an action plan which placed heavy emphasis on safety measures. Nevertheless, there was a virtual halt in new nuclear energy projects and by 1993 the nuclear share in total EC energy production had dropped to 14.3% and was still falling.

New and renewable energy sources. Greater financial support should be provided for the development of new technologies, such as mini-hydro plants for electricity generation, the use of biomass and waste, solar, geothermal and wind energy. These could together account for nearly 5% of consumption by the end of the century, in the view of the commission, which had by 1985 already provided grants to assist more than 500 demonstration projects, while EIB loans had been made available for the development of 100 of them. In 1991 a new research and technological development programme was launched with a budget of 157m ecus over five years.

Horizontal targets

Completion of the internal market. The market for oil products is already largely open, and little more can practically be done to open up the coal market any further, given the high cost of internally produced coal in relation to imports from countries such as Poland and the United States. There is, however, scope for increasing internal trade in the gas and electricity sectors through the encouragement of long-term contracts, cross-border investment and interconnections between national systems, such as France–UK and France–Italy, both of which have been assisted by EIB loans. In 1990 a more comprehensive programme was adopted for linking up energy networks throughout the Community.

Common pricing.   The EC has been increasingly active in ensuring that all energy sectors should follow common pricing principles which are transparent and realistic and should not distort competition between industries. For example, the Dutch gas industry was prevented from supplying cheap gas to horticulturalists which allowed them to heat their greenhouses more cheaply than their competitors in other EC countries. In 1990 a directive was adopted enforcing transparency in the pricing policies of electricity and gas suppliers.

Improved security of supply.   This is to be achieved by the development of competitive European production, diversification of imports, greater flexibility of consumption and effective contingency measures. Community legislation provides for the compulsory stocking of fuel at electricity plants, equal to 30 days' consumption and for oil stocks to be maintained at a minimum level equivalent to 90 days' consumption.

External relations.   The EU is seeking to capitalise on its bargaining power as a major customer of energy supplies, the Union absorbing some 14% of the world market. In 1989 the EC negotiated an economic co-operation agreement with the Gulf states, which have the world's largest oil reserves, and it maintains close relations with OAPEC, the Organisation of Arab Petroleum Exporting Countries. In the nuclear field long-term agreements with the principal uranium suppliers (Australia, Canada and the United States) assure a certain stability of supply. The commission is seeking to secure a greater degree of co-operation between member states on gas supply contracts. In the developing countries the Union is helping to disseminate new technologies (solar energy, energy saving, and so on) through some 60 aid programmes. (See also European Energy Charter, pages 194–5.)

Environmental protection.   Since 1989 the EC, in response to strong pressure from public opinion, has adopted a series of measures designed to reduce environmental damage caused by the energy sector. They concern the introduction of lead-free petrol, the reduction of toxic emissions from automobiles and large combustion plants, and the reduction of the sulphur content of heating oil and diesel fuel.

Regional development.   In addition to the grants and loans offered by the ECSC, the ERDF and the EIB for regional development projects, many of which are concerned with the energy sector, the special Valoren programme for improving the efficiency of energy resources in the less-favoured regions was launched in 1986. This programme, which was allocated 400m ecus, seeks to exploit the use of indigenous fuels (such as small peat and lignite deposits) as well as to promote the efficient use of energy. In 1996 the Valoren programme was incorporated in the EU's SAVE II programme, running from 1996 to 2000, to promote energy efficiency. Under this programme the commission now finances some 100 local energy agencies under the responsibility of local and regional authorities.

Technological innovation.   The EU is pursuing a major research, development and demonstration programme focusing on:

- nuclear safety (reactor security, waste management, control of fissile materials, protection against radioactivity, and so on);
- controlled nuclear fusion;
- solid fuels;
- new energy resources; and
- the efficient and environmentally friendly use of energy.

Much of the research is being pursued by firms and institutes in the different member states. In 1993, for example, under its Thermie programme (for the promotion of energy technology), the commission gave financial support amounting to 129m ecus to 137 different projects. The four research centres directly established by Euratom, at Karlsruhe in Germany, Ispra in Italy, Geel in Belgium and Petten in the Netherlands, now known collectively as the Joint Research Centre (JRC), do important work mainly in the field of nuclear safety and environmental protection. The EC's most ambitious undertaking, however, was the establishment at Culham in the UK of the Joint European Torus (JET), where all West European research into nuclear fusion is now concentrated. This is one of only four major programmes in the world, the others being in Russia, the United States and Japan. Co-operation and exchange of information agreements have been reached with each of these countries, and the four partners have agreed to the construction of an International Thermonuclear Experimental Reactor (ITER) under their joint auspices. This is seen as the next major step in a programme whose ultimate objective is the generation of electricity by more economic, cleaner and safer means than those provided by nuclear fission. By the end of 1999 a site had not been agreed for ITER, but the commission was optimistic that it would be within the EU.

Meanwhile, in 1991 the SAVE programme (Specific Actions for Vigorous Energy Efficiency) was launched, with the objective of reducing energy intensity per unit of GNP by 20% over the following five years. A series of actions to limit carbon dioxide emissions by improving energy efficiency was launched under this programme in 1993. Altogether 250 separate projects were supported at a total cost of 25.1m ecus, and in 1996 the SAVE II programme was launched with a mandate to continue and expand the work until the end of the century.

Energy white paper.   In December 1995 the commission adopted a white paper entitled "An Energy Policy for the European Union" which set out objectives until the end of the present century. The three pillars of the EU's energy policy in the future were defined as overall competitiveness, security of energy supply and environmental protection. This policy would be implemented mainly by means of integration of the market, management of the external dependency, promotion of sustainable development and support of energy research and technology. The first fruits of the white paper were directives aiming to secure the liberalisation and transparency of the markets for electricity and gas supply. The electricity directive was approved at the end of 1996 and the gas directive early in 1998.

However, with France consistently blocking moves to let foreign companies compete in national markets, the energy liberalisation plans seem to be heading nowhere. At the European Council in Barcelona in March 2002, France came under tremendous pressure to open its energy market, but with just one month until the French presidential elections, neither President Jacques Chirac nor Lionel Jospin, the prime minister and a presidential candidate, was ready to give much ground on this issue. However, the summit conclusions did move the slow process of energy market liberalisation forwards. France was able to sign up to opening the market in 2004 and introducing a range of measures that will make it easier for the hitherto frustrated power companies of Spain and Germany to get into the market.

Under the accord, EU leaders backed opening the market for commercial users of gas and electricity, around 60% of the market, in 2004. A decision on when to open up the politically more sensitive household sector was put off until 2003. The deal maintained, for a while at least, the unique protection enjoyed by Eléctricité de France, a state-owned energy giant. The compromise allowed France to claim that it had warded off a commission threat to deploy rarely used competition powers to open up the market by decree. The leaders also agreed to French demands for a new "framework directive on services of general interest", which would set out the scope for governments to intervene to ensure customers get a fair deal and high quality of service once markets are opened.

Trans-European Networks. A programme of Trans-European Networks (TENs) – in transport, telecommunications, training and energy – was announced by the commission in 1990. In particular, it contained proposals for energy interconnections in natural gas and electricity. Financial measures were proposed to promote private funding (particularly by meeting the costs of prior feasibility studies) and to ensure that higher priority is given to TENs in the future operation of the EU's budgetary and lending instruments. The commission's intention is that, as far as possible, funding should come predominantly from the private sector, but public funding, which might include Union support, will be required in certain cases. The Cohesion Fund, set up as a result of decisions taken at the Maastricht summit in December 1991, also provides some funding for TENs in the poorer Union states. The major EU contribution, however, is through loans from the EIB, which by 1998 totalled almost €27 billion, of which €3.9 billion was in the energy sector. The EDRF also provided subsidies for the energy projects amounting to €2.3 billion.

European Energy Charter

A major initiative towards international co-operation in energy supplies was launched by the Dutch prime minister, Ruud Lubbers, who, in 1989, proposed that an energy charter should be signed between the EC and the Soviet Union, under which Western know-how and investment would be made available to the Soviet natural gas and oil industries in exchange for the Soviet Union guaranteeing supplies to Western Europe over a lengthy period. The European Energy Charter was eventually signed in The Hague in December 1991 by the EC, 37 European and OECD states and 12 former Soviet republics. Its objective was to create a climate favourable to the operation of enterprises and to the flow of investment and technology by applying market-economy principles to the field of energy. Concrete co-operation focused specifically on:

- access to and development of energy reserves;
- market access;
- liberalisation of trade in energy;
- energy efficiency and environmental protection;
- safety principles and guidelines;
- research, technological development, innovation and dissemination;
- education and training.

In 1994 the signatory countries went on to sign a binding agreement, the European Energy Charter Treaty, which set out the general rules on trade in energy, conditions of competition, access to capital, transmission and transit, transfers of technology, environmental protection, intellectual property, conditions for investment and the procedure for settling disputes. The treaty came into force in 1998, by which time it had been ratified by 38 countires, including 13 EU member states.

ECSC treaty expires
When the European Coal and Steel Community (ECSC) was established in 1951, the coal and steel industries, which were regarded as the "basic industries", held a dominant place in the West European economy. This is now much less true, though both industries remain significant factors. The steel industry, in particular, has been transformed in the past three decades, and the Community was largely instrumental, first in its rapid growth and subsequently in its sharp decline.

The ECSC treaty expired on July 23rd 2002. Well before the treaty ran out, the levies on coal and steel production were phased out, as they were yielding far more than was needed to meet the social costs of the run-down of the two industries. By 2001, the total budget of the ECSC was €168m, compared with €339m 14 years earlier.

However, the commission decided to maintain the strict rules on state aid for the European iron and steel industry. It adopted guidelines in February 2002 banning regional investment aid and rescue and restructuring aid to the steel sector after the expiry of the ECSC treaty. As for the other types of state aid – for environmental protection purposes or for research and development activities – the steel industry will be subject to the same horizontal rules as the other sectors of the economy. The commission also decided that closure aid for this sector, under the same strict conditions that applied under the 1996 Steel Aid Code, remain compatible with the single market.

The expiry meant the treaty's assets were transferred to the EU, as provided for in a protocol annexed to the Nice treaty. The revenue from these assets and liabilities is now used exclusively for research in the sectors related to the coal and steel industries.

26 Transport

Slow progress on common transport policy ...

The Rome treaty, in Article 74, envisages the creation of a common transport policy, but for the first 24 years of the EC's existence progress in this direction was so slow that in September 1982 the European Parliament brought proceedings against the Council of Ministers in the Court of Justice for failing to carry out its obligations under the treaty. The action was partially successful. The court held that the council had infringed the treaty by failing to ensure freedom to provide services in international transport and to lay down conditions for the admission of non-resident carriers to national transport in the member states. The court declined, however, to take cognisance of the absence of a common transport policy as such, since the treaty did not define that policy with sufficient clarity to enable the court to pronounce on it. It did, however, recommend the council to work continuously towards the progressive attainment of a common transport policy.

... speeds up after court ruling

Following the court's ruling there was a significant acceleration of council decision-making in the transport field, partly in the context of the adoption of a timetable to complete the EC's internal market by 1992. In 1991 a report entitled "Transport 2000 and Beyond" was adopted, setting objectives for an integrated continent-wide transport system, involving EC assistance in linking national networks and in improving links with central and eastern Europe. Transport is estimated to provide 6.5% of the EU's gross national product, and it employs more than 6m people. Its importance in the economic integration of Western Europe can hardly be overestimated. In 1983 the European Commission established a series of broad policy targets.

- Greater integration of national transport policies.
- A better climate of competition between and within different forms of transport.
- Greater productivity and efficiency in the European transport system, partly through eliminating bottlenecks and bureaucratic restraints.
- Financial support for a series of major infrastructure projects of

Union-wide importance.
◩ A co-ordinated Union approach to safety, technical harmonisation, environmental protection and working conditions in
the transport industry.

In 1995 the commission adopted an action programme for 1995–2000,
laying down guidelines for a common approach to transport. The guidelines adopted cover the following areas: "Improving quality by developing integrated transport systems based on advanced technologies
which also contribute to environmental and safety objectives; improving the functioning of the single market in order to promote efficiency,
choice and the user-friendly provision of transport services while safeguarding social standards; broadening the external dimension by
improving transport links between the EU and third countries and the
access of EU businesses to transport markets in other parts of the
world." A further action programme for 2000–04 put much more
emphasis on the environmental dimension.

Although the commission has sought to implement a global policy,
applying common principles to the different forms of transport – all of
which compete with each other to a varying degree – it has for the most
part had to adopt a sector-by-sector approach.

Roads

It is in road transport that the commission has made the most persistent
attempts to secure the adoption of EC policies, and it has often had to
wait for many years before the Council of Ministers was able to agree
on the proposals which it had put forward.

In September 2001, the commission unveiled a white paper on a
common policy in the transport sector for the following decade,
focusing on reversing the escalating demand for road transport. The
130-page paper included a range of measures covering pricing, revitalising railways and waterways as alternative modes of transport to
roads and targeted investment in trans-European transport networks.
It pinpointed unequal growth in the different modes of transport;
congestion on some main roads and busy rail lines, within towns
and at airports; the impact on the environment or citizens' health; and
the lack of road safety. With the number of cars tripling in the previous 30 years, and with an increase of 3m cars a year, the commission warned that Europe's transport system was heading for gridlock.
It noted that road carriers made up 44% of goods transport compared

with just 8% for rail, and that by 2010, without substantial initiatives, heavy goods vehicle traffic will increase by 50%, compared with 1998. If nothing is done to reverse the growth in traffic, the commission predicted that by 2010, carbon dioxide emissions will rise by about 50% compared with 1990 levels. It proposed a harmonised tax on diesel for commercial use at a rate higher than the current EU average, a measure designed to bring environmental benefits and allow hauliers from different EU states to compete on more equal terms. The white paper included 60 measures aimed at shifting goods off congested roads, cutting pollution, boosting transport technology and improving safety.

Road safety. Some 50,000 people are killed and 1.5m injured each year in road accidents. A string of directives has harmonised standards for brakes, lighting, windscreens, sound levels, and so on. After a 20-year delay, agreement was reached in 1984 for common standards on weights and dimensions of commercial vehicles. The maximum lorry weight was then set at 40 tons (38 tons in the UK and Ireland). A further agreement on maximum axle weights for articulated lorries was reached in 1986 (11.5 tons, but 10.5 tons in the UK and Ireland). Also 1986 was declared Road Safety Year, and the commission drew up an action programme including infrastructure improvements and measures relating to road signs, vehicle safety and the behaviour and training of drivers. Subsequently, directives were adopted on:

- technical vehicle inspection;
- lorry suspension systems;
- the fitting of speed limitation devices in lorries and coaches;
- limiting the risks involved in the carriage of dangerous goods;
- restricting drivers' hours.

Frontier crossing. Delays and bureaucratic checks at internal frontier crossings had been a major source of expense and an undoubted barrier to intra-EC trade. Under the 1992 programme, progressive steps were taken to remove this barrier. From January 1st 1988 a single administrative document (SAD), also valid for crossing into EFTA countries, replaced up to 70 different forms previously required for lorries crossing internal EC borders. On January 1st 1993 the SAD was withdrawn and frontier controls on goods at all internal EU borders ceased.

International transport of goods. This had traditionally been restricted by quota and by licence. Up to 1985 only some 40% of road freight was liberalised, but under an agreement reached by the Council of Ministers in June 1986 the remainder of the trade is being progressively opened up to free competition. By 1993 all quota restrictions ended, but it was only by June 1998 that full freedom to operate transport services in other member states (cabotage) will be granted. Meanwhile, the commission has established a more rational pricing system, publishing a scale of reference tariffs which is periodically revised.

Employment in road transport industry. Since 1974 the Community has established conditions for employment in the road transport industry, notably in terms of professional ability and training. Maximum driving periods have been established for each day and each week as well as obligatory periods of rest. Observance of these rules is controlled by a tachograph (known pejoratively as "the spy in the cab") which records the driving and resting time and speeds of heavy goods vehicles.

Railways

Community action regarding the railways has mainly focused on their troubled finances, which have steadily deteriorated in the face of increasing competition from road, air and waterway transport. The gap between revenue and costs has caused large deficits. These have been bridged by subsidies, which have placed considerable burdens on national budgets. In many cases these subsidies are a recognition of non-commercial duties imposed by the state, such as low fares and the continuation of loss-making lines in thinly populated areas.

Since the early 1960s the Community has tried to balance competition between rail and other forms of transport. Rules on financial competition have been harmonised to take account of public service obligations, capital and operating subsidies. The financial involvement of governments has been made more transparent without being generally reduced. In 1975 the Council of Ministers laid down guidelines for financial recovery and a clearer definition of relations between the railway companies (almost all of which were publicly owned) and government authorities.

To boost the productivity, efficiency and quality of rail services, the commission suggested in 1981 the laying down of multi-annual programmes, notably for investment in infrastructure and rolling stock, the re-examination of public service obligations and the extension of combined rail–road services under the umbrella of a specialised international company with independent powers. This suggestion has not, so far, been adopted by the Council of Ministers. The commission has since tabled further proposals for an improved capital structure for rail companies and a better sharing of infrastructure costs (those for roads and waterways are normally financed by national budgets).

By 1996 the commission had decided that a much more radical strategy was necessary if the Union's railway system was not to shrink inexorably, and in particular to lose out to road transport on the long-distance carriage of goods, where it should enjoy a competitive and environmental advantage. In July 1996 it published a white paper entitled "A Strategy for Revitalising the Community's Railways", which contained far-reaching proposals on railway finances, the introduction of market forces into rail, public service provision and the integration of national rail systems. The most striking proposal was for the rapid construction of a network of rail "freeways" which would facilitate the speedy transport of freight on a continental basis. The white paper included a map illustrating the routes that these freeways would take. One, starting at Liverpool, would continue through London, the Channel tunnel, Lille, Paris, Lyon and Madrid to Lisbon. Another would continue eastward from Lille through Hanover, Berlin, Warsaw and eventually to Moscow. Another eastward link would run through Brussels, Cologne, Munich, Vienna and Budapest, and a north–south link would run from Stockholm to the heel of Italy. By 1999 the member states had still to react to the white paper proposals which, if they are to be effective, need to be implemented with a minimum of delay.

Transport infrastructure

The EC has played an important role in helping to finance transport infrastructure projects, ranging from roads and motorways to bridges and tunnels, ports and airports, canals, the upgrading or electrification of railways and the purchase of more comfortable and economic equipment (aircraft, high-speed trains, and so on). Nearly 20 billion ecus had been loaned by the EIB up to 1993 and a comparable amount had been expended in grants by the European Regional Development Fund. Projects in the UK which have benefited include Manchester and Birmingham airports, the Tyne-Wear metro, the Manchester light railway, the second Severn bridge and the ports of Ramsgate and Harwich.

Trans-European Networks (TENs). In 1990 the commission published proposals for assisting the development of TENs in transport,
energy and telecommunications. So far as railway development is
concerned, a master plan was published for a high-speed network by
the year 2010, including 9,000km of new lines, 15,000km of modified
track and 1,200km of links between main lines. In addition, it identified 15 key links, often frontier links, where implementation essential
to the smooth operation of the European network presents a number
of difficulties. It also anticipated rapid progress in the technical com-
patibility of equipment. The priorities adopted by the commission
were as follows.

- A study of the problems raised by the 15 key links mentioned.
- Major links: the northern route, Paris–London–Brussels–
  Amsterdam–Cologne, with connections to other member states;
  the southern route, Seville–Barcelona–Lyon–Turin–Milan–Venice,
  with onward connections to Tarvisio and Trieste, and from
  Madrid to Lisbon and Oporto.
- Improved communications with Ireland: the Dublin–Belfast–
  Crewe and Dublin–Belfast routes.

The EU, through the EIB, had already assisted in the financing of the
Channel Tunnel, which will be a crucial element in the high-speed rail
network. Altogether, by the end of 1998, the EIB and other bodies had
provided around 48 billion ecus for investment in TENs. Projects
financed by the EIB, under public-private partnership arrangements,
during 1997–98 included the new Elbe Tunnel for Hamburg, Spata Airport and the Elefsis-Stravros section of the Patras-Athens-Thessaloniki
motorway in Greece, Malpenso Airport in Italy, and the M6 motorway
extension and Manchester Metrolink in the UK.

The commission has initiated a parallel study on future prospects for
a Union motorway network and has advocated EU financial support for
three types of projects.

- Linking up existing networks: the Brenner route across the Alps
  from Italy to northern Europe; links across the Pyrenees:
  Toulouse–Barcelona (through the Puymorens tunnel, completed
  in 1994), Toulouse–Madrid and Bordeaux–Valencia (through the
  Somport tunnel, completed in 1995).
- Improving communications with outlying regions: the road link

to Ireland (between Crewe and Holyhead), the Brindisi–Patras–
Athens route and the Madrid–Lisbon link.
- Other links to improve communications with the EU's
  neighbours: the Athens–Evzoni–former Yugoslavia route (held up
  because of war), and connections with Scandinavian countries
  via the Aalborg–Fredrikshavn motorway and Fehmark link.

Inland waterways

Inland waterways play an important role in heavy industrial trade in
several parts of the EU, the most notable of several large waterway systems being formed by the River Rhine and its tributaries. Since 1976 member states have agreed to a mutual recognition of each other's decisions
on the navigability of waterways, and since 1982 the Council of Ministers
has laid down technical specifications for waterway craft. In 1991 the
council adopted a directive liberalising cabotage (international competition for the carriage of goods or passengers within other member states)
and others on the mutual recognition of boatmasters' certifications, cock-
pit crew licences and driving licences.

The commission has taken the initiative in:

- moves to scrap overcapacity, financed by national governments;
- setting up a market monitoring system;
- drawing up an international agreement securing free competition
  once the Rhine–Main–Danube canal is completed and mutual
  access is provided for vessels from East European waterways.

Shipping

Few Community agreements had been reached on sea transport before
1986, despite the importance of this sector to the EC's trade. Around 95%
of its external trade is carried by sea, which also plays an important role
in intra-EU trade, in part because three member states do not have a
common land frontier with the rest of the Union. It is in the interests of
the EU to keep the shipping industry open to international competition,
but it was only in December 1986 that the Council of Ministers agreed
most of the elements of a common shipping policy which should enable
the EU to use its collective bargaining power in such a way as to
strengthen its opportunities to compete on the world market. Four regulations were approved, which came into effect in July 1987.

Competition.   This regulation set out precise directions as to how the

EC's general rules of competition should be applied to the maritime transport sector. Transport had previously been excluded from a 1962 regulation which had defined competition rules for most other economic sectors.

Predatory pricing by third countries.   This provided for a coordinated response, allowing the EC to take anti-dumping measures against the countries or companies concerned. A complaints investigation procedure was instituted, and provision made for the imposition of provisional or definitive duties on the country's vessels.

Cargo reservations.   This regulation provided for a co-ordinated EC response to third countries which reserve a portion of their trade to their own vessels. Countermeasures which may now be applied include the imposition of permits for loading, carrying or discharging, the introduction of quotas or the imposition of taxes or duties.

Freedom to provide services.   Community vessels are now free to ply between member states and between member states and third countries. Member states are forbidden to enter agreements with third countries which would restrict access for the vessels of other member states.
A fifth regulation, which would allow vessels from member states to compete for the coastal trade of other member states (cabotage) and would effectively have completed the common shipping policy, was, however, shelved. This opened up a division between the more northerly EC countries which are strongly in favour and certain southern states which would like to continue with their national restrictions. In particular, Spain was reluctant to allow other member states to compete for trade between mainland Spain and the Canary Islands, and Greece wished to remain in a position, in the event of Turkish accession to full membership of the EC, to exclude its ships from plying between the Greek islands. Agreement in principle on the liberalisation of cabotage was eventually reached in 1991, but it will still be several years before full international competition becomes a reality.
In the wake of the tanker disasters at La Coruña and the Shetland Islands, the European Commission and the Council of Ministers mapped out, in 1993, an EU policy on safety at sea to underpin the work of individual member states, and to ensure more effective implementation of international regulations. The commission prepared directives or regulations to:

- lay down common rules for ship inspection;
- enforce a minimum level of training for crews;
- regulate the ballast requirements for oil tankers;
- set up a European vessel reporting system;
- regulate the carrying of dangerous or polluting goods.

Several other EU initiatives were adopted in 1998, including common safety rules for roll-on, roll-off ferries and high-speed passenger craft services; a proposal to improve port reception facilities for ship-generated waste and cargo residues; and directives to impose on all vessels operating within the Community (including those flying the flags of third countries) the working hours laid down by the International Labour Organisation, to apply certain international safety standards for passenger vessels, and to register all persons sailing on board passenger ships.

Tougher shipping rules were announced in 2000 in the wake of the Erika oil tanker spill off the French coast, when the 25-year-old single-hull vessel broke in two, releasing 100,000 tonnes of oil and damaging 400km of the Brittany coast. The first package of measures, known as Erika I, is supposed to toughen up port inspections, introduce better controls for ship classification societies and gradually phase out single-hull tankers, replacing them with safer, double-hull versions. The second package, Erika II, emphasises training for crews, establishes a European pollution damage fund to provide compensation of up to €1 billion for victims and sets up a European Maritime Safety Agency. The main duties of the agency are to support and monitor member states' compliance with maritime safety rules, evaluate the effectiveness of the rules, collect data and audit maritime classification societies.

Airways

Air transport was for many years the sector on which the Community had the least impact, and where its competition rules remained largely a dead letter. The entire system was controlled by a series of inter-governmental and inter-airline agreements, which effectively excluded competition and led to some of the highest air fares in the world, substantially greater, in particular, than on routes of comparable distance in North America. Before 1986 EC action had been largely restricted to the adoption of directives on co-operation in accident inquiries, the reduction of noise from aircraft and helicopters and the opening of routes between certain regional centres in the Community.

In April 1986 a ruling from the Court of Justice gave the commission the green light to force the pace. In a case involving the French travel firm Nouvelles Frontières, which had challenged price-fixing regulations under the French Civil Aviation Code, the court ruled that the EC general competition rules were applicable to air transport and that member state governments have an obligation under the Rome treaty not to approve air fares if they know that they result from an agreement or concerted practices between airlines. In the absence of a specific regulation applying the competition rules to air transport, the competence for deciding whether an air fares agreement contravenes the treaty's competition rules rests with the commission (under Article 89) and the anti-trust authorities of the member states (Article 88). Subsequently, the then competition commissioner, Peter Sutherland, threatened legal action against ten leading European airlines if they did not terminate or drastically amend their price-fixing agreements. After having stalled for several months, the ten airlines indicated in April 1987 that they were willing to comply. The introduction of competitive fares, however, still depended on the abrogation or amendment of bilateral agreements between the airlines and their own national governments, only a minority of which were prepared to contemplate such a radical departure.

Simultaneously with its legal initiative, the commission sought to secure a political compromise which would enable at least a partial liberalisation of fares to be implemented. After lengthy and tortuous negotiations such a compromise – involving discount fares, capacity sharing, the entry of new competitors on established routes, regional to hub airport connections, the right to pick up and put down passengers at intermediate points, and the conditions under which block exemptions to EC competition rules should be granted – was agreed in principle by the Council of Transport Ministers in June 1987. It was, however, immediately vetoed by Spain, on the ground that the inclusion in the agreement of Gibraltar as a UK regional airport compromised the Spanish claim to sovereignty over the Rock.

The Spanish veto was lifted in December 1987 following a bilateral deal with the UK over the use of Gibraltar airport. The compromise agreement came into force in January 1988. In 1991 the commission adopted a third liberalisation package designed to introduce full competition between European airlines after 1993. The principle that airlines should be allowed to set their own prices on international routes was agreed by the EC in March 1992, but there was a virtual impasse on timing, with the UK and the Netherlands demanding free markets from the end of 1993 while France and the others held out for a six-year "transition period". A four-year compromise was finally agreed in June 1992, and since March 1997 airlines have been free to set their own fares and to operate anywhere within the EU.

The principal beneficiaries of the agreement are the Union's fast-growing private airlines, which have lower overheads and can charge lower prices than most state-owned organisations. The opponents of liberalisation, however, won enough "safeguards" to keep new competitors out. In an attempt to prevent a fall in profitability such as hit American airlines following deregulation in the 1980s, EU governments can complain to the commission if an airline proposes to charge too little for tickets.

The commission's 1999 plans for a "single European sky" to improve air traffic management have been consistently delayed – again by British and Spanish differences over Gibraltar airport. Ironically, both countries, which formed a powerful alliance in favour of liberalisation at Lisbon, strongly back the proposal in principle. The plan aimed at co-ordinating air traffic control as a necessary first step towards liberalisation of the airline market and, it is hoped, fewer delays and cheaper fares. In March 2002, with the issue still not resolved, leaders at the Barcelona European Council committed themselves to create the single European sky by 2004. The proposals came after a report showed that one-fifth of European flights take off late.

Attempts by the commission to negotiate liberalisation agreements with third countries, in particular the United States, have been frustrated by the refusal of some member states, notably the UK, to allow it to negotiate on their behalf. Consequently, the United States has been able, to some extent, to pick and choose among EU governments and to play one off against the other, with the prospect that the overall outcome will be less favourable to European airlines and consumers than would otherwise be the case. In February 2002, a preliminary finding from the EU's Court of Justice called into question the basis of all bilateral agreements signed by member states since the creation of the single EU aviation market nearly ten years earlier. The commission sued eight EU countries, and the court indicated that the central feature of such agreements between the United States and individual EU member states over access to European airports was illegal. US open skies accords have been signed by 56 countries. In a preliminary assessment, a court advocate-general said the current open skies agreements involved "a case of discrimination based on nationality" that was illegal under the EU treaty.

The ruling means that in future all EU airlines will be given access to EU airports, leading to much greater pan-European competition on lucrative transatlantic routes. The EU will negotiate such treaties with non-EU countries, which should lead to carriers within member states merging freely to create a much-needed consolidation in an industry riddled with overcapacity and inefficiency.

Galileo

In March 2002, the €2.5 billion Galileo satellite programme was approved, offering a European and primarily civilian alternative to the dominant American global positioning system (GPS) which was developed largely for military purposes. Galileo, initially based on 30 satellites, will pinpoint the locations of users such as car drivers and airline pilots to within 1 metre, compared with the 100 metres on offer from GPS. The satellite's UN-approved frequencies are adjacent to those of GPS, making US co-operation indispensable if technical conflicts between the systems are to be avoided. However, GPS is free to commercial users whereas Galileo will charge a fee. Galileo should cover extreme latitudes that GPS misses, overcome the poor availability that GPS suffers in urban areas and make it possible to study from space tectonic movements in earthquake zones or analyse the level of rivers and lakes. It is expected to create 150,000 jobs and generate over €11 billion in annual revenue for EU companies after its launch in 2008. Like the Ariane space rocket and Airbus programmes, Galileo was hailed as helping the EU to narrow the innovation gap with the United States. There have been regular spats between the EU and the United States, with the Pentagon complaining that the system could interfere with the signals of the military-run GPS. But EU leaders had objected to relying on an American system whose services could – and on occasion have been – withdrawn.

27 Fisheries

A common fisheries policy was envisaged by Article 38 of the Rome treaty, on similar lines to the common agricultural policy. Yet no proposals for such a policy were produced before 1966, and it was another 17 years before the policy was finally put into place.

Initial fisheries policy causes problems

In 1970 an attempt was made by the six original member states to assert the principle of free access to Community fisheries, but the decisions taken then by the Council of Ministers were limited in scope. A common market organisation for fish was created, including price-support mechanisms and measures to protect the Community market. To modernise the sector and ensure equal terms of competition within it, the Community was given the task of co-ordinating the structural policies of the member states and of supplementing them with financial interventions of its own.

The timing of these decisions was unfortunate, as they occurred during the closing stages of the entry negotiations with Denmark, Ireland, Norway and the UK, all important fishing nations. It appeared that the original six members had determined to settle the issue to their own advantage before the new member states had a chance to exert their own influence. Consequently, Norway turned down the entry terms its government had negotiated in a closely fought referendum. Many observers regarded the fisheries policy as a decisive factor which swung the vote against membership. Opinion was appeased in the other three applicant states by a last-minute agreement that all members could, until the end of 1982, restrict fishing within a six-mile coastal limit, and in certain areas a 12-mile limit, to vessels which traditionally fished in those waters.

Exclusive fishing zones extended

Well before the 1982 deadline was reached it became apparent that a more comprehensive approach would be necessary if fishing resources in EC waters were to be conserved. From 1975 onwards a number of countries on the Atlantic coastline, including Iceland, Norway and Canada, extended their exclusive fishing zones to 200 nautical miles. These limits were subsequently to be endorsed by the international

Convention on the Law of the Sea. The effect was to turn out of these waters many EC boats and also trawlers from third countries, many of which now concentrated their efforts on the North Sea, which was seriously threatened with overfishing.

In 1977, in self-defence, the Community also extended its fishing limits to 200 miles, leaving itself in charge of a huge expanse of sea, in which competition between member states' fishermen was intensifying. Within these limits there was fierce argument, particularly involving the UK, over the extent to which member states could claim permanent and exclusive rights in their coastal waters.

Common fisheries policy agreed

The European Commission tabled proposals as early as 1976, but it was only at the beginning of 1983, following hard fought negotiations in which Denmark, in particular, had found great difficulty in reaching agreement with its partners, that a common fisheries policy (CFP) was finally concluded. Its main provisions are as follows.

Fishing zones. In principle the Union's waters are open to all EU fishermen within a 200-mile limit from the Atlantic and North Sea coasts, but within narrower limits in the Mediterranean and Baltic seas. Member states are, however, allowed to retain limits up to 12 miles from their shores, within which fishing is reserved for their own fleets and for boats from other member states with traditional rights. In addition, fishing in an area beyond 12 miles around the Orkney and Shetland islands, for potentially endangered species, is subject to a system of Union licences. These measures apply for 20 years, but may be reviewed after ten.

Fish stocks. These are conserved and managed by fixing total allowable catches (TACs) which are agreed annually by the Council of Ministers for all species threatened by overfishing. They are divided into quotas for each member state.

Conservation. Based on scientific advice, conservation measures consist mainly of limits on fishing in certain zones, minimum mesh sizes for nets and, in certain cases, minimum sizes for fish landed. With the agreement of the commission, member states may apply extra conservation measures of their own, but these must not discriminate against other member states.

Surveillance. Measures such as obligatory logbooks, port inspections, aerial controls, and so on, are applied by the member states, under the supervision of the commission, which has a team of inspectors for this purpose.

Marketing. Standards as regards quality, size, weight, presentation and packing are applied throughout the Union, largely through the agency of producer organisations, but subject to inspection by the commission. Guide prices are set by the Council of Ministers with "withdrawal" prices set at 70–90%, the Union compensating fishermen for catches withdrawn from the market. Export refunds are available when, as is usually the case, the guide and withdrawal prices are higher than world prices. If European supplies prove insufficient, customs duties on imports can be suspended, as has happened in recent years with tuna and cod.

International relations. Reciprocal agreements, permitting limited access to each other's waters and markets have been made with several other countries, such as Norway, the Faeroes, Canada and the United States. Other agreements with developing countries in Africa and the Indian Ocean permit EU vessels to fish in their waters in exchange for financial and technical assistance.

EU is world's fourth largest producer

The accession of Spain and Portugal in 1986 doubled the number of fishermen in the Community (now about 300,000), and increased the tonnage of the fishing fleet by about 65% and total catches by 30%. The EU is now the world's fourth largest producer. Spain and Portugal were required to adapt their fishing policies to the CFP, with mutual access being provided to several fishing zones, the number of which was to be reviewed by 1995. During the negotiations for Norwegian membership of the EU in March 1994, however, it was agreed that Spain and Portugal should have full access to EU waters as from January 1st 1995.

At the same time the Community stepped up its financial aid for restructuring the fishing fleets – with grants available for the scrapping of surplus capacity, the construction and modernisation of boats, the development of aquaculture and improvements in processing and marketing. In 1998 the EU adopted a regulation banning the use of driftnets by all vessels in EU waters except the Baltic and by all EU vessels in other waters. It came into effect on January 1st 2002, and was accompanied by social measures and compensation for the fisher-men concerned.

The CFP is based to a large extent on the model of the CAP, but it is far less expensive. The total cost for 2001 was around €1 billion, or around 1% of the entire budget.

Reform of the CFP is due to take place before the end of 2002. Until now, the discussions have raised concerns from all sides – fishermen, fish processors, environmentalists and consumers – that the current mechanism is wasteful and encourages cheating. Indeed, from the middle of the 1990s, the European Commission began pushing for more conservation measures, claiming that if current trends in fishing contin-ued, stocks would soon be exhausted. The sensitivity of the issue was raised during the "Greenland halibut war" between Spanish fishermen and Canadian authorities off the coast of the Grand Banks, a region where Canadian fishermen had been forced to stop fishing cod because of a dramatic collapse in stocks. Within the EU, fleet-cutting programmes were adopted – the so-called multi-annual guidance programmes (MAGPs) – which included tough sanctions for member states that failed to meet their targets.

28 Environment

There was no legal provision in the Rome treaty for a common EC policy on the environment, other than the general authority given by Article 235 enabling the Council of Ministers, acting unanimously, to take appropriate measures to achieve any of the objectives of the Community. This gap, reflecting the lack of interest in environmental matters in the 1950s, was remedied by the Single European Act, which in Article 25 set out a threefold aim for action on the environment:

- to preserve, protect and improve the quality of the environment;
- to contribute towards protecting human health;
- to ensure a prudent and rational utilisation of natural resources.

Programmes adopted from 1973

It is not surprising that, in the absence of any earlier definition of EC competence in this area, the Community's environment policy evolved in an ad hoc and incremental manner. It was not until 1985, for example, that the Council of Ministers drew up a work programme for obtaining information on the state of the environment and natural resources in the Community. Nevertheless, from 1973 onwards the council adopted a series of five-year action programmes which gradually broadened out from immediate responses to serious pollution problems to an overall preventive strategy for safeguarding the environment and natural resources. The most recent, the ten-year Sixth Environment Action Programme, was agreed in March 2002. The main areas in which EU measures have so far been adopted include the following.

Water pollution. A number of directives have been approved dealing with the protection of water, surface and underground, fresh and salt. Quality standards have been set for bathing water, drinking water, fresh water suitable for fish life and water used for rearing shellfish. The discharge of toxic substances is strictly controlled, with limits set for mercury, cadmium, lindane, DDT, pentachlorophenol and carbon tetrachloride, and specific rules for the control and gradual reduction of dumping of titanium dioxide, which causes "red sludge". The Union is a participant in several conventions designed to reduce pollution in international waterways such as the River Rhine, the North Atlantic, the North Sea and the Mediterranean.

Atmospheric pollution.   Despite the adoption of a series of directives on such topics as the discharge of sulphur dioxide, the use of chloro-fluorcarbons (CFCs) in aerosol cans and the control of pollution from certain industrial premises, progress has been slow in what are widely regarded as the two key areas: pollution from large combustion plants, particularly power stations, and the emission of gases from motor vehicles. Both of these are blamed for widespread damage to forests through acid rain and for a variety of threats to public health. In March 1985 the council reached agreement concerning the lead content of petrol (which provided that unleaded petrol would be generally available in the Community from October 1st 1989), but it was only in July 1987, that – under the majority voting provisions of the Single European Act – a series of regulations on automobile exhaust emission was adopted. A substantial work programme has been initiated by the European Commission to study the greenhouse effect and to find ways to limit the heating-up of the atmosphere. Specific measures are also envisaged to reduce pollution by such substances as photochemical oxidants.

Noise.   Directives have been adopted fixing maximum noise levels for cars, lorries, motorcycles, tractors, subsonic aircraft, lawnmowers and building-site machinery. The noise level of household equipment must be stipulated on its packaging, and proposals are under consideration concerning helicopters and rail vehicles.

Chemical products.   Particularly since the Seveso accident in northern Italy in 1977, which resulted in the contamination of a large area by a highly toxic dioxin, increasingly stringent measures have been taken to reduce the risks arising from the manufacture and disposal of chemical substances. As long ago as 1967 a directive was adopted relating to the classification, packaging and labelling of dangerous substances. Two 1973 directives control the composition of detergents, while since 1986 there has been a European Inventory of Existing Chemical Substances, which lists all chemical products on the market, enabling them to be subject to a general procedure for notification, evaluation and control. Other measures ban the use of certain substances in pesticides, and strictly control the manufacture and use of PCBs and PCTs (the substances involved in the Seveso accident), and of asbestos. In an attempt to prevent further major accidents and to limit their consequences, a directive of June 1982 imposes on manufacturers in all member states the obligation to inform the authorities about substances, plants and possible locations of accidents.

Following the Bhopal tragedy in India there has been strong pressure, particularly in the European Parliament, for a further tightening up of control measures. Concern about the depletion of the ozone layer, which protects the earth from ultraviolet rays, led the Community to adopt a series of measures to bring about a substantial reduction of CFCs and other substances thought to be responsible for this phenomenon.

Waste disposal.   Since 1975 Community rules have been in force concerning the collection, disposal, recycling and processing of waste, of which the EU produces more than 2 billion tons every year. Specific measures have also been taken in individual areas, such as waste from the titanium oxide industry, waste oils, the dumping of waste at sea and radioactive waste. Recommendations have been made on the reuse of old paper, cardboard and drinks containers.

Nature protection.   The EU is a member of the 1979 Berne Convention on the conservation of wildlife, and has also recommended member states to adhere to the 1950 Paris Convention on the protection of birds and the 1971 Ramsar Convention on Wetlands. The Council of Ministers has adopted several directives on the conservation of wild birds, on banning the importation of products made from the skins of baby seals (following a mass campaign in which the European Parliament played a crucial role) and on the control and restriction of scientific experiments on animals. Financial support is given to projects to conserve natural habitats, and further proposals were planned under the fourth action programme (1988–92) to protect fauna and flora.

Broadening the scope of environmental policy

By the early 1990s there was a widespread feeling that the EC should adopt a much more determined and systematic approach to environmental management. The June 1990 summit in Dublin called for action by the Community and its member states to be developed on a co-ordinated basis, in keeping with the principles of sustainable development and giving priority to preventive measures. The creation of a European Environmental Agency was agreed, but its establishment was delayed by failure among the member states to agree on where it should be sited.

In 1991 there was a considerable broadening of the scope of EC environmental policy, which became inextricably linked to overall economic policy-making. Commission initiatives were seen to be necessary to bring about the integration of environmental considerations into other policy areas including agriculture, the internal market, transport and energy. Linked closely to energy policy issues and in response to the urgent problem of global warming, the commission proposed a package of measures to limit carbon dioxide emissions and to improve energy efficiency and security of supply. It proposed a carbon dioxide/energy tax as a means of attaining the target of stabilising emissions at 1990 levels by 2000. The council approved the commission proposals in principle, but it is far from certain that the energy tax proposal will go ahead. European industrialists believe that they will lose price competitiveness against their main rivals in Japan and the United States unless a comparable tax is also levied in these two countries. This issue was discussed at the UN Earth Summit in Rio de Janeiro in June 1992, where the EC took a leading role in proposing a worldwide approach to the reduction of carbon dioxide emissions.

Also in 1991 the Council of Ministers adopted the LIFE programme, designed to provide financial incentives for priority projects in the environmental field. The most recent programme, the €640m LIFE III, covers the period 2000–04. The EU has also recently adopted measures on:

- the EC Norspa project (to protect the environment in the coastal areas and waters of the Irish Sea, North Sea, Baltic Sea and north east Atlantic Ocean);
- waste water;
- a Community eco-label;
- the protection of natural habitats;
- pollution by lorries.

The Treaty on European Union agreed at the Maastricht summit in December 1991 incorporated a new section on the environment in the Rome treaty, substantially extending EU competence. However, a number of issues were reserved for unanimous decision in the Council of Ministers rather than by qualified majority voting, which the commission would have preferred. The Amsterdam Treaty of June 1997 elevated the promotion of "a high level of protection and improvement of the quality of the environment" into a specific Community objective, and extended the co-decision powers of the European Parliament into some, though not all, environmental issues.

At the United Nations conference on Climate Change at Kyoto in December 1997 the EU committed itself to reducing total greenhouse gas emissions by 8% by 2010, compared with 1990 levels. In June 1998 the Council of Ministers agreed on the contribution to be made by each member state towards meeting this target. Much of the subsequent work of the Union in this field has been focused on a range of measures to restrict the use of substances that deplete the ozone layer. However, although the EU has remained committed to the Kyoto process, George Bush confirmed when he became president of the United States in 2001 that he would not sign up to the treaty. Despite this setback, the EU continued with negotiations, and by early 2002 EU member states had begun their national ratification procedures.

29 Justice and home affairs

Until the Delors era, the Community steered clear of justice and home affairs issues, accepting these were essentially the prerogative of member states. The Maastricht treaty changed this: the creation of the European Union – erected on three supposedly separate pillars – implied a specific role for justice and home affairs. It reflected concerns that as internal frontiers disappeared, external borders would be strengthened, and that implied increased co-operation between the interior and justice ministries. The Maastricht treaty provided a framework for this co-operation. It provided a new structure with a permanent secretariat and named the actors and joint instruments for dealing with sensitive issues.

Although some working structures are unwieldy, consistency has been improved. With the entry into force of the Treaty of Amsterdam, civil law matters, asylum and immigration became Community matters, with police and judicial co-operation in criminal matters remaining within the third pillar. Since then, co-operation has developed fast, accelerated by continuing debates on immigration and security concerns following the September 11th 2001 attacks in the United States. The rules now try to guarantee the free movement of EU citizens and non-EU nationals, while promising public security by combating terrorism and all forms of organised crime, including human trafficking, sexual exploitation of children, vehicle, arms and drug trafficking, corruption and fraud. With regular council meetings of justice and home affairs ministers, it is easy to forget that this was once a no-go area.

Informal beginnings

In 1957, the Treaty of Rome set the free movement of persons as one of its objectives, but it failed to deal with border crossings, immigration or visa policy. Freedom of movement was viewed in purely economic terms and concerned only workers. But by the 1970s, the desire to extend this freedom to everyone and the growing importance of certain problems – such as cross-border organised crime, drug trafficking, illegal immigration and terrorism – encouraged member states to seek informal co-operation in justice and home affairs.

Member states were already co-operating at various levels: bilaterally, regionally (within the Council of Europe, for example) and globally

(Interpol and the UN). The 1967 Naples convention on co-operation and mutual assistance between customs administrations set out the first framework for dialogue between member states. From 1975 onwards, intergovernmental co-operation slowly began to develop outside the Community's legal framework for dealing with immigration, the right of asylum and police and judicial co-operation. Informal arrangements were set up to swap experiences, exchange information and expertise, and develop networks to improve contacts between member states. The Trevi Group met initially to discuss terrorism and internal security, but it extended its scope in 1985 to cover illegal immigration and organised crime. In parallel, 1984 saw the first regular informal meetings of justice and home affairs ministers, every six months, to discuss issues such as police, judicial and customs co-operation, and the free movement of people.

The Single European Act in 1986 marked a turning point in intergovernmental co-operation. Article 8a (renumbered Article 7a in the Maastricht treaty and Article 14 in the Amsterdam treaty) creates a single market based on four fundamental freedoms: the free movement of goods, capital, services and persons. But freedom of movement for all – European citizens and non-European nationals – obviously implied scrapping border controls. Resistance from certain member states on this issue was overcome by promises of flanking measures to strengthen external frontiers and draft European asylum and immigration policies. New working parties were set up after the Single European Act: the ad hoc immigration group in 1986, the European Committee to Combat Drugs (CELAD) in 1989 and the Mutual Assistance Group (MAG) on customs in 1992.

However, they were still outside the Community framework, and progress on developing the justice and home affairs policy stuttered. This prompted France, Germany and the Benelux countries to sign the Schengen Agreement in 1985 and the Schengen Convention in 1990. This was designed to abolish internal border checks, improve controls at external borders and harmonise arrangements relating to visas, asylum and police and judicial co-operation (see pages 114–5).

The Maastricht treaty

It was the Maastricht treaty that revived the process, establishing justice and home affairs as a third pillar to the structure of the European Union (see page 40). The new form of co-operation covered nine areas considered to be of common interest: asylum policy; the crossing of external borders; immigration; combating drug addiction; combating international fraud; judicial co-operation in civil matters; judicial co-operation in criminal matters; customs co-operation; and police co-operation. It incorporated the existing working parties into a complex five-tier structure: specific working parties, steering committees, a co-ordinating committee set up under Article K4 of the EU treaty, the Committee of Permanent Representatives, and the Council of Justice and Home Affairs Ministers.

But the third pillar's decision-taking mechanisms, based on those of the common foreign and security policy, quickly created problems, owing to a blurred distinction between the provisions contained in the Treaty of Rome and EU treaty. Should drugs issues fall into the net of Community health policy or that of co-operation on justice and home affairs, which covers trafficking and drug dependency? Should questions of asylum, immigration and external frontiers be dealt with in the context of freedom of movement of persons, in a Community framework?

The Amsterdam treaty

From an institutional perspective, the third pillar as constructed by the Maastricht treaty offered only a limited role for the institutions and no real control over decisions taken by the member states. So changes were made by the time the Treaty of Amsterdam was negotiated in 1997. The new treaty defined the area of freedom, security and justice more precisely, as well as trying to improve the balance of the various institutions. It boosted the areas of common interest and inserted a new title in the treaty: "Visas, asylum, immigration and other policies related to the free movement of persons". This covers external border controls, asylum, immigration and judicial co-operation in civil matters, bringing these areas under the first pillar, where they can be the subject of EU directives, regulations, decisions, recommendations and opinions.

Police and judicial co-operation remain under the reshaped third pillar, however, to which the Amsterdam treaty has added the prevention and combating of racism and xenophobia. Some changes have been made to decision-making: joint actions are replaced by the framework decisions, which are legal instruments similar in spirit to directives and the corresponding implementing measures.

Co-operation in the field of justice and home affairs, unlike other policies, puts more weight on the member states and limits the powers of the European Commission, the European Parliament and the Court of Justice. The commission does not have sole right of initiative, sharing this role with the member states. The treaty does, however, give it the right of initiative in all justice and home affairs areas. The Treaty of

Amsterdam creates a distinction between the free movement of persons and the establishment of an area of freedom, security and justice. This means that policies on visas, asylum, immigration and judicial co-operation in criminal matters have been made Community matters, making it possible to use Community instruments such as regulations, directives, decisions, recommendations and opinions.

The area of freedom, security and justice enables the Schengen agreements to be brought within the framework of the EU. The measures already taken under these agreements have been added to the established body of EU law in either Title IV or Title VI of the EU treaty in accordance with a decision taken by the Council of Ministers. To avoid the repetition of exclusive inter-governmental collaboration on the lines of Schengen, Title VI of the EU treaty now provides that member states intending to establish closer co-operation between themselves may be authorised to do so within the EU framework. The UK, Ireland and Denmark indicated in various protocols to the Treaty of Amsterdam that they do not wish to participate fully in all the measures relating to the area of freedom, security and justice (all have since adopted the Schengen rules). Conversely, Norway and Iceland have concluded an association agreement to co-operate with the Schengen area.

In July 1998 the European Commission published a communication on the area of freedom, security and justice setting out the basis, form and main objectives. The Vienna European Council of December 1998 endorsed a council and commission action plan which stressed the need for a European law-enforcement area, improved co-operation between national judicial and police authorities, a more effective Europol and an overall strategy on migration, asylum and the reception of refugees. At the Cologne European Council of June 1999, it was decided to draw up a charter of the basic rights of EU citizens which was adopted at the Nice summit in December 2000, although it was not formally incorporated into the Rome treaty.

At the Tampere European Council in October 1999, EU leaders asked the commission to produce a scoreboard listing all the measures to be taken in the next five years and keeping progress under review. The aim is to develop an open and secure European Union, compliant with the Geneva Refugee Convention and other relevant human rights instruments, and to improve European citizens' access to justice throughout the EU.

There were further changes when the Treaty of Nice was negotiated in December 2000. This shifted voting to qualified majority on asylum, civil law, the free movement of legal third-country nationals, frontier controls, illegal immigration and repatriation. In 2000, the EU also set up a €216m four-year European Refugee Fund to help member states cope with the influx of displaced people. In May 2001, justice and home affairs ministers agreed penalties of no less than eight years in prison for people convicted of smuggling and harbouring illegal immigrants. They also agreed to swap information among criminal investigation agencies to combat money-laundering, allowing foreign investigators access to bank accounts in countries with strong banking secrecy laws if they can demonstrate the information they are looking for has substantial value. The EU also set up a "Eurojust" unit with powers to combat cross-border organised crime.

Recent developments

The difficulties surrounding asylum revolve around the inability of member states to agree on the very concept of political refugee. So far there has been little movement on questions of minimum guarantees to be granted to asylum applicants in the event of expulsion and their rights during examination of an asylum application or an appeal. Naturally, these are sensitive political questions, perceived as directly affecting the sovereignty, security and people in member states, especially since political cultures, legal systems and administrative traditions can vary enormously. The different interpretations of rules at the end of 2001 led to dramatic attempts by immigrants gathered in Calais to try to seek asylum in the UK by jumping on Eurostar trains travelling into the Channel tunnel.

Earlier, in 2000, the discovery of the bodies of 58 Chinese immigrants in a truck in Dover led to a more intense discussion on issues of human trafficking. By March 2002, justice and home affairs ministers had adopted a new EU-wide fingerprint database for asylum seekers. This is seen as an important instrument in stamping out illegal immigration and so-called asylum shopping. The new Eurodac system should allow immigration services to check the fingerprints of asylum seekers against records held by other EU countries.

One of the most visible results of co-operation in justice and home affairs is the European Police Office, Europol, to improve police co-operation between the member states in order to combat serious international crime. Based in The Hague, Europol enables personal information to be exchanged, collected and analysed at European level. This has been followed by the creation of new co-operation bodies, such as the European Police College and the Police Chiefs Task Force.

September 11th 2001

In the wake of the September 11th 2001 attacks in the United States, ambitious plans were announced for sweeping anti-terrorist measures, including Europe-wide arrest warrants. Proposals for a new network of anti-terrorism liaison officers, a bigger role for Europol and closer collaboration on security precautions were backed by EU leaders who met in Brussels at an emergency summit on September 21st.

Until then, efforts to combat terrorism inside the EU were hampered by differences in law in member states: only six had laws referring to terrorism or terrorists; the rest used more general laws to prosecute suspects. The new agreement defined terrorism broadly, covering cyber and environmental attacks, and included a two-tier penalty system of eight years' imprisonment for those who commit terrorist acts and 15 years for the leaders of terrorist groups. The EU also agreed measures to force courts to freeze and transfer criminals' assets on request from a court in another member state.

The European arrest warrant was agreed in principle at the Laeken European Council in December 2001, and there was a January 2004 deadline for implementation. This will speed up extradition within the EU; it also differs from the current system in that there will be a minimal role for ministers. It will apply to 32 diverse crimes, including terrorism, trafficking in human beings, corruption, rape and racism.

30 Consumers

Cinderella of the EU

To some extent consumer policy has been the Cinderella of the EU. It was not mentioned in the Rome treaty, and it took years of campaigning by consumer organisations, often backed by pressure from the European Parliament, before practical steps were taken to ensure that consumer issues were considered on a serious continuing basis. The turning point came at the EC summit meeting in Paris in 1972, when the heads of government decided that economic development must be accompanied by an improvement in the quality of life. This meant that the Community should pursue an active consumer policy. Three important steps followed over the next few years.

- The creation of a service, and then a directorate-general, for the environment and consumer protection, within the commission.
- The creation of a Consumers' Consultative Committee (CCC).
- The adoption by the Council of Ministers, in April 1975, of a first consumer information and protection programme. Five basic consumer rights were enunciated: the right to safeguards for health and safety; the right to economic justice; the right to redress for damages; the right to information and education; and the right to consultation. These rights were to be implemented by concrete measures and also taken into account in other Community policies, such as agriculture, the economy, social affairs and the environment.

Consumers' Consultative Council

The CCC (renamed Consumers' Consultative Council in 1989) was appointed and serviced by the commission. It consisted of 39 members, including representatives from each of four major European consumer organisations:

- the European Consumer Bureau (BEUC);
- the Committee of European Community Family Organisations (Coface);
- the European Community Consumer Co-operatives (Euroco-op);

◪ the European Confederation of Trade Unions (ETUC).

The commission gives annual grants to each of these bodies and tries to bring them into closer contact with equivalent European organisations representing manufacturers, distributors and advertising agencies. The CCC, which was reconstituted as the Consumer Committee in 1995, is consulted from the outset on any commission work in areas which touch on consumer interests, and may also give opinions on its own initiative.

Extending consumer choice

An important judgment by the Court of Justice in 1979 had a major significance in extending consumer choice. This was in the "Cassis de Dijon" case, and it reaffirmed in principle that all goods legally manufactured in a member country must be allowed into others. The judgment found that national technical regulations, even if applied equally to domestic and imported goods, must not be allowed to create a barrier to trade except for overriding reasons such as the protection of public health or consumer interests.

It was not until 1983 that EC ministers responsible for consumer affairs met for the first time. They are now established participants in the Council of Ministers, meeting several times each year and addressing themselves to a steady stream of proposals put up by the commission. Decisions taken so far in the consumer field can be divided into three broad categories:

◪ the health and safety of consumers;
◪ protecting consumers' economic interests;
◪ consumer information and education.

Health and safety

It is in this category that most progress has been made. Measures adopted have covered the following areas.

Foodstuffs.   European lists of permitted substances and purity standards have been established for foodstuff additives, such as colourings, anti-oxidants, preservatives, emulsifiers, stabilisers and gelifiers. Pesticide residues in fruit and vegetables and erucic acid in oils and fats for human consumption have been limited to maximum levels. Regulations also govern the production of honey, fruit juice, tinned milk, cocoa and

chocolate, coffee and chicory extracts, mineral waters, jams and mar-
malades and chestnut purée, and specialist foodstuffs such as products
for special diets. Directives are in force relating to the labelling of foodstuffs, specifying ingredients, quantity and the date by which they
should be consumed. A ban has been imposed on the use of animal
growth promoters which contain certain substances with hormonal or
thyrostatic effects.

Dangerous substances.   Directives control the classification, marketing and labelling as well as the use of many toxic substances such as
pesticides, solvents, paints, varnishes, printers' ink, glues and asbestos.

Pharmaceuticals.   The testing, patenting, labelling and marketing of
pharmaceutical products are all controlled by EU directives.

Other products.   EU directives regulate, for safety reasons, such products as cosmetics, textiles (where the main concern is to prevent the use
of inflammable material), toys and a number of other manufactured
products. Several hundred directives have been approved for the purpose of standardising tools, component parts and finished products in
manufacturing industry, with a view to increasing the efficiency and
competitiveness of European firms, but since 1985 a new approach to
standardisation has been adopted. Since then new directives have concentrated only on laying down safety specifications and have relied on
the mutual recognition of national standards where no European standards exist. The commission does, however, give financial support to the
two bodies responsible for setting European standards, CEN and Cen-
elec, and has given them remits to draft European standards concerning,
in particular, toys, pressure vessels, gas appliances and information
technology.

Warning system.   In March 1984 the Council of Ministers established a Community system for the rapid exchange of information
on dangerous products. This warning system allows the authorities of
one member state rapidly to draw the attention of all the others to
serious incidents and allow action to be taken to protect the health
and safety of consumers. A pilot project is also in operation monitoring accidents caused by consumer goods in order to reduce or prevent accidents of this type, which cause more injuries than either
road or work accidents.

Protection of consumers' economic interests

Action to protect the economic interests of consumers has been slower because of difficulty in achieving agreement within the Council of Ministers on proposals put forward by the commission. A number of directives have, however, been adopted in recent years on the following.

Misleading advertising. Consumers can complain to the courts, which are empowered to require advertisers to prove the accuracy of their claims.

Consumer credit. All credit agreements are to be in writing, be easily understandable and clearly indicate the real interest rate charged.

Door-to-door sales. This directive is designed to protect consumers against hard selling techniques, and allow them time to have second thoughts.

Airlines. A regulation which came into force in April 1991 requires airlines to pay financial compensation to passengers who are delayed through being "overbooked" on commercial flights.

Product liability. Potentially the most important EC decision affecting consumers was the adoption in August 1985 of a directive on product liability, which came into force in 1988. It imposed a strict liability on producers for damage caused by defects in their products, and it was adopted only after several years of campaigning on behalf of the victims of unforeseen side-effects of pharmaceutical products. Under the directive member states may impose a limit to the liability, but this must be at least 70m ecus.

Consumer information and education

In addition to the directives controlling the labelling of foodstuffs and dangerous substances, others require electrical household equipment to be marked with its estimated energy consumption and food to be marked with unit prices (by the kilogram or litre). Measures are also proposed to extend price marking to goods other than food. A three-year action plan, adopted in 1990, comprised 22 further measures in four main areas:

◪ consumer representation;
◪ health and safety of consumers;
◪ commercial transactions involving consumers;
◪ consumer information and education.

A second three-year plan, launched in 1993, focused on two important areas:

◪ consolidation of EU legislation, with the adoption of directives on cosmetic productions and on unfair terms of trade;
◪ selective priorities designed to raise the level of consumer protection and to make consumers more aware of their rights, notably by encouraging access to justice, by creating a European guarantee and after-sales service scheme, and by adopting transfrontier financial services.

The plan also aimed at better integration of consumer policy within other EU polices. A third three-year plan, covering the years 1996–98, focused on changes induced by technological development and the changing face of the European Union resulting from its enlargement. Attention was to be concentrated on ten priority areas, including financial services, food products, public utility services and more openness towards the countries of Central and Eastern Europe and the developing countries. In 1998–99 a European Young Consumer competition was launched on the theme of "explaining the euro". A fourth action plan, covering the years 1999–2001, largely consisted of a continuation of the objectives of the third plan. Meanwhile, three new directives were adopted: on product price indication, injunctions and consumer credit.

The commission is active in promoting a wider awareness of the results of comparative tests on consumer goods, better co-operation between the testing organisations and more information for consumers on the action taken on their behalf. It sponsors frequent conferences on consumer issues, supports experiments on consumer education in schools and gives subsidies to national consumer groups to support local consumer information programmes.

31 Education

Education has always been regarded as an area where national traditions and methods – which are extremely varied – should be respected and, indeed, fostered. Any attempt to standardise teaching, structures, methods or syllabi, it is accepted, would be misplaced. There was little reference to education in the Rome treaty, except for the need for mutual recognition of diplomas (Article 57) and vocational training (Articles 41 and 118).

Six-point programme adopted in 1976

Since 1974, however, there has been increasing recognition of the need for closer co-operation between the member states in educational matters. Accordingly, in February 1976 the Council of Ministers adopted a six-point Community programme which covered the following.

1 Improved cultural and vocational training for migrant workers and their children.
2 Better mutual understanding of the different European educational systems.
3 The collection of basic documentary information and statistics.
4 Co-operation in higher education.
5 The improvement of foreign-language teaching.
6 The equality of opportunity of access to all forms of education throughout the Community.

Subsequently, the programme was extended to include measures to improve the vocational training of young people and to ease the transition from school to workplace. Since 1980 there has been increasing concern about youth unemployment resulting, for example, in the decision in 1983 to earmark 75% of the Social Fund for measures aimed at improving job opportunities for young people aged under 25 (see pages 178–80).

Policy mostly takes form of recommendations

With a few notable exceptions EC policy has taken the form of recommendations to member states rather than of legislation requiring action by them. The main exception concerned efforts to ease freedom of

movement in jobs and professions with training and other requirements, where a long series of directives ensured that by the beginning of
1993 a comprehensive formula existed for the mutual recognition of
educational diplomas and the right to practice any trade or profession in
all member states. Another directive, adopted in 1977, concerned the
schooling of the children of migrant workers within the Community. It
required member states to set up reception classes, specialised training
for teachers and education in the language and culture of their country
of origin.

More typical, however, was the Community's approach to promoting
a wider knowledge of EC languages. In June 1984 ministers from the
member states committed themselves to a programme that aimed at
encouraging a working knowledge of two languages apart from the
mother tongue before the statutory leaving age. There is no guarantee,
however, that all member states will make an equivalent effort to
achieve this clearly desirable objective. Similar agreements have been
reached to promote:

- student and teacher mobility;
- education in European current affairs;
- the transition from school to working life;
- education for the handicapped;
- literacy campaigns; and
- new information technologies.

Eight important projects
Direct action by the Community itself has been limited, but there has
been a marked increase in activity over recent years. A few projects are
worthy of mention.

Eurydice.   This information service network has been in operation
since 1980, with access to educational administrators in all member
states, and to a wider public since 1982. It consists of a computer-based
databank, containing a mass of information about educational developments throughout the EU.

**Erasmus (European Community Action Scheme for the Mobility of
University Students).**   A project first proposed by the European
Commission in 1985, which foresaw that by 1992 some 10% of the stu-
dent population (that is 150,000 students) should spend an integrated

period of study in another EC country. A slimmed-down version was eventually approved by the Council of Ministers in 1987, which meant that fewer than 45,000 students benefited during the first three years. In 1990 the budget was more than doubled, and the programme is now steadily building up. A parallel programme called **Science** encourages the mobility of research workers. In 1990 a trans-European mobility scheme for university students called **Tempus** was established to extend the benefits of the Erasmus programme to students from the new democracies of Central and Eastern Europe. **Tempus II** provided support for the restructuring of the higher education systems of these countries, and allowed states from the former Soviet Union to participate. It was to run from 1994 to 1998. In 1995 the Erasmus and Tempus programmes, together with the Lingua programme (see below), were combined in the more comprehensive **Socrates** programme, with a budget of 850m ecus over the five years 1995–99 and €1.85 billion for 2000–06. This is open to the candidate member states in eastern and southern Europe, and to Iceland, Liechtenstein and Norway, as well as the 15 member states. In 1998 financial assistance was granted to 1,627 inter-university co-operation programmes, and 200,000 students and 35,000 teachers received a grant to spend time studying or teaching in another country. The **Youth** programme, with a budget of €520m for 2000–06, is intended to help young people by supporting training and voluntary service outside their country. The commission says it should also boost a sense of European solidarity, fostering a spirit of initiative, enterprise and creativity. In 2001, almost 11,500 projects involving organisations from 50 countries qualified for Youth funding. The projects brought together some 130,000 young people. Youth also brings together a number of existing actions within a single instrument, in particular the Youth for Europe programme and the European Voluntary Service.

Comett.   A programme, since 1990 also open to EFTA countries, to stimulate and strengthen co-operation between universities (including all post-secondary training establishments) and industry.

Lingua.   Started in 1990, Lingua contributes to the financing of scholarships, exchanges and teaching materials in order to promote the training of teachers in foreign languages as well as the learning of languages in higher education, vocational training and industry.

Eurotechnet.   This programme encourages the exchange and dissemination of experiences, the creation of European networks of demonstration projects and co-ordination of research on vocational training for new technologies.

European University Institute.   This post-graduate institution, set up in Florence in 1976, offers courses in history and civilisation, economics, law and political and social sciences.

European Centre for the Development of Vocational Training. Established in Berlin in 1975, the purpose of this centre is to foster the development of vocational training and in-service training of adults at Community level. The EU also established in 1995 its **Leonardo da Vinci** programme for supporting vocational training in the member states. Its annual budget in 2000 amounted to €143m, and it supported projects involving 1,500 partners.

The European Schools.   Ten schools offer an international syllabus, in which part of the teaching is in a language other than the pupil's native tongue, leading to a European baccalauréat, which provides admission to universities throughout the EU. Mainly intended for the children of people working in EU institutions, the schools are open to other pupils. The schools are in Luxembourg, Brussels (three) and Mol in Belgium, Varese in Italy, Karlsruhe and Munich in Germany and Culham in the UK.

32 Women's rights

The position of women within the Union has substantially improved since the EEC was first established, although they are still some way from removing all the disadvantages from which they suffer, and from achieving full equality with men. By the end of 1995, of the EC's estimated total working population of 148m, some 61m were women (79% of these were in services, 17% in industry and 4% in agriculture). Over the preceding 25 years the proportion of women in the workforce had steadily risen, from under 35% to 42%, but women were still heavily concentrated in certain sectors and job categories that were often vulnerable, less highly qualified, lower paid and with fewer promotion prospects. Above all, women predominated in part-time employment (80%, although this had come down from 90% ten years earlier), and there is a higher proportion of women among those unemployed than among the working population as a whole.

EU has helped improve women's status

There can be little doubt that the Union itself has been instrumental in improving the status of women. Article 119 of the Rome treaty stipulates that "each member state shall ... ensure and subsequently maintain the application of the principle that men and women should receive equal pay for equal work". It goes on to spell out the principle in some detail, stipulating that "pay" means "the ordinary basic or minimum wage or salary and any other consideration, whether in cash or in kind, which the worker receives, directly or indirectly, in respect of his employment from his employer". The article goes on to state that: "Equal pay without discrimination based on sex means:

- that pay for the same work at piece rates shall be calculated on the basis of the same unit of measurement;
- that pay for work at time rates shall be the same for the same job."

Despite the seeming lack of ambiguity in these provisions, it was necessary for the Council of Ministers to adopt several further measures before all the member states took adequate action to ensure their implementation. Five directives in particular were adopted.

Main directives concerning women's rights

February 1975. Member states are obliged to revise their laws so as to exclude all discrimination on grounds of sex; particularly in systems of occupational classification. Under this directive, all workers believing themselves to be victims of discrimination must have the right and the possibility to take their case to a tribunal, and be protected against any wrongful dismissal if they do so.

February 1976. Member states are obliged to ensure equal treatment in regard to working conditions and access to employment, training and promotion. Here, too, provision was made for individuals to have recourse to justice without putting their jobs at risk. Any person believing themselves to be wronged can lodge a complaint with a national tribunal or other competent body. In the event of a dispute over the interpretation of Community law the European Court of Justice will decide the question. In one important case brought by a Belgian air stewardess, the court ruled that women employees could not be compulsorily retired at a lower age than men.

December 1978. Any discrimination in statutory social security schemes covering risks of illness, disability, old age, accidents at work, occupational illness, unemployment and family allowances is rendered illegal.

July 1986. Discrimination in occupational pension schemes to be eliminated by 1993.

End 1986. Direct or indirect discrimination against independent women workers (including agricultural workers) was to be eliminated by the end of 1989 (or 1991 in some cases). The directive also included further provisions regarding maternity and social security.

Series of action programmes put forward

In addition to these directives, the European Commission has put forward a series of action programmes to the Council of Ministers, which have been adopted in the form of recommendations (that is they are not mandatory on the member states).

The fourth action programme, covering the years 1996–2000, foresaw particular emphasis on gender equality in the following fields: integration of equal opportunities into other policy areas; equal treatment under occupational social security schemes; burden of proof; equal pay; sexual harrassment; and reconciliation of work and family life.

The fifth programme, covering the period 2001–05, had three priority areas:

- combating gender inequality in economic, political, civil and social life;
- altering roles;
- eliminating stereotypes.

In tandem with this, EU ministers adopted a €50m programme designed to assist awareness-raising programmes and improve the collection of data.

Educational initiatives to encourage equal opportunities

In the belief that the roots of sexual discrimination may lie in the educational system, the commission has launched several initiatives to encourage sexual equality by removing elements which stereotype the sexes from an early age and cut off girls from career choices more readily open to boys. In June 1985 the EC's education ministers approved an equal opportunity programme, concerned mainly with:

- training those in charge of education and increasing their awareness;
- getting a better mix of men and women in teaching jobs;
- improving career guidance;
- eliminating stereotypes from educational material.

In vocational training, the European Centre for the Development of Vocational Training (Cedefop) is increasing its research and promotional activity, much of which focuses specifically on problems facing women; for example, those seeking to return to work after a long period. National governments are encouraged to make use of possibilities offered by the European Social Fund, which co finances numerous programmes for training, re-employment and first-time employment that are open without discrimination to men and women. It also helps to finance specific training programmes for women, particularly for non-traditional occupations.

Specialist services
The commission maintains two specialist services which enable it to monitor the development of women's issues on a continuing basis and to produce a steady stream of policy proposals.

The Women's Employment and Equality Office.   Responsible for drawing up and implementing Union policy, and for seeing that equality problems are taken into account in devising and implementing programmes in other policy areas.

The Women's Information Service.   Maintains constant contact with women's groups, associations and movements and informs them about Union activities.

Violence against women
In 1997 the European Parliament adopted a resolution on the violation of women's rights and another on the need for a Europe-wide campaign of zero tolerance of violence against women. It called for 1999 to be designated "European Year against Violence against Women" and for respect for women's rights to be written into all agreements with non-member countries. The EU's Daphne programme, from 2000 to 2003, has an annual budget of €5m and tackles all forms of violence against women and children.

Sexual harrassment
In April 2002, tough new rules to combat sexual harassment at work were agreed, and a number of other changes were made to the EU's sex equality laws. The new rules oblige employers to introduce preventative measures against sexual harassment in the workplace and to provide information to workers about equal treatment of men and women in the organisation.

A dearth of women commissioners
Given the apparent devotion of the EU to sexual equality, it is surprising that no women members at all were appointed to the European Commission until 30 years after its creation. The second Delors Commission, which took over in January 1989, did have two women members – Vasso Papandreou and Christiane Scrivener – as well as 15 men. The two-year commission appointed for 1993–94, however, included only one woman – Mrs Scrivener – and 16 male members. The Santer Com-

mission, which took office in January 1995, included four women among its 20 members. It established a special group of commissioners, chaired by Jacques Santer himself, with the specific task of ensuring that an "equal opportunities" element was incorporated into the full range of EU policies. It was also concerned to ensure that women candidates were not disadvantaged in the commission's own recruitment and promotion policies. Subsequently, there was a marked improvement in the recruitment of women at all levels except the highest, where of 33 directorates-general and services only one was headed by a woman. The Prodi Commission, which took office in September 1999, and which included five women, immediately announced that it would give a priority to increasing the proportion of women in higher management posts.

Summit commitments

Equal opportunities are regularly upheld at the highest level. At the Barcelona European Council in March 2002, leaders said the EU should remove disincentives for female labour force participation. They also said that by 2010 childcare should be provided for at least of 90% of children between three years old and the mandatory school age, and at least one-third of children under three.

33 Culture and the media

The work of the EU in the cultural sphere was for many years minimal, partly because of a desire to avoid duplicating the activities of the Council of Europe,[1] which has always seen the protection and development of the European cultural heritage as one of its principal functions. The development of new technologies, which are revolutionising the television and film industries and making a mockery of purely national boundaries, has caused a reassessment to be made, as substantial economic and social interests are involved which largely transcend the limited and purely voluntary framework of the Council of Europe. The commission has concluded that it must henceforward play the pivotal role in marshalling a European response to the commercial and cultural challenge in this sphere, which is spearheaded by American and Japanese interests.

Areas of concentration

The EU's budget for cultural affairs is small, apart from assistance for the development of advanced television services. Since 1973 a small unit within the commission has been responsible for producing proposals and for implementing those which the Council of Ministers approve. There are four main areas:

- free trade in cultural goods;
- the improvement of conditions for artists;
- widening the audience for culture; and
- the conservation of the Community's architectural heritage.

Support and training for artistic workers

Apart from films and television programmes, the EU has been mainly concerned with removing barriers to artistic workers exporting their talents and output from one EU country to another. The temporary tax-free export of the tools of an artist's trade (musical instruments, cameras, and so on) has been facilitated, and the commission is drawing up proposals to ensure the free export of works of art, except for strictly defined "national art treasures" which would be exempted. It is also seeking to establish a European information centre to keep a record of stolen works of art, making it more difficult for thieves to dispose of stolen items.

Research sponsored by the commission has revealed that a large number of cultural workers are unemployed, and that many others earn less than they need to live. They are forced to take a second job or abandon their art. It has proposed a number of measures to strengthen their economic position. These include:

- the harmonisation of national laws governing copyright to creative artists and performers;
- a share in public subsidies for playwrights and composers;
- "resale rights" to artists guaranteeing them a percentage of the proceeds every time their works are sold;
- the payment of royalties on works in the public domain to funds which could be used for welfare payments to artists or for arts sponsorship.

Specific social security and tax improvements have also been proposed, but member states have been reluctant to agree to directives in this field, and so far the Council of Ministers has confined itself to making recommendations to member states.

The commission has used the limited funds at its disposal to support a number of schemes for training young artists, including assistance for young musicians in Siena and Dublin, violin makers in Cremona, composers at the University of Surrey and dancers in Brussels. Grants are available to retrain ballet dancers as instructors, while EU support has been available for both classical and jazz youth orchestras and the Wiltz Festival in Luxembourg, which involves actors, singers, musicians and dancers from five member states. Some assistance has also been given for the training of cultural workers and local cultural employment by the ERDF.

Efforts to widen the cultural audience

In recognition of its responsibilities towards a wider Europe, European Cultural Months were held in Cracow (Poland) in 1992, Graz (Austria) in 1993 and Nicosia (Cyprus) in 1995. The next cities chosen were Valletta (Malta) and Linz (Austria) in 1998. The commission also acted as a sponsor of the Quincentenary exhibition held in Seville in 1992, and similarly supported Expo '98 in Lisbon in 1998. Other efforts include:

- financial support since 1982 for the translation of great works of contemporary literature, mainly from the lesser spoken languages such as Danish, Dutch and Greek;

- sponsorship of the European Theatre in Milan and Paris;
- a European Film Festival held each year in a different city;
- a variety of events held in the city that the commission designates each year as European culture city (Athens 1985, Florence 1986, Amsterdam 1987, Berlin 1988, Paris 1989, Glasgow 1990, Dublin 1991, Madrid 1992, Antwerp 1993, Lisbon 1994, Luxembourg 1995, Copenhagen 1996, Thessaloniki 1997, Stockholm 1998, Weimar 1999). In 2000, to mark the millennium, nine cities were designated: Avignon, Bergen, Bologna, Brussels, Helsinki, Krakow, Prague, Reykjavik and Santiago de Compostella. Subsequent choices are Rotterdam and Oporto in 2001, Bruges and Salamanca in 2002, Graz in 2003, Genoa and Lille in 2004, and Cork in 2005.

Conservation of monuments and buildings

Largely as a result of pressure from the European Parliament, funds have been made available, in the form of interest-rate subsidies and capital grants as well as loans through the EIB, for conservation work on monuments of EU-wide importance or buildings in underdeveloped regions whose restoration would bring economic benefits, especially through tourism. The first beneficiaries, in 1982–83, were the Milos Museum in Greece, the Doges' Palace in Venice and the Parthenon in Athens. Twelve more projects were approved in 1984, and a further 13 in 1986. These 13 give a clear indication of the broadening scope of the Community's support in this field, and its extension to important sites in all 12 member states.

- The remains of Greek ramparts behind the Marseille Bourse.
- The Forum in Rome.
- Charlemagne's palace chapel in Aachen cathedral.
- The abbey of Santa Maria do Bouro at Amares (Portugal).
- The Church of St Nicholas at Edam (Netherlands).
- The Stavronika monastery on Mount Athos (Greece).
- The naval arsenal at Rochefort (France).
- The house of the Dukes of Brabant in Grand Place, Brussels.
- The Georgian Castletown House at Celbridge (Ireland).
- The Temple of Piety at Studley Royal Gardens near Ripon.
- The Danish Museum of Decorative Arts at Copenhagen.
- The archaeological and industrial site at Differdange (Luxembourg).
- The Alhambra at Granada.

A number of other sites have subsequently been added to this list. In 1997 six were directly assisted from the EU's budget: the Acropolis, Mount Athos, Lisbon, Coimbra, Santiago de Compostella and Venice (the Fenice theatre).

Books and reading

In 1989 the Council of Ministers approved a programme of support for books and reading, which included eight priority measures.

- A guide for authors and translators.
- A programme for the publication of statistics in the book sector.
- A European literary prize.
- A prize for the best translations of literary works.
- Scholarships for literary translators.
- The conservation of books made from acid paper and use of "permanent paper".
- A study of export aid measures for books.
- A campaign for raising awareness of books and reading.

A more ambitious programme in support of books and reading, known as the **Ariane** programme, was adopted in 1996, along with the **Raphael** programme to ensure public access to the movable and non-movable cultural heritage and the **Kaleidoscope 2000** programme to support trans-European cultural initiatives. The **Culture 2000** programme 2000–04, with a total budget of €167m, replaces these three cultural programmes.

In 1998 the commission drew up plans for a greatly enhanced level of participation under the first European Community framework programme in support of culture (2000–04). It adopted a budget of €167m to be spread over the five years.

Films and television

The commission's initiatives regarding films and television were prompted chiefly by the prospects offered by the development of direct broadcasting by satellite and the extension of cable networks. In November 1986 the Council of Ministers approved a commission proposal that the member states should adopt the MAC-packet "family" of standards developed by European industry and the European Broadcasting Union. They are compatible with each other and allow better sound and vision reproduction, the simultaneous use of one visual channel and several sound channels (multilingual programmes), and gradual evolution to-wards high-definition television (HDTV). The adoption of the commis-sion's proposals would, it was hoped, prevent repetition of the PAL and SECAM television receiver fiasco which left EC countries with two in-compatible systems.

In 1991 agreement was reached between the commission and all sides of the audio-visual industry (cable and satellite operators, broad-casters, equipment manufacturers and producers) on a five-year pro-gramme which should have led to all new television services and any new satellite transmissions using the MAC standard of HDTV. All large television sets produced after 1992 should have been able to receive MAC transmissions, and the commission pledged to spend 100m ecus a year over five years to assist the simultaneous transmission of PAL and SECAM programmes on MAC, and to support the start-up of new MAC broadcasts.

Yet renewed hesitancy by manufacturers, and the development by Japanese and American researchers of new digital systems that threat-ened to supersede the MAC system, led member states to have second thoughts, and in 1993 the policy was dropped. In its place the Council of Ministers agreed an action plan for the introduction of advanced televi-sion services in Europe with a budget of 228m ecus over four years, at least half of which would be spent on programme production. The fi-nancial support was intended to compensate for extra costs incurred by the introduction of a new 16:9 format for television, both for new shoots and for reformatting old material. The plan also set standards for digital and non-digital transmissions.

In 1989 a directive entitled "Television without Frontiers" was adopted, which came into force in October 1991. This directive, which is mandatory on member states, made it illegal for them to impede the transmission of programmes from other EC countries provided they con-form with the requirements of the directive. The directive covers:

- advertising breaks;
- the duration of advertising;
- ethical questions;
- sponsorship;
- protection of minors;
- the right of reply;
- the production and distribution of European audiovisual works.

The directive, which was denounced as discriminatory by the US government, also calls on member states to try to ensure that at least 50% of air time is devoted to programmes originating within the EC and that at least 10% of their programming budgets is devoted to European works from independent producers.

The commission also produced an action programme entitled **Media** (1991–95) to support the European film industry, in relation to both production and distribution. It designated 1988 as European Cinema and Television Year in the hope of stimulating supportive action by the member states, but the results were disappointing. The **Media II** programme (1996–2000) envisaged assistance on a much larger scale. During that time, it had backed the development and promotion of 3,600 European works (films, TV films, documentaries, animation, multimedia), including Sheka Kapur's "Elizabeth", Damien O'Donnell's "East is East", Lars von Trier's "Dancer in the Dark", Roberto Benigni's "La Vita e Bella", and Claude Berri's "Asterix". In four years, the number of European films distributed outside their country of production increased by 85% (from 246 films in 1996 to 456 in 1999). Media Plus (2001–05) has a budget of €400m. It includes an annual award: the first Media Prize was handed out at the Cannes Film festival in 2000 for "East Is East".

Sport

The European Union has become increasingly involved in sport. The 1995 Bosman ruling on football transfers is the most widely known ruling by the European Court of Justice. It outlawed transfer fees for out-of-contract players, thus aligning football rules with standard EU employment contracts. UEFA and FIFA, respectively the European and world football authorities, were slow to accept the ruling and initially hinted that EU law had no jurisdiction over them. But they eventually accepted the ruling, and in March 2001, FIFA's package covering transfers, training and compensation for breached contracts was approved by the commission. The Bosman ruling also ended the quotas of national players in club teams, heralding a spectacular growth in foreign-player transfers throughout Europe.

Other EU actions in sport include:

- becoming involved in the launch of the World Anti-Doping Agency (WADA), the body set up by the International Olympic Committee to drive out drug cheats. As well as being instrumental in providing funding, the commission took observer status in the agency;

◪ designating 2004 as the European Year of Education through Sport;

◪ examining the licensing and management of motor racing, which the commission's competition authorities have suggested is a closed shop;

◪ working with UEFA to ensure that the broadcasting rights for the Champions League are sold on a fair basis and do not constitute a market-sharing arrangement.

Note

1   The Council of Europe, founded in 1949, brings together 40 countries, including the 15 EU and four EFTA countries, Cyprus, Malta, San Marino and Turkey, and most of the countries of Central and Eastern Europe and the European republics of the former Soviet Union, which were accepted into membership during the 1990s. Its purpose is to achieve greater unity between its members to safeguard and realise the ideals and principles which are their common heritage and facilitate their economic and social progress. It has produced some 140 conventions and agreements, many in the cultural field, but these are not binding on the member states. Its most significant contribution is in the human rights field, through the work of the European Commission of Human Rights and the European Court of Human Rights, both of which work under its aegis.

34 Citizens' rights and symbolism

The European Union continues to be rather a remote concept to most people. In so far as they think about it at all, it is regarded as a matter for governments, specialist committees and for experts. Although there is a fairly general appreciation (which is stronger in the original six member states than in the others) of the economic benefits that the Union has brought, there is little feeling that the EU affects citizens in their everyday life.

Committee for a People's Europe formed

It was in order to help create such a feeling, and to foster sentiments of loyalty and solidarity among the mass of the population in the member states, that the EC heads of government, at the Fontainebleau summit in June 1984, decided on the appointment of a Committee for a People's Europe, which would suggest ways of strengthening the identity and improving the image of the Community. The committee, which consisted of personal representatives of each of the heads of government and of the president of the European Commission, was chaired by an Italian, Pietro Adonnino. It produced two reports, which were approved in principle by further summit meetings in March and June 1985. These contained a series of proposals for actions, some of a largely symbolic character, for protecting and extending the rights of EC citizens. Some of the proposals were new, others were designed to give fresh impetus to ideas which had been languishing, sometimes for many years, in the maw of the Community's decision-making process.

Adonnino reports ...

The first Adonnino report proposed a number of immediate steps on the following:

- the simplification of border formalities;
- duty-free allowances;
- tax exemptions for books and magazines;
- taxation of frontier workers;
- a general system for the recognition of diplomas;
- the equivalence of diplomas;
- the right of abode.

The second and final report put forward both specific proposals and longer-term objectives which would make the Community more real in the eyes of its citizens. These proposals cover special rights for citizens, culture, information, youth, education, exchanges and sport, voluntary work to assist developing countries, health, social security, drugs and twinning schemes. It constituted more of a miscellaneous shopping list of desirable measures than a coherent plan of action.

... call for special citizens' rights
The special citizens' rights which the Adonnino committee called for included the following.

The right to participate in Euro-elections under equal conditions. Electoral procedures should be made uniform, as the European Parliament has requested, and as is required under Article 138 of the Rome treaty. Where Community citizens are travelling or living abroad at the time of the poll, they should have the right to vote in their home country or country of residence.

The right of self-expression and assembly. This should be granted to Community citizens on the same terms as nationals of the host state.

Permanent residents in another member state. Numbering about 5m, these people should have the right, after a period of time, to vote and stand in local elections. They should also have the right to be consulted on issues which affect them, such as housing or foreign language teaching.

Border region residents. Taken in the widest sense, 48m people should have the right to be consulted when the neighbouring country is contemplating developments which could affect them such as major public works, reorganisation of transport or measures affecting ecology, safety or health.

The right of all Community citizens to enjoy full benefits of Community policies. In cases where these conflict with national regulations, the citizen can seek redress in the courts. Things would be easier for ordinary people, however, and their legal rights would be underpinned, if member states ensured the total, straightforward and rapid implementation of Community law. It would also help if this law was itself codified and simplified. In all cases superfluous legal provisions should be abolished.

The right to better access to the administration.   First, the citizen's right of petition should be strengthened and simplified, as the European Parliament has demanded. A European ombudsman or mediator, or, as the Parliament had requested, a mediating commission, would examine citizens' complaints and could help them to obtain redress.

The right to adequate information on efforts to develop the EU. The Community institutions and member states should co-operate more closely in informing their citizens of the historic reasons for the creation of the Community and the importance of current efforts to develop it further. The same applies to explaining the implications of EC policies and their impact on people's everyday life.

European passport holders.   The holders of EU passports (see below) should have the right to benefit from the assistance of the embassy or consulate of another member state when visiting a foreign country where their own country is not represented.

During 1986 and 1987 the commission tabled legislative proposals to meet most of the points listed in the two Adonnino reports, and the major part of the People's Europe programme was implemented by the target date of 1992 which the Community set for the completion of the internal market.

Areas of particular difficulty

Frontier controls.   Fears about drug peddlers, terrorism and illegal immigrants have made some member states, particularly the UK, reluctant to ease or abolish controls at internal EU frontiers. This led five countries – France, Germany and the three Benelux states – to sign the Schengen Agreement (see pages 114–5) to eliminate their own frontier controls before the 1992 deadline and to align their immigration and visa requirements for citizens of non-EU countries. The majority of member states, and even countries such as Iceland and Norway which are outside the EU, subsequently subscribed to the Schengen Agreement, although Ireland and the UK remain outside, and are likely to continue to do so for the foreseeable future. Under the Amsterdam treaty, the Schengen Agreement was incorporated in the European Community and it is now mandatory on all member states except the UK and Ireland, which have secured opt-outs.

Euro-election procedures.   The demand for a uniform procedure for elections to the European Parliament has still not been met, largely because of the refusal of former UK Conservative governments to agree to introduce proportional representation. The Labour government elected in May 1997 conceded the point, and the elections to the European Parliament in June 1999 were held under different systems of PR in all 15 member states. This development has removed the pressure for a uniform system, and it seems unlikely that one will be adopted in the near future.

EU citizenship

Despite the progress made in implementing the Adonnino proposals, the Spanish government argued that a specific treaty commitment should be made establishing the right of all persons holding the nationality of a member state to citizenship of the European Community. The Treaty on European Union, agreed at Maastricht in December 1991, accordingly contained provisions establishing citizenship of the European Union. It guaranteed the rights of free movement and residence, the right of EU citizens to vote and stand as candidates in municipal elections and European Parliament elections, in countries of residence other than their own, and to equal consular protection in third countries where their own countries were not represented. The right of all citizens to petition the European Parliament was also inscribed, and the Parliament was directed to appoint an ombudsman empowered to receive complaints from any citizen concerning alleged maladministration by EC institutions. The commission was instructed to report every three years on the application of this part of the treaty, and the Council of Ministers was empowered, acting unanimously, to adopt provisions to strengthen or add to the rights inscribed therein.

Attempts to introduce common symbolism ...

One factor which has retarded the development of popular loyalties to the European Union has been the absence of common symbolism, a lack which the commission and the national governments have made increasing attempts in recent years to rectify.

... include an EU flag ...

Since 1986 the European Union has had a common flag, which is flown at national and international functions and ceremonies, as well as on other occasions when public attention needs to be drawn to the existence of the Union. This flag, which contains a crown of 12 five-pointed stars on an azure background, had already been used since 1955 by the Council of Europe. It is now shared with the Council of Europe.

... anthem ...

The Council of Europe also shares the European anthem, for which the words of Schiller's "Ode to Joy", set to Beethoven's Ninth Symphony, have been chosen. (This is a cut above most national anthems – of which both words and music are almost uniformly banal – but it remains to be seen whether it will catch the public imagination.) May 9th, the date of Robert Schuman's birth in 1886, was also chosen in 1986 as Europe Day, with the hope that it would be celebrated as a public holiday in each member state.

... passport ...

Since 1974 slow progress has been made towards achieving a common European passport. In 1981–82 the member states reached agreement on a uniform model. The format is 88mm $\times$ 124mm, the colour is Burgundy red, and the heading is now "European Union", followed by the name of the member state. The date set for its introduction was January 1st 1985, but only three countries, Denmark, Ireland and Luxembourg, respected this deadline. Most other member states started issuing the new style passports (which will progressively replace the old national passports on renewal) later on in 1985, but it was not until 1989 that European passports were being supplied in all member states.

... and driving licence

In 1980 the Council of Ministers adopted a directive on the introduction of a Community driving licence, which was implemented in two stages. Since 1983 there has been mutual recognition in each member state of each others' licences, which since then have been issued on the basis of theoretical examinations, practical tests and medical requirements conforming to common specifications. Since January 1st 1986 driving licences issued by member states conform to a Community model, which meets the requirements of the 1968 Vienna International Road Traffic Convention, so that they are valid in non-EU countries which subscribe to this convention.

35 Aid and development

Part Four of the Rome treaty, comprising Articles 131–136, provided for the association with the Community of the former colonial territories of Belgium, France, Italy and the Netherlands. It said:

> This association shall serve primarily to further the interests and prosperity of the inhabitants of these countries and territories in order to lead them to the economic, social and cultural development to which they aspire.

EU–ACP relations are governed by conventions

Initially, this provision applied mainly to former French territories in Africa, nearly all of which became independent in the early 1960s; subsequently, former UK, Spanish and Portuguese territories also became eligible. At first only 18 countries were involved, and they were known collectively as the Associated African States and Madagascar (AASM). Now 78 in number (including South Africa, which was admitted, on a qualified basis, in April 1997), they have been known since the mid-1970s as the African, Caribbean and Pacific (ACP) states (see Appendix 7).

Relations between these countries and the EU have been regulated by a series of conventions concluded at periodic intervals. The first two were signed at Yaoundé (capital of Cameroon) in 1963 and 1969, and they set the pattern for the four subsequent ones, signed at Lomé (capital of Togo) in 1975, 1979, 1984 and 1989. On the one hand, provision was made for duty-free access to the EU for almost all the products of the ACP countries, without any reciprocity being required; on the other, development aid was made available, both in the form of grants from the European Development Fund (EDF), which was set up for this purpose, and of low-interest loans from the EIB. About 10% of the total aid programmes of the EU member states is channelled through the Union, and the bulk of it goes to the ACP countries, although India is the largest single recipient.

The EU–ACP conventions have broken new ground in four ways. They have:

- given stability to co-operation links by creating a legal framework, based on a contract negotiated for a fixed period of years between two groupings, each comprising a large number of independent states;

◪ established a single contract between regional blocs, excluding economic and ideological discrimination and taking account of the special problems of countries which are severely under-developed and those of enclaves and islands;

◪ created common institutions allowing a permanent dialogue and largely responsible for the implementation of the development programmes: a joint assembly of MEPs and ACP representatives, an ACP–EU Council of Ministers and a Committee of Ambassadors;

◪ instituted a global approach covering all aspects of co-operation: financial aid, trade concessions, stabilisation of export earnings, agricultural and industrial assistance.

Altogether some 99.5% of the goods exported to the EU by the ACP countries are admitted free of customs duties, the main exceptions being farm produce in direct competition with EU produced items protected by the CAP. A special deal has been negotiated for sugar, of which the EU has contracted to buy an annual quota of 1.4m tons at high EU prices, despite the surplus production of sugar beet in the Union. This concession was originally made to offset the loss of Commonwealth preferences by several ex-UK colonies. However, ACP textile exports are sharply restricted by the operation of the Multi-Fibre Arrangement (see page 108).

Development aid has grown substantially ...

The amount of development aid has grown substantially from one convention to the next, but so has the number of recipients. Under the fourth Lomé Convention, which covers the years 1990–2000, the total sum made available for the first five years was 12 billion ecus, although not all of this was spent. In 1995 it was agreed that 14.625 billion ecus should be allocated for the period up to 2000, the bulk of it in the form of grants and soft loans. An additional sum of 127.5m ecus, to cover 1997–99, was made available for South Africa in 1997. A particular feature of the second, third and fourth Lomé Conventions has been the inclusion of a stabilisation fund (known as Stabex), which compensates countries heavily dependent on one or more staple products for severe fluctuations in their export earnings. Altogether 48 basic commodities are included, and in recent years over 400m ecus have been paid out of the fund annually to more than 30 ACP countries. A similar system, Sysmin, applies to mineral products. It provides finance for the upkeep or reconstruction of mining installations during periods when their operation is curtailed by unforeseen circumstances. Table 29 shows the breakdown of Lomé development expenditure in 2001.

Table 29 **Lomé IV: development expenditure, 2001a**

Sector	€m
National and regional indicative programme	869.40
Structural adjustment	215.46
Sysmin	0.28
Emergency aid	17.76
Aid for refugees	41.29
Risk capital	366.97
Interest rate subsidies	8.30
Other and new initiatives	21.36
Total	**1,540.82**

a Provisional figures.
Source: European Commission

... but the emphasis has changed

The third and fourth Lomé Conventions changed the emphasis of the EDF by focusing much greater attention on rural and agricultural development, and on the financing of concerted programmes rather than of individual projects. The EDF also supports cross-border regional development projects to assist small and medium-sized enterprises and "micro-projects" of local importance. It aims to take a bigger interest in the restoration of natural equilibria: the struggle against drought and desertification, and so on.

The EIB provides long-term loans from its own resources, with a 3% interest-rate subsidy paid by the EDF. It also finances or part-finances feasibility studies for industrial projects, including those involving small and medium-sized business, agro-industry, mining, tourism and energy; and productive infrastructure such as ports, railways, water supplies and telecommunications.

The EDF has established in Brussels a Centre for the Development of Industry (CDI), which is managed and staffed by nationals of both ACP and EU countries. Its principal function is defined as "to help to establish and strengthen industrial enterprise in the ACP states, particularly by encouraging joint initiatives by economic operators of the European Community and the ACP states". Co-operation is also to be extended in areas such as energy, shipping and fisheries, as well as in social and cultural fields: the development of the human resources and cultural identity of ACP countries and assistance for workers and students from ACP countries in Europe.[1]

In June 2000, the 20-year EU–ACP Agreement was signed in Cotonou, Benin, after 18 months of negotiations. The deal, known as the Cotonou Agreement, replaced the Lomé Convention, and focused on poverty alleviation, aid and stronger political, economic and trade co-operation. The 15 EU member states and the 78-member ACP group (56 of which are WTO members) together represent more than 650m people. Through a €13.5 billion EDF commitment covering the agreement's first five years, the EU will support the ACP governments in their attempts to create a balanced macroeconomic situation, expand the private sector and improve both the quality and coverage of social services. The agreement is valid for a period of 20 years and will be open to revision once every five years.

In April 2002, the commission adopted a negotiating strategy for Economic Partnership Agreements (EPAs) between the EU and 76 ACP countries, designed to translate the EU's relations based on unilateral preferences – provided for by the Cotonou Agreement – into more "balanced relations". The strategy outlines EPA negotiations between September 2002 and January 2008. The resulting agreement will come into force in 2008, with a 12-year transition period to 2020. The new EPAs would enhance duty-free access to the EU market for exporters in the ACP countries, while simultaneously dismantling barriers that prevent European goods and services from entering their markets.

Other forms of assistance to developing countries

The Lomé conventions are not regarded by the EU primarily as a charitable venture. The self-interest of the Union, which is heavily dependent upon the supply of a host of commodities and raw materials from developing countries, is deeply involved in the maintenance of a stable world economy and the orderly and rapid development of poorer countries. Although it had chosen to give priority to the associated ACP countries through the EDF, the EU also spends a substantially larger amount (some €4.9 billion in the 2001 budget) on other forms of assistance to developing countries. Apart from trade concessions under the generalised system of preferences (see page 108), this falls into three main categories.

Emergency aid.   The Union sends foodstuffs to countries which request assistance in coping with serious food shortages. Emergency aid is also sent to countries devastated by natural catastrophes or other crises. In 2001, some €455m was spent on food aid, largely in supplying grain, as well as sugar, dairy products and vegetable oils, to sub-Saharan Africa and Asia. Emergency aid went notably to Rwanda and Burundi, Bosnia and Chechnya. Such aid, much of it channelled through non-governmental organisations, is administered by the European Community Humanitarian Office (ECHO), created in 1991. In 2001, a total of €473m was distributed through ECHO for humanitarian aid. In recent years numerous emergency aid operations have been launched, particularly to assist the victims of famine and war in countries such as Afghanistan, Kosovo, North Korea, Rwanda, Burundi, Ethiopia, Sudan, Somalia, Angola, Mozambique and Liberia, as well as in former Soviet republics such as Tajikistan, Armenia, Azerbaijan and Georgia. The assistance is not entirely disinterested: it helps to reduce the surplus food stocks of the CAP. Funds are, however, also provided for special programmes to help poor countries overcome their food production problems, and to assist the work of non-governmental organisations.

Phare and TACIS.   In July 1989 EC farm ministers allocated some 110m ecus of food aid to Poland, in response to an appeal from the Western economic summit, which had just been held in Paris, for the European Commission to co-ordinate emergency aid to Poland and Hungary. This assistance was primarily motivated by a desire to encourage these two countries' progress towards democracy. It was followed up by a more comprehensive programme of development aid to the countries of Eastern Europe, administered by the EC on behalf of the OECD countries (the group of 24), and known as the Phare Programme (Poland and Hungary – Aid for Economic Restructuring. Phare in French means "beacon"). A similar programme, entitled TACIS (Technical Assistance for the Commonwealth of Independent States), was launched for the former states of the Soviet Union and Mongolia in 1991. By 1998 nearly 9.4 billion ecus had been spent under the two programmes (see Figure 9 and Figure 10 on page 256), and an increasing budget had been agreed for the remaining years of the century.

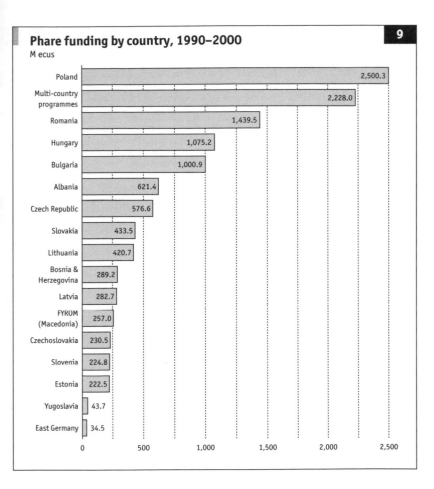

Phare funding by country, 1990–2000

M ecus

Country	M ecus
Poland	2,500.3
Multi-country programmes	2,228.0
Romania	1,439.5
Hungary	1,075.2
Bulgaria	1,000.9
Albania	621.4
Czech Republic	576.6
Slovakia	433.5
Lithuania	420.7
Bosnia & Herzegovina	289.2
Latvia	282.7
FYROM (Macedonia)	257.0
Czechoslovakia	230.5
Slovenia	224.8
Estonia	222.5
Yugoslavia	43.7
East Germany	34.5

Aid to non-associated countries. The EU has concluded a series of agreements with Asian countries, such as India, Pakistan and Bangladesh, as well as with Latin American countries, under which development aid amounting in 2001 to €900m is provided. Similar development aid is provided to Mediterranean countries in the Maghreb and Mashreq, and to Israel, under financial protocols attached to co-operation agreements with these countries. Some 2,375m ecus was allocated for 1991–95. Largely because of pressure from southern member states, the aid programme for third countries in the Mediterranean region was sharply increased for the period 1995–99, to reach approximately two-thirds of the amount expended in the countries of Central

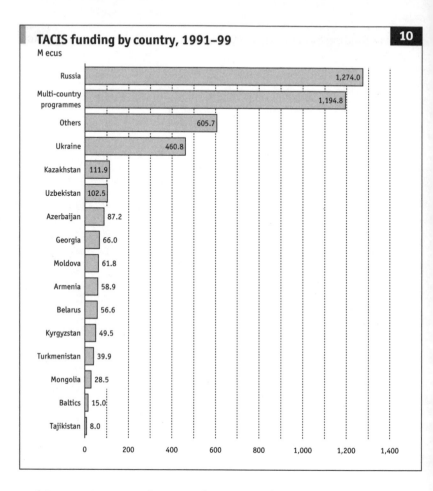

TACIS funding by country, 1991–99 · **10**
M ecus

Country	M ecus
Russia	1,274.0
Multi-country programmes	1,194.8
Others	605.7
Ukraine	460.8
Kazakhstan	111.9
Uzbekistan	102.5
Azerbaijan	87.2
Georgia	66.0
Moldova	61.8
Armenia	58.9
Belarus	56.6
Kyrgyzstan	49.5
Turkmenistan	39.9
Mongolia	28.5
Baltics	15.0
Tajikistan	8.0

and Eastern Europe. After 1999, however, when the amounts allocated included pre-accession aid to the countries negotiating EU membership, the proportion fell to less than one-third. The yearly amounts are shown in Table 30.

Considerable scope for expansion and improvement

When all the different EU programmes for assisting developing countries are added together they appear to amount to a considerable effort, and it is true that the EU devotes a larger slice of its GDP to development aid than either the United States or Japan. In the early years of the 1990s it was providing 47% of total world aid, compared

Table 30 **EU assistance to Central and Eastern Europe and to third countries in the Mediterranean, 1995–2002 (m ecus)**

	Countries of Central & Eastern Europe	Mediterranean third countries
1995	1,154	550
1996	1,235	900
1997	1,273	1,000
1998	1,397	1,092
1999	1,634	1,143
2000	3,174	1,127
2001	3,240	896
2002	3,328	861
Total	16,435	7,569

Source: Council of Ministers

with 20% by the United States and 17.8% by Japan. However, it should be emphasised that only three EU member states – Denmark, the Netherlands and Sweden – have reached the UN target of devoting at least 0.7% of their GDP to aid programmes. Moreover, some EU policies – notably the CAP – which encourages the dumping of EU food surpluses on world markets, sometimes in direct competition with farmers from developing countries, and even the food aid programme itself may add considerably to the problems of developing countries. The EU's aid programmes have also been criticised for being geared to the interests of EU firms, which receive the bulk of the contracts awarded, and which may gain more from them than the intended beneficiaries. Despite the achievements of the EU's development policies, there remains enormous scope for both expansion and improvement before they come anywhere near the full realisation of their objectives

Europe aid

In 2000, Chris Patten, European external relations commissioner, announced plans to replace the sprawling, chaotic and wasteful system of EU overseas aid management with a single new service named "EuropeAid". Patten admitted that the commission's efforts to administer the annual €10.2 billion in EU aid were a shambles, but insisted this was mainly because of a chronic lack of staff and resources. He also reproached the member states for putting undue pressure on the commission to announce bold packages of aid even if delays and bureaucracy meant it could take years to deliver. In 2000 the backlog of unpaid commitments to aid recipients worldwide was around €20 billion, and the average delay over the previous five years for disbursements of payments was around four-and-a-half years. He noted that EU member states and the World Bank have between four and nine officials for every €10m of aid, compared with the commission's 2.3 officials. EuropeAid, which became operational in January 2001, is responsible for managing the entire project cycle in all geographical areas except the candidate countries.

Note

1 Assistance under the Lomé conventions is also available to Overseas Countries and Territories (OCTs) still associated with member states (see Appendix 7 for full list). Overseas territories which have the status of provinces or departments of a member state (such as the Azores, Madeira, the Canary Islands and the French overseas departments) are not eligible. Instead they receive assistance from the European Regional Development Fund (ERDF).

36 Foreign, defence and security policy

The Rome treaty made no mention of foreign policy, as distinct from foreign-trade policy, and progress towards co-ordinating the foreign policy of the member states has been slow and largely informal. It is, however, one of the few fields where progress, however limited, has been virtually continuous – at least since 1969 – and each year has seen somewhat closer co-operation among the member states than the previous one.

Davignon Report provided basic framework

Foreign policy co-operation (long known as "political co-operation" in EU circles) really dates in an organised sense from The Hague EC summit of December 1969, when it was decided to ask top national officials to report on the possibilities of achieving a degree of co-operation in foreign affairs. A committee presided over by Etienne Davignon (then a Belgian foreign office official, later a leading EC commissioner) drew up a report which recommended a system to "harmonise points of view, concert attitudes and, where possible, lead to common decisions".

The Davignon Report was accepted, and with a number of adaptations over the years it provided the basic framework for "political co-operation" by EC countries during the 1970s and 1980s. It proposed that the EC foreign ministers should meet at least twice a year to discuss foreign policy matters. In practice, they now normally meet at monthly intervals, and more often at times of crisis. For a number of years, largely due to French insistence during the Gaullist and post-Gaullist period, a sharp distinction was drawn between meetings held on political co-operation (which were normally convened in the capital city of the country currently holding the presidency of the Council of Ministers) and those on "normal" EC business,[1] which were in Brussels or Luxembourg. Over the years this distinction has become looser, and it is now quite common for both types of business to be transacted at the same meeting.

As well as the foreign ministers, each member state has designated a leading diplomatic official, known as the political director, who is specifically responsible for foreign policy co-operation between the 15 member states. The political directors meet every month, and each is assisted by a more junior official, known as the European correspondent, who is responsible for day-to-day communications. They are

linked by a special telex system, and exchange more than 5,000 tele-
grams each year. With the development of e-mail, the interaction has
become a great deal more intense and can best be described as a continuous process. The organisation of political co-operation is assumed by
the foreign ministry of the country currently holding the presidency.
However, under the Single European Act, which formalised political co-
operation for the first time, a small secretariat was established in Brussels in 1987 to provide back-up support and ensure greater continuity.

Commitment to joint foreign policy formalised ...

The Single European Act formally committed the member states to
"endeavour jointly to formulate and implement a European foreign
policy" (Article 30). It also (Article 2) regularised the position of the European Council, or the regular series of summit meetings of heads of government, which had been meeting three times a year since 1973, and
twice yearly since 1986. The European Council meetings had played a
considerable role in promoting political co-operation, and foreign policy
issues invariably occupy a prominent, and sometimes the predominant,
place on the agenda. To a significant extent, they have provided an
opportunity for the European members of the Western alliance to co-
ordinate their positions, and thus enable them to adopt a more equal
posture vis-à-vis the United States, which dwarfs each of them on a one-
to-one basis.

... but development hindered by member states' own interests

A number of factors, however, have seriously inhibited this development. One has been the neutrality of Ireland, which has largely prevented the EU from playing the role of the European end of NATO (there
is also the fact that three European NATO members – Norway, Iceland
and Turkey – are not members of the EU). Furthermore, both Denmark
and Greece, although they belong to NATO, have had severe inhibitions
about discussing matters of Western security within an EU framework.
Denmark, because of its policy of seeking to restrict the EU's authority to
those matters specifically referred to in the Rome treaty; Greece, because
under the Papandreou government it adopted a position less critical of
the Soviet Union (and of the radical Arab states) than that of its NATO
allies.

Three of the larger EU members – Germany, France and the UK –
have also on occasion been reluctant to subordinate their independent
interests to those of the Union. Before German unification in 1990 the

West German government, because of its economic links with East Germany and its desire to keep open doors to closer co-operation with the East German regime and to do nothing to hinder prospects, however remote they then seemed, of eventual unification, often took a slightly softer position in relation to Eastern Europe than the other member states. After unification it continued to be notably more willing than its allies to accommodate the former Soviet Union and to consider economic aid on a large scale. By 1992, however, the cost of unification had become so great that German resistance hardened to paying the lion's share of aid to the rest of Eastern Europe. France and the UK both have worldwide interests, largely arising from their colonial pasts, and each has shown itself rather more nationalistic in its approach than the majority of other member states.

For these reasons, the European Council – and the EU foreign ministers' meetings – have not formally assumed the role of the "general staff" of the European end of the Western alliance that might otherwise have been expected. Informally they have come rather nearer to it. For example, defence matters are supposed to be excluded from the agenda (as distinct from the "political and economic aspects of security"), but there is no doubt that they have been discussed several times. On these occasions, the Irish prime minister or foreign minister has kept silent. He might more logically have left the meeting temporarily, but nobody has wished to make an issue of the matter, and in practice the neutral status of Ireland has not been noticeably compromised by the attendance of its ministers. Nevertheless, the Community felt inhibited from shouldering responsibilities in the defence field, and this led in 1984 to an attempt to breathe new life into the moribund Western European Union (WEU) as a forum for discussing defence in a West European context.

Co-operation has been achieved in some respects

In practice foreign policy co-operation within the EU has manifested itself in three main aspects.

Presenting a common EU position. A serious effort has been made for the 15 countries to speak with one voice in international fora. Thus the foreign minister of the country holding the presidency now speaks on behalf of all the member states in the general debate which opens each session of the United Nations in September. During the course of the year the 15 EU ambassadors to the UN are in constant conclave and take a lot of trouble to ensure that all the EU countries vote together in divisions in the General Assembly. As well as in the UN, it has become the practice for the country holding the presidency to present a common EU position at other international conferences, notably the Conference on Security and Co-operation in Europe (CSCE), arising out of the 1975 Helsinki agreement. Since 1992 this body has been known as the Organisation for Security and Co-operation in Europe (OSCE). Its membership of 53 states includes all European countries, plus the United States and Canada.

Imposing sanctions. Common action has been taken in the imposition of economic sanctions. These have been imposed by all or most EU members, in concert, on at least nine separate occasions.

- Against Southern Rhodesia in 1965, following a UN resolution.
- Against Iran after the taking of American hostages in 1980.
- Against the Soviet Union and Poland after the imposition of martial law in Poland in 1981 (Greece declined to apply the sanctions).
- Against Argentina during the Falklands War in 1982 (Italy and Ireland discontinued the sanctions halfway through the war).
- Against Israel after the invasion of Lebanon in 1982.
- Against South Africa in 1986 (the UK was initially unwilling to participate, but eventually agreed to do so after the original package of measures had been considerably watered down).
- Against Iraq, following its invasion of Kuwait in August 1990, in accordance with the resolutions of the UN Security Council.
- Against Serbia and Montenegro during the fighting in Croatia and Bosnia-Herzegovina in 1991–95.
- Against Serbia before, during and after the Kosovo conflict, from 1998 onwards.
- Against Zimbabwe in 2002, following evidence of violence and massive irregularities in the presidential election.

It is arguable that none of these attempts at applying the EU's economic clout for a political purpose had the desired effect. What they perhaps did achieve was to cement the EU countries' habit of working together in foreign policy and to strengthen their sense of common purpose.

Taking initiatives. The EU heads of government have taken a number of initiatives during their periodic meetings in the European Council. Statements and declarations have been made on East–West relations, the Middle East, the Iran–Iraq War, Afghanistan, Poland, Central America and South Africa, with no apparent effect at all, even though some of them (such as the Venice declaration on the Middle East which was taken to imply a role for the PLO in the peace process) were widely publicised at the time. A persistent weakness of these statements is that they have generally been purely declaratory, and no serious attempt has been made to follow them through.

New impetus towards common foreign policy ...

The collapse of communism in Eastern Europe, which had as one of its many consequences the unification of Germany, followed by the Gulf war against Iraq, gave a fresh impetus towards a common foreign policy. On the one hand, the then German chancellor, Helmut Kohl, felt that it was necessary to tie Germany into a closer European federation if its neighbours' fears about unification were to be allayed. On the other hand, the serious differences that emerged among the member states before and during the Iraq war emphasised how far the EC had to go before it presented a single face to the outside world.

... reinforced by Maastricht treaty

Steps towards a common foreign, defence and security policy were thus major items on the agenda of the inter-governmental conference on political union, which opened in December 1990 and reported to the Maastricht summit in December 1991. The Treaty on European Union, which was agreed at the summit, did contain far-reaching provisions, although they did not go as far as Germany and most of the other member states would have preferred. A more cautious approach, based substantially on the principle of unanimity rather than majority voting, prevailed, largely at the bidding of the UK government. It was, however, agreed that the whole question should be reviewed at a further conference beginning in 1996, when Germany and its supporters hoped that a more thorough-going approach will be adopted. When this inter-governmental conference reported in June 1997 to the Amsterdam summit it was not in a position to put forward any radical proposals, and the Amsterdam Treaty (see page 41) did not represent a conspicuous advance on that of Maastricht.

The Maastricht treaty pledged the "Union and its member states" to put into effect a common foreign and security policy (CFSP). This was to be pursued by establishing systematic co-operation between member states, gradually implementing joint action. The member states are required to inform and consult each other within the Council of Ministers on matters of foreign and security policy, and the council will adopt common positions where necessary. Member states are to ensure that their national policies conform to the common positions, and are to co-ordinate their action within international organisations. The European Council is to define general guidelines for "joint action" and the council will decide, by unanimity, whether an area or issue should be the subject of joint action. The detailed arrangements for the implementation of joint action will be decided by qualified majority (that is, 62 votes in favour out of 87, cast by at least ten member states – see page 55).

The treaty states that the CFSP should include all questions relating to the security of the European Union, including the eventual framing of a common defence policy, which might in time lead to a common defence. Decisions on security with defence implications would, in the meantime, be implemented on request by the Western European Union. Previously, although there had been a substantial overlapping of membership, relations with the WEU had been complicated by the fact that not all the EC member states belonged to it. At Maastricht a parallel meeting of WEU ministers agreed to admit any EC member states that applied. Greece joined the existing nine members of the WEU, but Denmark, Ireland, Austria, Finland and Sweden chose instead to become WEU Observer States. Only Denmark of these five is a member of NATO. In order to facilitate future co-ordination between the EU and the WEU it was also agreed at Maastricht that the latter's headquarters should be transferred to Brussels.

The treaty specifically gave authority to the country holding the rotating presidency of the Council of Ministers to act on the EU's behalf, which it had often done informally in the past. It effectively gave it the responsibility for organising the CFSP, assisted where appropriate by the preceding and successive presidencies (the so-called "troika") and by the commission. It also laid down that the European Parliament must be kept regularly informed by the presidency, be consulted on broad policy questions and be permitted to question the council and make recommendations. The actual decision-making process of the CFSP would, however, be entirely inter-governmental, with the other EC institutions excluded. This process is known as Pillar Two of the EU.

The treaty also provided for co-operation between the member states on the following matters relating to security:

- asylum policy;
- rules governing crossing of member states' external borders;
- immigration policy;
- conditions of entry and movement by third-country nationals;
- conditions of residence including family reunion and access to employment for third-country nationals;
- combatting unauthorised immigration and residence by third-country nationals;
- combatting drugs;
- combatting fraud;
- judicial co-operation in civil matters;
- judicial co-operation in criminal matters;
- customs co-operation;
- police co-operation on information exchange within a European Police Office (Europol).

These subjects, known collectively as Pillar Three, were also to be dealt with on an inter-governmental basis.

There was widespread disappointment that the Maastricht Treaty provisions did not prove effective, and a number of changes were incorporated in the Amsterdam treaty in June 1997. They included the following.

- The appointment of a High Representative, intended to be a major political figure, for the CFSP. He would act as secretary-general of the Council of Ministers, with a deputy to take charge of day-to-day management, and would have at his disposal a new Policy Planning and Early Warning Unit.
- A new "troika", consisting of the president of the Council of Ministers, the high representative and the president of the commission (or his nominee).
- Unanimity would be retained for substantive decisions, but there would be a possibility for "constructive abstention by member states which do not want to participate in a joint action, but have no wish to prevent a 'willing majority' from acting together".
- Many of the issues consigned to Pillar Three would be transferred back to Pillar One, and would in future be subject to normal EC procedures. The Prodi Commission established a separate directorate-general for Justice and Home Affairs, and at the Tampere summit in October 1999 EU leaders called for the creation of an area of "freedom, justice and security".

The appointment in September 1999 of Javier Solana, formerly secretary-general of NATO and foreign minister of Spain, as the EU's High Representative, gave a new impetus to the development of the CFSP. This was followed up at the Helsinki summit the following December with a series of decisions that should lead to an increase of the overall power and influence of the EU in international affairs.

The principal decision was that the EU should effectively take over the responsibilities of the 50-year-old Western European Union (WEU), which was largely defunct, although it still existed on paper. The EU leaders decided that the Union needed its own military force to back up the CFSP. The aim was to assemble within three years a rapid reaction force (RRF) of 60,000 troops, which would be available within 60 days for deployment to a crisis area up to 2,500 miles away with the ability to stay in place for at least a year.

The missions that the force would fulfil were the so-called Petersberg tasks, enumerated at a WEU conference at Petersberg, Germany, in June 1992:

- humanitarian and rescue tasks;
- peacekeeping tasks;
- tasks of combat forces in crisis management, including peacemaking.

Such missions are normally carried out by NATO. The largely unspoken justification for having a separate EU force was to cover situations in which NATO (and, more particularly, the United States) did not wish to be directly involved, but was nevertheless sympathetic.

A new institutional basis was established for controlling the RRF. The Political and Security Committee (PSC) was established at ambassadorial level, with twice-weekly meetings in Brussels. It replaced the former Political Committee, which met far less frequently and whose members were based in their own capital cities. The PSC is flanked by a military committee, chaired for a three-year term by a four-star general, initially General Gustav Haglund from Finland. The 140-strong military staff is headed by General Rainer Schuwirth from Germany.

The objective was to have the RRF operational within three years, but, despite a dispute with Turkey about the conditions under which NATO equipment and planning resources could be loaned to the new force, it was declared "partially operational" at the Laeken summit one year early, in December 2001. The first operations are expected to be in the Balkans, where EU military and police personnel may well progressively replace NATO troops, both in Macedonia and in Bosnia-Herzegovina.

The member states held two "capabilities conferences" in 2000 and 2001, at which pledges were made of troops and equipment for the force. There was little difficulty in finding the numbers of troops needed, but there were significant shortfalls on the equipment side, mainly of air-lift and sea-lift capacity, communications equipment and headquarters units, intelligence-gathering satellites and aircraft, and precision-guided weapons. It was clear that, for the foreseeable future, the RRF would be heavily dependent on NATO assistance in any large scale combat missions.

The changes effected since the Amsterdam treaty, and those currently proceeding, should help to bring greater coherence to European foreign policy. So long as the unanimity rule is maintained for the CFSP, however, it is unlikely that the EU will be able to play as effective a part on the world stage as its economic power, military potential and wealth of democratic experience would warrant.

Note

1   The foreign ministers form the so-called "general affairs council" which is regarded as the most senior of the various manifestations of the Council of Ministers. As such they often meet to discuss matters unrelated to foreign affairs, sometimes arbitrating on issues which overlap the competences of departmental ministers, sometimes discussing particularly knotty problems, sometimes acting as direct deputies to the heads of government.

4
SPECIAL PROBLEMS

37 Enlargement

It was, from the outset, envisaged that other European countries besides the original six member states would subsequently be admitted into the European Community. Article 237 of the Treaty of Rome stated, in part: "Any European state may apply to become a member of the Community". This general invitation was, however, qualified by the preamble to the treaty which referred to the original members' resolve to strengthen peace and liberty and called upon "the other peoples of Europe who share their ideal to join in their efforts". This wording has subsequently been taken to mean that only countries with a democratic form of government are eligible to join. A further implied condition is that the economies of applicant states should be sufficiently developed to enable them to meet the obligations of membership and to be able to compete effectively within a free market.

Successful applicants

In 1961, and again in 1967, the UK, Denmark, Ireland and Norway made applications to join. On both occasions the UK was eventually vetoed by France, and the other three countries withdrew their applications. In 1969 a third approach was made, and new negotiations began with the four applicants which resulted in treaties of accession being signed in 1972. The three smaller applicant countries submitted the treaties to referenda, which produced majorities in favour in both Denmark and Ireland. France also held a referendum which showed a majority in favour of enlargement, but the Norwegian referendum resulted in a narrow majority against joining the Community (53:47 per cent). Denmark, Ireland and the UK became full members on January 1st 1973, although a transitional period of five years was allowed for adjusting tariffs, and for staggering various other membership provisions regarding, for example, agriculture and budgetary contributions. The UK did not hold a referendum on its entry to the Community, but following the election in 1974 of a Labour government the entry terms were partially renegotiated, and membership was subsequently confirmed by a majority of more than 2:1 in a referendum held on June 5th 1975.

Greece, Portugal and Spain were effectively excluded from membership during the years that they languished under dictatorships. Greece, which had already negotiated associate status with the EC several years before the military coup which overthrew its democratic regime in 1967, lost no time in applying for full membership after democratic government was restored in 1974. Its application was tabled in 1975, and Greece became the Community's tenth member on January 1st 1981. There was a five-year transition period for aligning import duties and for most parts of the common agricultural policy. A seven-year period, ending on January 1st 1988, was allowed for peaches and tomatoes, and also for the free movement of workers.

Portugal and Spain also applied for membership within a year or two of the Portuguese revolution of 1974, and the death of General Franco in 1975. Their membership negotiations were a great deal longer and more complicated than those with Greece, partly because of initial French reluctance but also because Spanish membership, in particular, was likely to cause greater problems for the existing member states. Agreement was finally reached in May 1985 and treaties of accession were signed on June 12th 1985, to take effect, after ratification by all the existing members as well as by Spain and Portugal, on January 1st 1986. In this case the transitional period was for seven years, ending on January 1st 1993, but for a number of sensitive agricultural products it lasted for ten years up to January 1st 1996. Freedom of movement for workers was not to come fully into effect for seven years, and in the case of Luxembourg (which already had a large population of immigrant Portuguese workers) for ten years.

Unsuccessful applicants

Turkey, which is recognised as a European state despite having 96% of its land area in Asia, and which signed an association agreement as long ago as 1963, officially applied for membership in April 1987, as did Morocco, which had made an unofficial approach three years earlier, in July 1987. Morocco claimed to be a democratic state with organic links with Europe, but was politely told that it was not eligible. The Turkish application was officially referred to the commission, for an opinion on its acceptability, as provided by the Rome treaty and as had occurred with all previous applications. In the past the commission verdict had always been favourable and membership negotiations had subsequently been opened. In this case, however, the commission reported that Turkey was not yet ready for membership, both because its economy was insufficiently developed and because its democracy had not been fully established. It was politely suggested to Turkey that its application should be shelved indefinitely. This rebuff did not deter the Turkish government, which in November 1992 announced that it wished to proceed to a full customs union with the EU, as had been foreshadowed in the original association agreement. The target date that the Turks set themselves was 1995.

Despite much scepticism, and some reluctance by the European Parliament to give its approval, the customs union came into effect on December 31st 1995. It will be a severe test for Turkish industry, which will have to face the full effect of competition from manufacturers within the EU. Yet the Turkish government welcomes this challenge as it believes that it will give an essential spur to the efficiency of Turkish enterprises. A provisional report by the commission on the working of the customs union, after the first ten months in October 1996, concluded that it was too early to assess the long-term effects, but the early indications seemed promising. There had been a sharp rise of EU exports to Turkey in the early months of 1996, while Turkey's exports to the EU had also risen, but not so sharply. Turkey has attracted a considerable amount of West European investment in recent years, and – since the end of the Cold War – has been seen as an important trading link with the countries of the former Soviet Union and its satellites in the Balkans, the Caucasus and Central Asia. The Turks believe that the more their country becomes economically involved with the EU the more difficult it will become for the Union to refuse it full membership. In practice, however, Turkish accession is unlikely in the foreseeable future and, indeed, will not take place unless three conditions are met.

1 A sustained improvement in Turkey's human rights record.
2 A solution to the Cyprus dispute, involving the withdrawal of Turkish troops.
3 The consolidation of Turkish democracy.

Two other Mediterranean countries which have association agreements with the EU – Malta and Cyprus – applied for membership in 1990. Both could probably have adapted easily enough to the requirements of membership, but they were given no early opportunity to do so. As far as Cyprus was concerned, there was a strong feeling that membership would be inappropriate so long as the northern part of the island continued to be under Turkish military occupation. Both countries also suffered from EU doubts as to whether such small nations could effectively take on the burdens of membership. However, as Luxembourg, a founder member, has a similar population to Malta and a

GUIDE TO THE EUROPEAN UNION

much smaller one than Cyprus, it was difficult to advance this as an argument against admitting them. The Copenhagen summit, in June 1993, adopted a more encouraging approach, and approved the sending of positive signals to both countries. These foresaw that the membership application of Cyprus would be re-examined in January 1995, in the light of the progress made in settling the Turkish Cypriot problem, and that an intensive dialogue would be held with Malta which would help prepare it for integration into the EU. Later, both countries received an assurance that negotiations on membership could commence within six months of the conclusion of the inter-governmental conference of 1996–97. The Maltese application was, however, put on ice by the newly elected Labour government in December 1996, only to be reactivated in September 1998 following its defeat in a subsequent election.

Two events gave a strong impetus to expanding EU membership, which had looked as though it would stabilise for many years after the accession of Spain and Portugal in 1986: the 1992 programme to complete the single European market and the collapse of Soviet communism.

Negotiations with EFTA countries

The launch of the 1992 programme (see Chapter 16) caused immediate ructions in the seven EFTA countries. These had all negotiated industrial free trade agreements with the EC in the 1960s, but they were afraid that they would be left out of the opportunities that the creation of a single European market would provide.

A two-year negotiation led to an agreement to form a European Economic Area (EEA), due to come into effect on January 1st 1993. Yet in the process of the negotiations most of the EFTA countries concluded that they were being asked to make so many concessions that they might as well go the whole hog and apply for full membership. Austria had already decided to do this before negotiations began and Sweden put in its application in 1991. Finland and Switzerland followed suit early in 1992. Norway still had traumatic memories of the 1972 referendum which narrowly rejected membership at the same time as Danish, Irish and UK entry. Its government, in the face of sharply divided public opinion, hesitated before taking the plunge, but finally put in an application at the end of 1992. Meanwhile, the Swiss voters narrowly rejected membership of the EEA in a referendum in December 1992. This led to a minor renegotiation of the terms of the agreement enabling it to come into effect after a delay of one year, on January 1st 1994, without Swiss participation. Consequently, the Swiss application for membership of the EU was put on ice, much to the chagrin of Swiss industry which believed it would have great difficulty in competing if Switzerland remained outside.

This left two EFTA countries: Iceland and Liechtenstein. The latter, with a population of 28,000 (less than one-tenth of Luxembourg's), can hardly aspire to full membership though since April 1995 it has been a member of the EEA. Iceland is obsessed with the need to retain full control over its fisheries resources and is not currently thinking of membership.

Negotiations with Austria, Finland, Sweden and Norway started early in 1993 and were successfully concluded in March 1994. Referenda were subsequently held in Austria in June, in Finland in September and in Sweden and Norway in November 1994. The first three produced majorities in favour, but Norwegian voters for the second time rejected EU membership (by 52.5% to 47.5%), so the number of member states increased from 12 to 15 in January 1995.

Few problems arose during the negotiating process. Each of the four applicant countries have high per head incomes and all will eventually become net contributors to EU funds. The main contentious issues related to agriculture, the environment, regional policy, transport (in particular the transit of goods vehicles over mountain roads in Austria), alcohol monopolies (in the three Nordic countries) and, in Norway's case, fisheries. Eventually final agreement was reached on the basis that the applicant states would conform to EU legislation, but with varying transition periods and a small number of special provisions to meet specific difficulties.

The problems anticipated by the traditional neutrality policies of Austria, Finland and Sweden largely disappeared with the end of the Cold War. In the event, each of these countries declared that, from the time of its accession, it would "be ready and able to participate fully and actively in the Common Foreign and Security Policy as defined in the Treaty on European Union" (the Maastricht treaty).

Obstacles for new members

New members who join the EU are required to accept not only all the provisions of the treaties (see Chapter 3), but also the entire *acquis communautaire* (that is, all the secondary legislation – directives, regulations and decisions – that has already been adopted under the treaties). Consequently, membership negotiations, which are nonetheless normally exhaustive and long drawn out, are mostly concerned with the length and nature of the transitional period during which the applicant state will have to modify its existing laws in order to conform, and which provisions shall be included in such transitional arrangements. If an accession treaty is concluded it must then be ratified by the parliaments of all the existing member states before it can come into effect. Since the Single European Act came into force in 1987 it has also been necessary for the European Parliament to ratify new accessions by the vote of an absolute majority of its members. The first time this occurred was on May 5th 1994 when, by a large majority, the membership applications of Austria, Finland, Sweden and Norway were approved.

Central and Eastern Europe

No sooner had the countries of Central and Eastern Europe broken free from the Soviet yoke in 1989–91 than they started to show a keen interest in joining the European Union. Some EU voices were raised against this, but in December 1991 association agreements were reached with Czechoslovakia, Hungary and Poland which specifically foresaw eventual membership. Similar agreements were later negotiated with Albania, Bulgaria, Romania, Slovenia and the Baltic states of Estonia, Latvia and Lithuania. The agreement with Czechoslovakia was later replaced by separate agreements with the Czech Republic and Slovakia. Slovenia also negotiated a similar agreement, and the remaining former Yugoslav republics, including what is left of Bosnia-Herzegovina, may qualify for comparable treatment in the future. Some or all of them may later aspire to full EU membership.

At the Copenhagen summit in June 1993 it was specifically affirmed that any Central or East European country that so wished could become a member of the EU "once it was able to fulfil the obligations associated with membership and meet the economic and political requirements". The first such countries to apply were Hungary and Poland in March 1994, and over the next two years they were followed by Bulgaria, the Czech Republic, Estonia, Latvia, Lithuania, Romania, Slovakia and Slovenia.

The commission reacted by producing a white paper in May 1995, setting out the preliminary steps the applicant countries should take to prepare themselves for membership. This bulky document, which contained hundreds of recommendations under 23 different policy headings, was intended largely as a checklist for the applicant countries to help prepare their administrations and adapt their legislation. At the same time, a great deal of technical assistance was provided to each of the countries under the Phare programme, to help minimise the pain that the process would inevitably entail. It was subsequently decided at the Florence summit in June 1996 that membership negotiations with the Central and East European applicants could start, at the same time as those with Cyprus, six months after the conclusion of the inter-governmental conference. The commission was asked to prepare its opinion on the suitability and preparedness of each of the candidates immediately after the conclusion of the IGC.

Accordingly, in July 1997 it published its opinion on the relative pre-paredness of the 11 candidate countries, concluding that membership negotiations should begin early in 1998 with six of them but that the other five were not yet ready to accept the obligations of membership. The commission's opinion was accepted by the EU heads of govern-ment at the Luxembourg summit in December 1997, and negotiations were opened with Cyprus, the Czech Republic, Estonia, Hungary, Poland and Slovenia the following March. Bulgaria, Latvia, Lithuania, Romania and Slovakia were encouraged to continue with their prepara-tions and were assured that these would be monitored on an annual basis and that if they made sufficient progress they too could be included in the process. In the meantime they were invited to an annual European conference of all EU member and applicant states, the first of which was held in London in March 1998. Turkey was also invited, but was offended at not being given the same assurances as the other can-didates, and boycotted the conference.

Separate, but parallel, negotiations were started with the six favoured candidates, and at the Helsinki summit, in December 1999, EU leaders gave the go-ahead for entry talks with Bulgaria, Latvia, Lithuania, Malta, Romania and Slovenia to begin early in 2000. Long and laborious nego-tiations continued, and by the end of 2001 four of the second batch of candidates had caught up with the earlier starters. Bulgaria and Roma-nia, however, were significantly behind. At the Laeken summit in December 2001, a target was set to complete negotiations with the ten leading candidates by the end of 2002, with the aim of bringing them into membership in time to participate in the European Parliament elec-tions in 2004. Another aim was to open all 30 chapters of the negotia-tions with Bulgaria and Romania during 2002, with the unofficial expectation that they would join by January 1st 2007.

By May 2002, the leading candidates had "provisionally closed" up to 27 of the 30 chapters, leaving only the tricky dossiers of agriculture, regional policy and the EU budget to be resolved. The EU side was determined to keep the short-term cost of enlargement well within the limits set at the 1999 Berlin summit for EU expenditure for 2000–06. The candidate countries, and Poland in particular with its large agricultural population, considered the terms offered to be mean, and were making strenuous attempts to obtain a more generous settlement. The chances of the EU making substantial improvements in its offers did not appear good, but there was guarded optimism that agreement would be reached with all ten candidates by the time of the Copenhagen summit, scheduled for December 2002.

At the Helsinki summit, it was finally signalled to Turkey that it, too, was a candidate for eventual membership, while spelling out the conditions it would have to meet before negotiations could begin. The Turkish government announced early in 2002 that it was embarking on an ambitious programme of political and economic reforms to meet the EU's pre-requisites for membership, and aimed to begin negotiations during 2003 – an optimistic but not totally unrealistic scenario. During the Kosovo conflict Albania and Macedonia entertained hopes that they might be accepted as fast-track candidates as a reward for their support for the NATO campaign. This will not happen, although they received pledges of considerable economic and technical assistance. In the long run, they – as well as Bosnia, Croatia and even Serbia – will undoubtedly be accepted as candidates, though it will be many years before they are able to qualify for membership.

After the Central and East European states may come six former Soviet republics in Europe – Armenia, Azerbaijan, Belarus, Georgia, Moldova and Ukraine – all of which have already signalled an interest by applying to join the Council of Europe. It is early days so far as they are concerned, but if by the end of the first decade of the 21st century they have consolidated their democracies and developed their economies – two big ifs – some at least of them may be knocking at the EU's door. Many Russians, too, would like to see their country join the EU eventually, but this is more problematical. Russia's vast size, its large land area in Asia and its former (and possibly future) status as a great power all mitigate against its acceptance as a cosy member of the club. It is more likely that some kind of exclusive treaty relationship – comparable to that which NATO has sought to negotiate with Russia – will develop out of the partnership and co-operation agreement signed with Russia in 1994. A free-trade agreement with Russia is a possibility, but probably not in the near future.

Further west, three prosperous western democracies, Iceland, Norway and Switzerland, could all secure membership with little ado if they (and their electors voting in referendums) decide that they want to. A third Norwegian application may not be long delayed, and Icelandic opinion is moving strongly in favour. Switzerland is more problematic, but it is unlikely to remain permanently excluded.

The Community, which started with six members in 1958, now has a membership of 15 and a population of 370m. By 2008, half a century after its birth, it could well have 27 members and a population of 450m. Ten years later there could be over 40 members, not including Russia but otherwise embracing the entire continent of Europe, and a total population approaching 700m. This may seem scarcely credible, and many would no doubt deeply regret the sea change in the nature of the Union which such an expansion would imply. Yet the logic of the Treaty of Rome and the way in which the EU has conducted itself so far point inexorably to a gradual but accelerating increase in membership.

38 The UK and the Union

The UK was a late entrant into the EC, and it has had an uneasy relationship with its partners for much of the time since it became a
member state in 1973.

A history of distrust

Even before 1973 there was a long history of distrust and disappointment, despite the evident desire of the original six members of the Community for UK membership. At the end of the second world war the
popularity and prestige of the UK was probably higher in Western
Europe than at any time before or since, and there was little doubt that
had the UK taken the lead in the movement for closer integration it
would have had a predominant influence on the shape and form of any
association that was formed. In the event, there was widespread dismay
and incomprehension at the UK's lack of interest in joining the Coal and
Steel Community in 1951 or in attending the 1955 Messina conference
which led to the creation of the EEC. The reasons behind this aloofness
– the continuing belief that the UK was a global rather than a European
power, that it had a special relationship with the United States, and that
its major trading as well as political links were with the Commonwealth
– were little appreciated beyond the English Channel. Furthermore, the
UK initiative in founding the European Free Trade Association (EFTA) in
1959 was widely seen as a spoiling device to reduce the impact of the
EEC which had been established the previous year.

Nevertheless, the UK's application to join the EC, when it finally came
in 1961, was warmly welcomed, and there was regret in all the member
states (including France itself) when President de Gaulle twice vetoed its
entry, in 1963 and 1968. It was only at the third time of asking that terms
of accession were finally agreed, in June 1971, following renewed negotiations between Edward Heath's Conservative government and the six
existing members.

Opposition to EC membership in the Labour Party

The long years of haggling had taken their toll in the UK, and a substantial degree of opposition to membership had built up. This affected both
major political parties, but in the Conservative Party, where it was
largely confined to a narrow, right-wing, nationalistic fringe, the party

leadership had little difficulty in isolating and containing its anti-EC members.

In the Labour Party internal divisions were more serious. The EC was depicted by left-wingers as a capitalist conspiracy opposed to the party's most basic objectives, while many trade unionists feared that food prices would rise as a result of the impact of the CAP. The pro-EC elements in the party, led by Roy Jenkins, held their ground against strong pressure to abandon their own deep convictions; 69 Labour MPs defied the party whip and enabled the membership terms to be approved by a good majority in the House of Commons. The damage done to the Labour Party by this dispute, particularly by the intolerant way in which it was conducted, was considerable, and undoubtedly contributed to the split which occurred a decade later when the Social Democratic Party was formed. Hostility within the Labour Party continued, but it was successfully defused, at least for a time, by the commitment that a Labour government would hold a referendum to determine whether the UK would remain a member. Following Labour's election victory in 1974, the terms of membership were renegotiated, the main change being the institution of a financial mechanism designed to prevent excessive UK budgetary contributions (although in the event it proved to be ineffective, see pages 13–14). A majority of the cabinet led by the prime minister, Harold Wilson, and the foreign secretary, James Callaghan (both of whom had voted against membership in 1971), were able to recommend the acceptance of the revised terms, despite the opposition of a large section of the Labour Party. In the referendum which followed, on June 5th 1975, a majority of just over 2:1 favoured continued UK membership, and the dispute seemed to be over.

It flared up again in 1979 when it was discovered, in the closing months of James Callaghan's Labour government, that – despite the renegotiated terms – the UK, which had now reached the end of its transitional stage of membership, was liable to pay an unacceptably high net contribution to the EC, probably exceeding 1 billion ecus in the following year (see pages 18–19). It fell to Mrs Thatcher's Conservative government, elected in May 1979, to attempt to secure a permanent abatement of the UK contribution. Mrs Thatcher played the leading part in the negotiations, which dominated the life of the Community and particularly the meetings of the European Council until a settlement was reached at the Fontainebleau summit in June 1984 (see page 20). In the meantime Labour Party hostility to UK membership was rekindled, and in the June 1983 general election campaign the party proposed a unilateral withdrawal, without even the possibility of a further referendum. Following Labour's heavy defeat in that election, and the replacement of Michael Foot by Neil Kinnock as party leader, the issue was quietly dropped. There was no mention of withdrawal in the Labour Party manifesto for the 1987 general election.

A year or so later, following a highly successful visit to the Trades Union Congress in 1988 by Jacques Delors, who fired the delegates with a vision of a Europe in which trade unionists would share fully in the fruits of the Community's future development, including the 1992 programme, both the trade unions and the Labour Party finally came round to see the EC in a positive light.

Mrs Thatcher reduced UK influence in the EC ...

This welcome development was balanced by a perverse reaction in the Conservative Party, which, under the leadership of Mrs Thatcher, became steadily more hostile to the EC from September 1988 onwards, when she delivered a widely reported speech at Bruges. This was hailed as a rallying call by all those who looked nostalgically back to the days when the UK was a world power and who were psychologically incapable of adjusting to current realities. Mrs Thatcher became especially hung up over questions of "sovereignty", which she and her supporters saw as a zero-sum concept, assuming that any accretion of power to EC institutions constituted an equal diminution of that of the member states. This ran directly counter to the prevailing view within the Community, which was that national sovereignty had been declining for many years, for reasons which had little to do with the growth of the EC, and that it was only by pooling their resources in a number of fields that the member states would be able collectively to achieve objectives which would be beyond their individual capacity.

In fact it is clear that Mrs Thatcher substantially reduced UK influence within the EC during her final years as prime minister by insisting that the UK took a negative or minimalist position on most proposals for new EC initiatives, even including those, such as the Lingua programme on foreign language teaching (see page 231), which would be of particular benefit to the UK. She seemed to glory in being in a minority of one at meetings of the European Council, and it was her behaviour at and after the Rome meeting in October 1990, which set a date for the beginning of stage two of EMU, that led to her being challenged for the leadership of the Conservative Party and her replacement by John Major.

... and John Major did not do any better

Major evidently did not share Mrs Thatcher's deep distrust of the Community, and spoke of his desire "to bring the UK into the heart of Europe". He promptly dropped her abrasive criticisms of the EC, but, conscious of her continuing influence within the Conservative Party, he continued to approach the proposals for EMU and "political union" with circumspection. By adopting a more reasonable negotiating approach, he was able to secure considerable changes in the two inter-governmental conferences, particularly in that on "political union", and a year after becoming prime minister he agreed to the Maastricht Treaty on European Union, but only on the basis of two opt-out clauses. One of these reserved the right of the UK not to take part in the third stage of EMU, with a European Central Bank (ECB) and a common currency. Few observers believed at the time that there was any serious possibility of the UK not participating in stage three, and the only lasting consequence of Mr Major's obduracy at Maastricht was likely to be the undermining of the otherwise strong claim of the City of London to house the ECB. This prediction proved correct when Frankfurt was subsequently chosen as the site for the European Monetary Institute, which is the forerunner of the bank. The other opt-out concerned the Social Charter (see pages 180–1).

These opt-outs were double-edged so far as Major was concerned. While not really appeasing the Euro-sceptics in his own party, they were profoundly unwelcome to the Labour and Liberal Democratic parties which otherwise were enthusiastic supporters of the Maastricht treaty. It was not, therefore, possible to depend on wholehearted support from the opposition parties during the long and difficult process of getting the ratification bill through both Houses of the UK Parliament. This was completed only in July 1993, after repeated alarms and a real risk that the government, with its slender parliamentary majority, might be swept away in the process. Major and his colleagues emerged shell-shocked from the experience and thereafter seemed to give overriding priority to keeping Tory Euro-sceptics happy. This led to a resumption of Thatcherite anti-EU rhetoric by ministers, and the UK once again allied itself with those wishing to obstruct further progress towards European integration. Major unwisely attempted to play to the anti-EU gallery in his party in March and April 1994, when he sought to maintain the size of the blocking minority in votes in the Council of Ministers at the same level as for 12 member states when the rules were being revised for the extension of membership to 16, with the anticipated accession of

Austria, Finland, Sweden and Norway. He encountered determined opposition from all the other member states except Spain, as well as from the European Parliament, and eventually had to make a humiliating climbdown in order not to jeopardise the accession of the four applicants, which had been a long-term UK aim.

Worse was to follow in June 1994, when at the Corfu summit Major vetoed the appointment of the Belgian prime minister, Jean-Luc Dehaene, as successor to Jacques Delors as president of the commission. This caused real offence, not only in Belgium but in the other member states as well, all of which had backed his appointment. The ostensible reason given for Major's action was that Dehaene was a "federalist", who believed in an important role for the state in economic decision-making. Actually, it was intended as a "macho" action to impress Tory backbenchers. It was to little avail: a few weeks later Major agreed without demur to the appointment of the Luxembourg prime minister, Jacques Santer, who blandly announced that his own views were identical to those of Dehaene.

Subsequently, the Conservative Party got itself into a hideous mess over the question of economic and monetary union, with a determined attempt by the Euro-sceptics to rule out UK membership definitively. Major resisted this pressure but at the cost of engaging in more and more anti-EU rhetoric, spurred on by large sections of the press which, although mostly foreign-owned (by Rupert Murdoch and Conrad Black), took an increasingly obsessive nationalistic line. Major's government also took a negative position in the inter-governmental conference, making it impossible for it to reach any agreed positions on serious issues before the UK general election on May 1st 1997.

Last chance for the UK?

The newly elected Labour government lost no time in emphasising that it intended to make a "fresh start" in relations with the European Union, and that although it would defend vital UK interests it would adopt a much more positive approach than its predecessors. Its first initiative, within a couple of days of the election, was to announce that it would end the UK opt-out and sign up to the Social Chapter at the earliest opportunity. This was probably the UK's last chance to end the damage caused by its previous semi-detached attitude to the Union, and to restore its influence as a leading player. Tony Blair and his ministers followed this up by adopting a much more conciliatory attitude in negotiations within the inter-governmental conference, enabling agreement to be reached at the Amsterdam summit in June 1998. The fact that the Amsterdam Treaty did not go so far towards greater EU integration as many people had hoped was not, for once, the fault of the British negotiators. Blair succeeded in dispelling within a few weeks the bad blood which had existed between the UK and its European partners over the preceding years, but there was great disappointment when later in the year Gordon Brown, the British Chancellor of the Exchequer, announced that the UK would not be one of the founder members of economic and monetary union (EMU). British ministers were subsequently reluctant to concede – what was evident to everybody else – that their influence in EU decision-making was bound to be reduced until such time as they finally took the plunge. It was especially painful for them to accept their exclusion from the ministerial Euro-11 (later Euro-12) committee set up to oversee the EMU process.

It is far from certain when, and even if, the UK will join the single currency. The Blair government has declared itself in favour in principle, but has repeatedly said that it would recommend entry only when five economic tests set by Gordon Brown had been satisfied. These tests were:

- Would joining EMU create better conditions for firms making long-term decisions to invest in the UK?
- How would adopting the single currency affect the UK's financial services?
- Are business cycles and economic structures compatible so that the UK and others in Europe could live comfortably with euro interest rates on a permanent basis?
- If problems do emerge, is there sufficient flexibility to deal with them?
- Will joining EMU help to promote higher growth, stability and a lasting increase in jobs?

Few, if any, of these tests are susceptible to precise measurement, and there is a large subjective – if not cosmetic – element to them. The government's decision will, in fact, be made on political rather than economic grounds.

Its overcautious attitude up to now has been affected by three important factors. First, opinion polls, which consistently showed majorities of two to one, or even more, against entry, even though 80% of voters expect the UK to have adopted the single currency by 2010. Second, the hostility of large parts of the press, particularly the *Sun* and the *Daily Mail.* Third, the opposition of the bulk of the Conservative Party. The last factor was greatly mitigated by the rout of the Conservatives in the 2001 general election after William Hague, then its leader, had made "Save the Pound" a central feature of his campaign. The government has since become less wary of the popular press, and the opinion polls have begun to improve, particularly following the exceptionally smooth introduction of euro notes and coins in the 12 euro nations in January 2002, although the "no" voters remain in a majority.

The government has pledged to give its ruling on the five economic tests by June 2003, and if it is favourable to recommend entry in a referendum. It now seems likely that the ruling will be brought forward by at least six months, with the likelihood of a referendum in May 2003. If so, it would follow in the wake of a similar Swedish referendum in March or April, which is predicted to produce a strong majority in favour of the euro, despite earlier Swedish misgivings.

Blair and his government really have no choice but to take the plunge if they want the UK to play a full part in Europe and to enjoy the influence to which they aspire. There is certainly still a serious risk of being defeated in a referendum, but if they fail to take this risk they will surrender any claim to be serious players on the European stage.

UK's hostility had many causes ...

That hostility to the EU and to UK membership had lasted so long cannot be explained by reference to a single cause. The UK's historical experience and the existence of the English Channel, which remained a powerful psychological barrier long after modern transport technology had reduced it to only a minor physical impediment, have undoubtedly had a substantial effect on UK attitudes. The power struggle within the Labour Party between left and right in the 1970s certainly contributed to perpetuating a conflict which might otherwise have been expected to die down much earlier. (Similar divisions in the Conservative Party, at a later period, between Margaret Thatcher and her critics, also contributed to sharpening controversy over Europe.) It was a cruel stroke of fate that the UK's eventual membership of the EC (which had been delayed for nearly a decade by de Gaulle's intransigence) coincided with the beginning of the economic crisis sparked off by the oil price rises of 1973. By this time the original six members had already enjoyed 15 years of prosperity during which they had been members of the EC, and much of that prosperity was attributed to the effects of membership. By contrast, virtually all the UK experience of membership has been during a period of economic difficulty. Many Britons came to regard the EC as a convenient scapegoat for the lack of economic success.

The UK has undoubtedly suffered from the fact that it was not a founder member and that several aspects of the Community to which it has most strongly objected, particularly certain procedures within the CAP, were already entrenched by the time its membership came to be negotiated. Although some modifications have been achieved, there is little doubt that a more acceptable framework, from the UK point of view, would have been adopted had UK influence been brought to bear from the outset. Similarly, many of the working methods of the Community (including the widespread use of French as a working language, which causes more problems for the notoriously monoglot UK than for most of its European partners) might have evolved differently, making the organisation a more comfortable working environment.

... but it has slowly adapted to EU membership

Yet the very real difficulties encountered at the outset of UK membership have been attenuated with time, and those Britons who have worked for the EU, or who have had professional dealings with it, have mostly shown sufficient adaptability to overcome their initial handicaps.

UK industry, in particular, has progressively adapted itself to membership. Whereas in 1972 only one-third of UK exports and imports were with the EC, by 1986 the proportion had grown to one-half and by 1995 to 57%. Had the UK not entered the EC in 1973, its economy would no doubt have developed in a different direction and sought whatever alternative opportunities, however limited, might have been available to it. These have now gone, and there can be little doubt that horrendous difficulties would arise if the UK were to leave the EU.

For all practical purposes the UK is in the EU to stay, and it would be folly to base national policies on any other foundation than the development of the Union in a manner designed to produce the maximum benefit for its members. The grudging and minimalist attitude often adopted by British ministers in their dealings with the EU was damaging to UK interests and undermined the UK's influence within the organisation. This is a lesson which does seem to have been learned by Tony Blair's ministers, and it is to be hoped that the days of the UK as an awkward "odd man out" are past.

39 The future

It is likely that a special meeting of the European Council will be held in Rome on 25th March 2007 to celebrate the 50th anniversary of the signing of the treaty to set up the European Economic Community (EEC). This will be a very different gathering from the one 50 years earlier, when the heads of state and government of France, West Germany, Italy, the Netherlands, Belgium and Luxembourg first assembled in the Italian capital. That cosy club of six West European neighbours will have expanded probably to at least 27 member states by 2007, and the population of the Community will have grown from less than 200m to more than 480m. The expansion in the scope of its activities has been equally impressive. What started out as an embryonic customs union, with a Common Agricultural Policy tagged on, has emerged as a leading economic actor on the world stage, whose policies have proliferated into many fields not mentioned in the original treaty.

The achievements of the EEC, and its successor the European Union, are too numerous to list in detail, but on the economic side two, in particular, stand out. First, the 1992 programme for completing the single market (see Chapter 16) was substantially concluded on time, and the bulk of the internal barriers that prevented the Community from operating as a single trading area were removed. Second, the member states committed themselves to economic and monetary union. The successful launch of the euro at the beginning of 1999 and the astonishingly smooth introduction of notes and coins in January–February 2002 leave little doubt that it will act as a further spur to European integration and may well, in time, come to challenge, if not surpass, the American dollar as the principal world currency.

A third major economic initiative was that launched at the Lisbon summit, in March 2000, to turn the EU into "the most competitive and dynamic knowledge-based economy in the world". It is a ten-year programme, which is being monitored each spring by special meetings of the European Council. The first was in Stockholm in 2001 and the second in Barcelona in 2002. At both of these progress was reported, but rather less than had been hoped, and a considerable acceleration is necessary during the remaining eight years if the Union is to meet its ambitious target.

Progress has been mixed, too, in the EU's objective of forging a common foreign and security policy, with sufficient military clout to back it up, without being heavily dependent on the United States. The EU's response to the end of the cold war was highly positive. It took the lead in providing moral and material support for the newly free countries of Central and Eastern Europe, to which it clearly acted as a powerful magnet. It was the EU that took the initiative in setting up the European Bank for Reconstruction and Development and subscribed more than half its $12 billion capital, while establishing the Phare and TACIS programmes see (Chapter 35), which have dispersed a substantial amount of economic, financial and technical aid. In so far as this has represented a continuation of the Marshall Plan, which rejuvenated Western Europe, it is the EU and not the United States that is providing the great bulk of the material assistance. The EU has also opened up the prospect of membership for the countries of Central and Eastern Europe. Eight of them (together with Malta and Cyprus) are currently well advanced with their applications, with the hope of securing entry by 2004, and Bulgaria and Romania should be able to follow with two or three years' delay (see Chapter 37).

The uncertain EU response to the break-up of Yugoslavia in 1991–92, when the combatants looked to the EU rather than to the Organisation on Security and Co-operation in Europe (OSCE, formerly the CSCE) to broker a peaceful settlement, underlined how unready the Union and its member states were to assume such a role. This story was largely repeated in Kosovo in 1998–99, and in both cases it required massive intervention by NATO, with the American contribution predominant, before the conflicts were resolved.

Since then the momentum towards a common European defence effort has significantly speeded up. The wastefulness of competing national research and manufacturing concerns, most of which are too small to compete successfully with their American rivals, has produced a spate of mergers, which will certainly continue. The moves to develop a European Defence and Security Policy, with its own Rapid Reaction Force (RFF), described in Chapter 36, offer a hopeful prospect. But the member states will have to do a great deal more – in terms of contributing to the equipment as well as the manpower of the RFF – before it is able to play an effective role in peacekeeping, let alone peacemaking, operations.

What will be the nature of the European Union of the future? Will there, for example, be "an elected president of Europe?", as the author was once asked in a television programme. "Yes, but probably not for at least another 20 years," he replied, and immediately asked himself whether he was not being unintentionally misleading. For what the interviewer no doubt had in mind, and what most viewers probably took the question to mean, was a presidential election on American lines, with the implication that the EU would evolve into a United States of Europe, with a similar division of powers to the United States of America.

This does not appear to be a likely, or even desirable, development. The 15 member states of the EU (and even the original six, which formed a more cohesive unit) are far more diverse than the original 13 colonies that came together at the Continental Congress in Philadelphia in 1774. Apart from language and cultural differences they are all sovereign states, several of them with hundreds of years of independence behind them, with distinct political, administrative and legal systems and widely differing historical experiences. In the early 1990s many people expected that some form of federal government for Western Europe would eventually emerge (and indeed saw the existing European Commission as the embryo of such a government[1]). It is more likely that the advance to a fully federal system will not take place, and that the present hybrid system of supranational institutions co-existing with member states that retain a considerable degree of sovereignty will continue, though with substantial modifications. This, it has been cogently argued[2], would be more in tune with public opinion, which wishes to see an effective EU but not one that tramples over national peculiarities and susceptibilities. The European Union, in this view, is not a federal state half-built, but an entirely new form of political system: "Network Europe", in which power is shared and dispersed around many centres.

Compared with past attempts at federation or confederation, and with contemporary efforts to bring neighbouring countries closer together in other parts of the world, the progress made during the nearly 50 years since the EU was founded is remarkable. Yet it is apparent that it will need to proceed further and faster over the next 50 years if Europe is to punch its full weight in a rapidly shrinking but fast developing world. This does not mean that more and more power should be concentrated in Brussels for the sake of enhancing the authority of the European Union. An over-centralised Europe is even less desirable than an over-centralised member state, of which there are a number already in the Union. What is required is a clear-headed attempt to identify those powers which, for the common good, can most effectively be exercised at a European level. These powers, and these only, should be vested in a European authority; all others (including probably some currently exercised from Brussels) should be retained by national governments or, in some cases, devolved downwards to regional or local authorities. This was recognised in the Maastricht treaty, which speaks of "an ever closer union ... where decisions are taken as closely as possible to the citizens".

It goes beyond the scope of this book, and certainly beyond the expertise of the author, to produce a definitive list of which powers are most appropriately exercised at which level. It is indeed evident that the balance will change over time. Already the Union has discovered that both natural and man-made forces have made nonsense out of national sovereignty in areas not originally regarded as appropriate for EU decision-making. Conservation of fish species in the North Sea is one striking example, as it is impossible to prevent the fish swimming round from one country's territorial waters to another. It was only when herrings had all but disappeared that the EU countries were able to agree that if conservation was to be attempted at all it had to be on a Union-wide basis. When trees in the Black Forest started to die in large numbers, partly because of chemical emissions in the UK, the need for an EU environmental protection policy – for which no provision had been made in the Rome treaty – was forcibly brought home to both national governments and public opinion. It is evident that the EU, as at present constituted, is not attuned to the assumption of some responsibilities now held at national level, but which would certainly be more appropriately exercised on a Europe-wide basis. Its popularity has undoubtedly slipped in recent years, as its great achievements in bringing peace and prosperity to a region previously wracked by internecine warfare have come to be taken more and more for granted. Although opinion polls continue to show majority support for the EU in the member states, and also among the candidate members, the level of enthusiasm has fallen, as illustrated by the record low turnout in the last European Parliament elections in 2000 and the negative results of EU-related referendums in Denmark and Ireland. There is a growing feeling that European integration has become an elite rather than a popular project, and that urgent steps need to be taken to bridge the gap.

It was this feeling that lay behind the decision of the Laeken summit, in December 2001, to appoint a broadly based convention to consider the next stage of EU reform before the inter-governmental conference (IGC) due in 2004. The convention was given 56 specific questions to consider, but it was also given wide discretion to discuss other proposals, including those emanating from citizens' organisations. Among the questions posed were: how should democratic legitimacy and transparency be increased; how should the president of the commission be chosen; does the Union need a simplified constitution; what role should national MPs play in EU decision-making; should there be more EU legislation or less?

The future strength and influence of the European Union will depend to a considerable extent on the wisdom and perspicacity with which the convention confronts these questions, and on how the member states react to their proposals when they frame the conclusions of the 2004 IGC. It is a challenge that they cannot afford to flunk. A Union that is unable to muster popular support will hardly be able to face the future with confidence.

APPENDICES

APPENDICES

1 Basic statistics of the member and candidate states

The following table, which has been compiled from information supplied by the Directorate-General for Economic Affairs of the European Commission and by the Union's Statistical Office (Eurostat), contains comparative data on the 15 member states and on the 13 candidate members compared with the United States and Japan. The figures refer to 1999, except where indicated.

	Total area (km^2)	Pop. ('000)	GDP per head PPS^2	Inflation^1 %	Unemployment rate (% of working pop.)	Total working pop. ('000)	Trade balance (€m)
EU-15	3,236,260	375,346	20,610	1.5	9.2	154,988	-19,034
Austria	83,860	8,083	23,178	0.9	3.8	3,678	-4,935
Belgium	30,520	10,214	23,343	1.0	9.1	3,987	13,456
Denmark	43,090	5,314	23,997	2.7	5.2	2,698	4,262
Finland	338,150	5,160	20,886	0.7	10.2	2,326	9,504
France	543,980	58,973	21,395	0.4	11.3	22,748	10,065
Germany	357,030	82,037	22,463	0.9	8.8	36,089	65,202
Greece	131,960	10,522	14,277	2.9	11.7	3,940	16,451
Ireland	70,300	3,735	23,226	3.8	5.7	1,582	23,027
Italy	301,320	57,613	20,449	1.5	11.3	20,618	12,730
Luxembourg	2,570	429	35,980	2.3	2.3	175	-2,837
Netherlands	41,530	15,760	21,713	1.7	3.3	7,210	11,651
Portugal	91,910	9,979	15,111	3.5	4.5	4,830	-14,480
Spain	505,990	39,394	16,953	2.9	15.9	13,773	29,004
Sweden	449,960	8,854	19,985	0.5	7.2	4,051	15,311
UK	244,100	59,280	20,348	2.5	6.1	27,283	-49,477
Bulgaria	110,990	8,211	4,749	2.6	17.0	2,989	...
Cyprus	9,251	665	17,082	1.3	3.6	290	-2,907[3]
Czech Republic	78,870	10,285	12,498	1.8	8.7	4,716	-1,979[3]
Estonia	45,227	1,442	7,682	4.5	11.7	615	-1,375[3]
Hungary	93,030	10,068	10,705	10.0	7.0	3,785	-8,218[3]
Latvia	64,589	2,432	6,169	2.1	14.5	998	-1,231[3]
Lithuania	65,300	3,700	5,786	0.7	14.1	1,613	-1,857[3]
Malta	315	387	8,800	2.1	5.3	138	-851[3]
Poland	312,685	38,654	7,806	7.2	15.3	14,940	-16,779[3]
Romania	238,391	22,458	5,682	45.8	6.8	11,022	-3,153[3]
Slovakia	49,035	5,395	10,279	10.6	16.2	2,432	-2,047[3]
Slovenia	20,273	1,986	14,964	6.1	7.6	886	-945[3]
Turkey	774,820	64,330	5,881	64.9[3]	7.6	...	-16,972[3]
Japan	377,835	126,451	24,921	-0.9	4.7	67,790	95,891[3]
US	9,629,091	271,626	36,116	1.5	4.2	140,185	-276,226[3]

1 GDP price deflator.
2 Purchasing power standard.
3 1998.
Sources: European Commission (Eurostat and Directorate-General for Agriculture); FAO; UNSO

2 Presidents of the High Authority and the Commission

Presidents of the High Authority of the European Coal and Steel Community (ECSC)
(merged with the European Commission on July 1st 1967)

1952	Jean Monnet
1955	René Mayer
1958	Paul Finet
1959	Piero Malvestiti
1963	Dino Del Bo

Presidents of the Commission of the European Atomic Energy Community (Euratom)
(merged with the European Commission on July 1st 1967)

1958	Louis Armand
1959	Etienne Hirsch
1962	Pierre Chatenet

Presidents of the European Commission
(and since 1967 of the combined European Communities)

1958	Walter Hallstein
1967	Jean Rey
1970	Franco-Maria Malfatti
1972	Sicco Mansholt
1973	François-Xavier Ortoli
1977	Roy Jenkins
1981	Gaston Thorn
1985	Jacques Delors
1995	Jacques Santer
1999	Romano Prodi

3 The Commission

Romano Prodi (Italy)
President

RESPONSIBILITIES
Secretariat general
Legal service
Media and communication

DEPARTMENTS
Secretariat General
Legal Service
Media and Communication
Service

Neil Kinnock (UK)
Vice-President for Administrative Reform

RESPONSIBILITIES
Overall co-ordination of
administrative reform
Personnel and administration
Linguistic services
Protocol and security

DEPARTMENTS
Personnel and Administration
DG
Inspectorate General
Joint Interpreting and
Conference Service
Translation Service

Loyola de Palacio (Spain)
Vice-President for relations with the European Parliament, and for Transport and Energy

RESPONSIBILITIES
Relations with the European
Parliament
Relations with the Committee of
the Regions, the Economic
and Social Committee, and
the Ombudsman
Transport (including trans-
European networks)
Energy

DEPARTMENTS
Transport DG
Energy DG

Mario Monti (Italy)
Commissioner for Competition

RESPONSIBILITY	DEPARTMENT
Competition	Competition DG

Franz Fischler (Austria)
Commissioner for Agriculture and Fisheries

RESPONSIBILITIES	DEPARTMENTS
Agriculture and rural development	Agriculture DG
Fisheries	Fisheries DG

Erkki Liikanen (Finland)
Commissioner for Enterprise and Information Society

RESPONSIBILITIES	DEPARTMENTS
Enterprise	Enterprise DG
Competitiveness	Information Society DG
Innovation	
Information society	

Frits Bolkestein (Netherlands)
Commissioner for Internal Market

RESPONSIBILITIES	DEPARTMENTS
Internal market	Internal Market DG
Financial services	Customs and Taxation DG
Customs	
Taxation	

Philippe Busquin (Belgium)
Commissioner for Research

RESPONSIBILITIES	DEPARTMENTS
Science, research and development	Research DG
Joint Research Centre	Joint Research Centre

Pedro Solbes Mira (Spain)
*Commissioner for Economic and
    Monetary Affairs*

RESPONSIBILITIES
Economic and financial affairs
Monetary matters
Statistical Office

DEPARTMENTS
Economic and Financial
    Affairs DG
Statistical Office

Poul Nielson (Denmark)
*Commissioner for Development
    and Humanitarian Aid*

RESPONSIBILITIES
Development aid and
    co-operation
Humanitarian aid

DEPARTMENTS
Development DG
Humanitarian Aid Office

Günter Verheugen (Germany)
Commissioner for Enlargement

RESPONSIBILITIES
Enlargement process including
    the pre-accession strategy

DEPARTMENT
Enlargement Service

Chris Patten (UK)
*Commissioner for External
    Relations*

RESPONSIBILITIES
External relations
Common Foreign and Security
    Policy
Delegations in non-member
    countries
Common Service for External
    Relations

DEPARTMENTS
External Relations DG
Common Service for External
    Relations

Pascal Lamy (France)
Commissioner for Trade

RESPONSIBILITY
Trade policy and instruments of
    trade policy

DEPARTMENT
Trade DG

David Byrne (Ireland)
*Commissioner for Health and
    Consumer Protection*

RESPONSIBILITIES	DEPARTMENT
Public health	Health and Consumer Protection
Consumer protection	DG

Michel Barnier (France)
*Commissioner for Regional
    Policy*

RESPONSIBILITIES	DEPARTMENT
Regional policy	Regional Policy DG
Cohesion fund	
Inter-governmental conference	

Viviane Reding (Luxembourg)
*Commissioner for Education and
    Culture*

RESPONSIBILITIES	DEPARTMENTS
Citizens' Europe	Education and Culture DG
Transparency	Publications Office
Education and culture	
Publications Office	

Michaele Schreyer (Germany)
Commissioner for the Budget

RESPONSIBILITIES	DEPARTMENTS
Budget	Budget DG
Financial control	Financial Control DG
Fraud prevention	Fraud Prevention Office

Margot Wallström (Sweden)
Commissioner for Environment

RESPONSIBILITIES	DEPARTMENT
Environment	Environment DG
Nuclear safety	

António Vitorino
  (Portugal)
*Commissioner for Justice and
  Home Affairs*

RESPONSIBILITY

Freedom, security, and justice

DEPARTMENT

Justice and Home Affairs DG

Anna Diamantopoulou
  (Greece)
*Commissioner for Employment
  and Social Affairs*

RESPONSIBILITIES

Employment
Social affairs
Equal opportunities

DEPARTMENT

Employment and Social Affairs
  DG

4 The Directorates-General and Services of the Commission

Since September 1999 the administration of the commission has been organised in 36 different services and directorates-general, as listed below.

Secretariat General
Legal Service
Press and Communication
Economic and Financial Affairs
Enterprise
Competition
Employment and Social Affairs
Agriculture
Transport
Environment
Research
Joint Research Centre
Information Society
Fisheries
Internal Market
Regional Policy
Energy
Taxation and Customs Union
Education and Culture
Health and Consumer Protection

Justice and Home Affairs
External Relations
Trade
Development
Enlargement
Common Service for External
    Relations
Humanitarian Aid Office –
    ECHO
Eurostat
Personnel and Administration
Inspectorate General
Budget
Financial Control
European Anti-Fraud Office
Joint Interpreting and
    Conference Service
Translation Service
Publications Office

5 Addresses of main EU institutions

European Parliament
Secretariat
Centre Européen, Plateau du Kirchberg
L-2929 Luxembourg
Tel. +352 43001

Council of the European Union
General Secretariat
Rue de la Loi 175
B-1048 Brussels
Tel. +32 2 2856111

European Commission
Rue de la Loi 200
B-1049 Brussels
Tel. +32 2 2991111

Court of Justice of the European Communities
Boulevard Konrad Adenauer
L-2925 Luxembourg
Tel. +352 43031

European Court of Auditors
12 rue Alcide de Gasperi
L-1615 Luxembourg
Tel. +352 43981

Economic and Social Committee
Rue Ravenstein 2
B-1000 Brussels
Tel. +32 2 5199011

Committee of the Regions
Rue Belliard 79
B-1040 Brussels
Tel. +32 2 2822211

European Investment Bank
100 boulevard Konrad Adenauer
L-2950 Luxembourg
Tel. +352 43791

European Central Bank
(formerly European Monetary Institute)
Kaiserstrasse 29
D-60311 Frankfurt am Main
Tel. +49 69 13440

6 Party groups in the European Parliament

The Euro-elections have been contested in each member state by the main national political parties. Within the Parliament, however, the elected members have joined together in transnational groups, and they sit in these groups rather than in national delegations, inside the chamber. There are currently seven of these, as well as some 27 MEPs who have declined to join any group and who sit as independents.

EPP/ED   The European People's Party and European Democrats, comprising Christian Democrat and Centre Right parties from all member states, including UK Conservatives and Irish Fine Gael members. It is the largest group in the Parliament and also includes Ulster Unionist MEP Jim Nicholson.

PES   The Party of European Socialists, comprising members from all EU states including the UK and Ireland.

ELDR   European Liberal, Democratic and Reformist Group, where the largest contingent is now from the UK. It includes one Irish independent, who is group leader.

Greens/   Comprises 38 MEPs from Green parties in 11 member
EFA   states, who have formed an alliance with ten European Free Alliance (EFA) MEPs from home rule parties in Scotland, Wales, Flanders, the Basque country, Galicia and Andalusia. The UK Greens
and Plaid Cymru are represented for the first time with two MEPs respectively.

EU/NGL   The Confederal Group of the European United Left/Nordic Green Left NGL Group, made up of representatives of Left/Green parties from Denmark, Finland, Germany, Greece, Italy, the Netherlands, Spain and Sweden as well as members of Communist parties from France, Greece and Portugal.

UEN   The Union for a Europe of Nations is pledged to defend the nation state, is led by 13 French national MEPs and is opposed to further integration. It includes six Fianna Fail members from Ireland, nine Italians from Mr Fini's Allianza Nazionale, one Danish member from the People's Party and two Portuguese members from the Partido Popular.

IND   The independents include Belgian and French National Front members, Italian radicals, regionalist members from the Freedom Party in Austria, a Spanish regionalist and Ian Paisley.

EDD   The Europe of Democracies and Diversities Group comprises six members from the French pro-hunting/defence of rural traditions group. three MEPs from the UK Independence Party, four anti-EU Danish members and three Dutch Calvinists.

Political groups in the European Parliament, April 2002

	EPP/ED	PES	ELDR	Greens/ EFA	EUL/ NGL	UEN	IND	EDD	Total
Austria	7	7	–	2	–	–	5	–	21
Belgium	6	5	5	7	–	–	2	–	25
Denmark	1	2	6	–	2	1	–	4	16
Finland	5	3	5	2	1	–	–	–	16
France	20	22	1	9	11	3	12	9	87
Germany	53	35	–	4	7	–	–	–	99
Greece	9	9	–	–	7	–	–	–	25
Ireland	5	1	1	2	–	6	–	–	15
Italy	35	16	8	2	6	10	10	–	87
Luxembourg	2	2	1	1	–	–	–	–	6
Netherlands	9	6	8	4	1	–	–	3	31
Portugal	9	12	–	–	2	2	–	–	25
Spain	28	24	3	4	4	–	1	–	64
Sweden	7	6	4	2	3	–	–	–	22
UK	37	29	11	6	–	–	2	2	87
Total	233	179	53	45	44	22	32	18	626

7 Overseas links with the EU

The 78 ACP states

African

Angola
Benin
Botswana
Burkina Faso
Burundi
Cameroon
Cape Verde
Central African
  Republic
Chad
Comoros
Congo (Brazzaville)
Congo (Kinshasa)
Côte d'Ivoire
Djibouti
Equatorial Guinea
Eritrea
Ethiopia
Gabon
The Gambia
Ghana
Guinea
Guinea Bissau
Kenya
Lesotho
Liberia
Madagascar
Malawi
Mali

Mauritania
Mauritius
Mozambique
Namibia
Niger
Nigeria
Rwanda
São Tomé & Príncipe
Senegal
Seychelles
Sierra Leone
Somalia
South Africa[1]
Sudan
Swaziland
Tanzania
Togo
Uganda
Zambia
Zimbabwe

Caribbean

Antigua & Barbuda
Bahamas
Barbados
Belize
Cuba
Dominica
Dominican Republic

Grenada
Guyana
Haiti
Jamaica
St Kitts & Nevis
St Lucia
St Vincent & The
  Grenadines
Suriname
Trinidad & Tobago

Pacific

Cook Islands
Federal States of
  Micronesia
Fiji
Kiribati
Marshall Islands
Nauru
Niue
Palau
Papua New Guinea
Solomon Islands
Tonga
Tuvalu
Western Samoa
Vanuatu

1 Qualified membership.

Overseas Countries and Territories (OCTs)

Denmark

Special relationship
Greenland

France

Territorial collectives
Mayotte
St Pierre & Miquelon
Overseas territories
New Caledonia & dependencies
French Polynesia
French Southern & Antarctic Territories
Wallis & Futuna Islands

Netherlands

Overseas countries
Netherlands Antilles (Bonaire, Curaçao, St Martin, Saba, St Eustace)
Aruba

UK

Overseas countries and territories
Anguilla
British Antarctic Territory
British Indian Ocean Territory
British Virgin Islands
Cayman Islands
Falkland Islands
Southern Sandwich Islands & dependencies
Montserrat
Pitcairn Island
St Helena & dependencies
Turks & Caicos Islands

8 The Maastricht, Amsterdam and Nice treaties

The **Treaty on European Union** was approved at the Maastricht meeting of the European Council on December 9th and 10th 1991, and signed in Maastricht on February 7th 1992. After ratification by the 12 national parliaments, it came into force on November 1st 1993.

The treaty, which is divided into six parts, and a long list of annexes and protocols, consists principally of amendments to the Rome treaty, in whose text it has been incorporated. The main provisions of the Maastricht Treaty are as follows.

1 The commitment of the Community to the achievement of economic and monetary union, including a single currency administered by a single independent central bank. This is to be achieved in three stages. The third stage, which will start no later than January 1st 1999, but perhaps as early as January 1st 1997, commits those countries which fulfil four specific criteria – relating to inflation, budget deficits, exchange rates and interest rates – to proceed to the adoption of a common currency. A protocol provides that the UK would not be obliged to enter the third stage of EMU without a separate decision to do so by its government and parliament.

2 The development of common foreign and defence policies, with defence issues initially subcontracted to the Western European Union, whose membership would be opened to all EC member states.

3 The introduction of union citizenship, defining the rights and obligations of nationals of the member states. These include freedom of movement, right of residence, the right to vote and stand as a candidate at municipal and European elections, and shared diplomatic protection outside the union.

4 EC powers in areas such as education and vocational training, trans-European networks, industry, health, culture, development co-operation and consumer protection were confirmed or extended.

5 The establishment of a Cohesion Fund to transfer resources from the richer to the poorer member states.

6 The strengthening of judicial, immigration and police co-operation between member states, largely on an inter-governmental basis.

7 An agreement by 11 member states, excluding the UK, to use EC machinery to implement measures arising from the Social Charter of 1989 concerning the protection of workers' health and safety, working conditions, information and consultation of workers, equal opportunity and treatment, and the integration of persons excluded from the labour market.

8 Institutional changes, including an extension of the legislative powers of the European Parliament, the increase in the commission's term of office from four to five years and the granting to the Court of Justice of the right to impose fines on member states for failing to implement its judgments.

The **Treaty of Amsterdam** was approved at the Amsterdam meeting of the European Council on June 16th and 17th 1997, and was signed, also in Amsterdam, on October 2nd 1997. It is divided into six sections and 19 chapters, with a substantial number of protocols, annexes and declarations. It consists mainly of amendments to the previous treaties, and was incorporated in the text of the Rome Treaty when it was ratified by the European Parliament and the 15 member states. It came into effect on May 1st 1999 following the receipt of the last instrument of ratification. Its main provisions are as follows.

1 Free movement of persons, asylum, immigration, the crossing of external borders and judicial co-operation in civil matters are brought within the Community framework (i.e. transferred from Pillar Three to Pillar One).

2 The Schengen Agreement, on opening of internal borders, is also brought within the Community framework.

3 The Protocol on Social Policy (the Social Chapter) is incorporated into the treaty and will apply to the United Kingdom and to all future entrants.

4 An employment chapter is added to the Treaty.

5 The provisions for a common foreign and security policy are strengthened, the Secretary-General of the Council of Ministers will become the High Representative for the CFSP and will form a "troika" with the Presidents of the Council and the commission.

6 The European Parliament's powers are extended, giving it the right to co-decision with the Council over the majority of EU legislation.

7 Qualified majority voting in the Council of Ministers is extended to

include research, employment, social exclusion, equal opportunities and public health.

8 The role of the President of the commission is upgraded. His appointment will need to be approved by the European Parliament and his assent will be needed for the appointment of the other members of the commission.

9 A new "flexibility" clause is added, enabling groups of member states to use the Community institutions to co-operate more closely on specific areas not within the exclusive competence of the EC.

The **Treaty of Nice** was approved at the Nice meeting of the European Council on December 11th 2000 and was signed, also in Nice, on February 26th 2001. Its main purpose was to provide for institutional changes within the European Union to pave the way for the expected adhesion of a substantial number of member states during the first decade of the 21st century. Parts of the treaty were due to come into effect only in 2005, with the remainder following ratification by the 15 member states and the European Parliament. By May 2002, 12 member states had deposited their instruments of ratification, but a referendum in Ireland on June 7th 2001 resulted in a "no" vote of 53.87% compared with 46.13% "yes". A further referendum in Ireland is expected in autumn 2002, and if this produces a "no" vote the Treaty will effectively be void. Its main provisions are as follows.

1 A reweighting of votes in the Council of Ministers to strengthen the position of the larger member states when new members, which are mostly small, join the Union.

2 The larger member states will give up their right to a second member of the commission. When EU membership reaches 27 or more, member states will no longer have an automatic right to nominate commissioners, who will be allocated on a rotation system in which all states, large or small, will be treated equally.

3 The number of seats in the European Parliament, both for the existing member states and for the 12 countries currently negotiating membership, is determined, giving a total maximum number of MEPs of 732. Membership numbers for other EU institutions are also agreed.

4 Qualified majority voting in the Council of Ministers is extended to over 30 more Articles of the Treaty of Rome, including notably the appointment of the president of the commission. The European Parliament's powers of co-decision are extended to ten more Articles.

5 Minor changes are made to the powers of the Court of Justice and the European Central Bank.
6 The scope of the "flexibility" clause of the Amsterdam treaty is extended.
7 There are new provisions to facilitate the implementation of the European Security and Defence Policy.

9 Abbreviations and acronyms

Like other international organisations, the European Union has spawned a goodly number of abbreviations and acronyms, sometimes derisively referred to as "Eurojargon". The following list cannot claim to be comprehensive, but it does seek to include all those in common usage, including several derived from non-EU organisations with which the Union has dealings. In some cases the acronyms are based on the French language version, which may explain why the words do not match the initials.

ACP	African, Caribbean and Pacific countries, parties to the Lomé Convention
ADAPT	Community initiative on adaptation of the workforce to industrial change
AFSJ	Area of Freedom, Security and Justice
Altener	Specific actions to promote greater penetration for renewable energy sources
ASEAN	Association of South-East Asian Nations
ASEM	Asia-Europe meeting
BC-Net	Business Co-operation Network
BEST	Business Environment Simplication Task Force
BSE	Bovine spongiform encephalopathy
CAP	Common agricultural policy
CBSS	Council of the Baltic Sea States
CCT	Common Customs Tariff
CEDEFOP	European Centre for the Development of Vocational Training
CELEX	Inter-institutional system of computerised documentation on Community law
CEN	The European Committee for Standardisation
CFSP	Common Foreign and Security Policy
CIS	Commonwealth of Independent States
CITES	Convention on International Trade in Endangered Species of Wild Fauna and Flora
Coreper	Committee of Permanent Representatives
CORDIS	Community Research and Development Information Service

COST	European co-operation on scientific and technical research
CREST	Scientific and Technical Research Committee
CRS	computerised reservation systems
CSF	Community support framework (structural funds)
EAGGF	European Agricultural Guidance and Guarantee Fund
EBRD	European Bank for Reconstruction and Development
EC	European Community
ECB	European Central Bank
ECE	European Commission for Europe (UN)
ECHO	European Community Humanitarian Office
ECIP	European Community Investment Partners
ECJ	European Court of Justice
Ecofin	Council of Economic and Finance Ministers
Ecu	European Currency Unit
EDF	European Development Fund
EEA	European Economic Area
EEC	European Economic Community
EEIG	European economic interest grouping
EFTA	European Free Trade Association
EIB	European Investment Bank
EIC	Euro-Info Centre
EIF	European Investment Fund
EMCDDA	European Monitoring Centre for Drugs and Drug Addiction
EMI	European Monetary Institute
EMS	European Monetary System
EMU	economic and monetary union
Erasmus	European Community action scheme for the mobility of university students
ERDF	European Regional Development Fund
ERM	exchange rate mechanism
ESA	European Space Agency
ESCB	European System of Central Banks
ESF	European Social Fund
Euratom	European Atomic Energy Community
EURES	European employment services
Euro	Basic unit in the single currency
EUR-OP	Office for Official Publications of the European Communities
Eurocontrol	European Organisation for the Safety of Air Navigation

Europol	European Police Office
Eurostat	Statistical Office of the European Community
Eurotecnet	Community action programme in the field of training and technological change
FADN	farm accountancy data network
FAO	Food and Agriculture Organisation (UN)
·FG	Financial Instrument for Fisheries Guidance
FORCE	programme for the development of continuing vocational training
FRY	Federal Republic of Yugoslavia
FYROM	Former Yugoslav Republic of Macedonia
G8	Group of eight major industrialised countries
GATT	General Agreement on Tariffs and Trade
GCC	Gulf Co-operation Council
GDP	Gross domestic product
GFCM	General Fisheries Council for the Mediterranean
GNP	gross national product
GNSS	global navigation satellite system
GSP	generalised system of preferences
IAEA	International Atomic Energy Agency (UN)
IBRD	International Bank for Reconstruction and Development (World Bank) (UN)
ICRC	International Committee of the Red Cross
IDA	interchange of data between administrations
IGC	Intergovernmental Conference
ILO	International Labour Organisation
IMF	International Monetary Fund (UN)
IMPEL	network for monitoring the implementation of Community environmental legislation
ISDN	integrated services digital network
ISO	International Organisation for Standardisation
ISPO	Information Society Project Office
ISTC	International Science and Technology Centre
ITER	international thermonuclear experimental reactor
ITU	International Telecommunications Union
JET	joint European Torus
JICS	joint Interpreting and Conference Service
JOP	Joint venture programme PHARE-TACIS
JRC	joint Research Centre
LDCS	Least developed countries

Leader	Community initiative concerning rural development
LIFE	financial instrument for the environment
Lingua	Programme to promote foreign language competence in the European Community
MEDA	financial and technical measures to accompany the reform of economic and social structures in the framework of the Euro-Mediterranean partnership
MEDIA	programme to encourage the development of the audiovisual industry
Mercosur	Southern Cone Common Market
NAFO	North-West Atlantic Fisheries Organisation
NATO	North Atlantic Treaty Organisation
NCI	New Community Instrument
NGO	non-governmental organisation
NPA	new partnership approach
NPT	Treaty on the non-proliferation of nuclear weapons
OAU	Organisation of African Unity
OCTS	overseas countries and territories
OECD	Organisation for Economic Cooperation and Development
OLAF	Anti-Fraud Office
ONP	open network provision
OSCE	Organisation for Security and Cooperation in Europe
PETRA	programme for the vocational training of young people and their preparation for adult and working life
PHARE	programme of Community aid for central and east European countries
PLO	Palestine Liberation Organisation
QMV	qualified majority voting
Rechar	Community initiative concerning the economic conversion of coal-mining areas
REGIS	Community initiative concerning the most remote regions
Resider	Community programme to assist the conversion of steel areas
RTD	research and technological development
SAPARD	Special Assistance Programme for Agricultural and Rural Development
SAVE	specific actions for vigorous energy efficiency
SEA	Single European Act
SIMAP	information system for public procurement

SLIM	simpler legislation for the internal market
SMES	small and medium-sized enterprises
SPD	single programming document (Structural Funds)
Stabex	system for the stabilisation of export earnings
Sysmin	system for the stabilisation of export earnings from mining products
TAC	total allowable catch
TACIS	programme for technical assistance to the independent States of the former Soviet Union and Mongolia
Target	trans-European automated real-time gross settlement express transfer
Tempus	Trans-European co-operation scheme for higher education
TENS	trans-European networks
UCLAF	Unit for the Co-ordination of Fraud Prevention
UN	United Nations
Unctad	United Nations Conference on Trade and Development
Unesco	United Nations Educational, Scientific and Cultural Organisation
UNHCR	United Nations High Commissioner for Refugees
UNIDO	United Nations Industrial Development Organisation
UNRWA	United Nations Relief and Works Agency for Palestine Refugees in the Near East
VAT	value added tax
WCO	World Customs Organisation
WEU	Western European Union
WFP	world food programme (UN)
WHO	World Health Organisation (UN)
WIPO	World Intellectual Property Organisation (UN)
WTO	World Trade Organisation

10 Chronology of major events concerning the European Union

1945	**May**	End of second world war in Europe.
1947	**June**	United States launches Marshall Plan to aid European reconstruction.
1948	**April**	Creation of the Organisation for Economic Co-operation (OEEC) to co-ordinate Marshall Plan assistance.
1949	**April**	North Atlantic Treaty signed, creating NATO.
1950	**May**	French foreign minister, Robert Schuman, proposes the pooling of French and West German coal and steel resources in a community open to other West European nations.
1951	**April**	Belgium, France, Italy, Luxembourg, the Netherlands and West Germany sign the Treaty of Paris, setting up the European Coal and Steel Community (ECSC).
1952	**May**	The same six countries sign a treaty to establish a European Defence Community (EDC), with a common European army.
	August	The ECSC established, with its headquarters in Luxembourg.
1954	**August**	French parliament refuses to ratify the EDC treaty, which is immediately abandoned.
1955	**June**	Negotiations begin at Messina for the creation of a European Common Market.
1957	**March**	Two treaties signed in Rome, setting up the European Economic Community and Euratom, by the six member states of the ECSC.
1958	**January**	The EEC and Euratom treaties come into effect. The EEC Commission is established, with its headquarters "provisionally" in Brussels.
1960	**January**	The Stockholm Convention established the European Free Trade Association (EFTA), linking the UK with Austria, Denmark, Norway, Portugal, Sweden and Switzerland.

	December	The OEEC is wound up and replaced by the Organisation for Economic Co-operation and Development (OECD), based in Paris.
1961	May	EFTA established, with its headquarters in Geneva.
	July	The EEC signs an association agreement with Greece. Ireland applies for EEC membership.
	August	Denmark and the UK also apply for membership.
	November	Membership negotiations open in Brussels.
1962	April	Norway applies for EEC membership.
1963	January	President de Gaulle vetoes UK membership; the other applicant states suspend their applications. Franco-German Treaty of Co-operation signed.
	July	Yaoundé Convention, providing for economic aid and trade concessions to 17 African states, formerly colonies of the EEC countries, is signed in the capital of Cameroon.
	September	The EEC signs an association agreement with Turkey.
1964	July	Common Agricultural Policy (CAP) comes into effect.
1965	June	Crisis in the EEC as France begins seven-month boycott of its meetings, refusing to be out-voted on issues it considered of great importance.
1966	January	France resumes its active membership, after negotiation of the "Luxembourg compromise", under which important issues were, in effect, to be decided by unanimity, irrespective of the provisions of the Rome treaty.
1967	May	Denmark, Ireland, Norway and the UK make second application to join the EEC. In view of de Gaulle's continued hostility, the applications are left on the table.
	July	The EEC is merged with the ECSC and Euratom to form a single European Community (EC).
1968	July	All internal tariffs removed within the EC, which established a common external tariff (CET).
1969	December	France's President Pompidou agrees with other EC leaders at a "summit" meeting in The Hague to consider an enlargement of EC membership.
1970	June	Membership negotiations open in Brussels with

		the four applicant states.
1972	January	Treaties of Accession signed between the EC and Denmark, Ireland, Norway and the UK.
	July	Free trade agreements signed with the six EFTA states which did not apply to join the EC.
	September	Norway turns down EC membership in a referendum (46% for, 54% against).
1973	January	Denmark, Ireland and the UK become full members of the Community.
	May	Norway signs free trade agreement with the EC.
1974	April	At request of the new UK Labour government, a "renegotiation" of the membership terms begins.
1975	February	First Lomé Convention, replacing the Yaoundé Convention of 1963, is signed, giving economic aid and trade concessions to 46 African, Caribbean and Pacific (ACP) states.
	June	Referendum in the UK shows a 2:1 majority in favour of staying in the EC.
		Greece applies for EC membership.
1977	March	Portugal applies for membership.
	July	Spain applies for membership.
1979	March	European Monetary System (EMS) established.
	June	First direct elections to the European Parliament.
	December	Row over UK budget contribution to the EC at the Dublin summit, when Mrs Thatcher demands "our money back".
1980	May	Provisional solution to UK budget problem, intended to last for three years.
1981	January	Greece becomes member of the EC.
1984	June	Second direct elections to European Parliament.
		At Fontainebleau summit agreement reached on reducing the UK budget contribution and on increasing the financial resources of the EC.
1985	January	Jacques Delors becomes president of the European Commission.
	June	At Milan summit agreement is reached on seven-year timetable to remove 300 barriers to the internal market, according to a programme devised by a British commissioner, Lord Cockfield. An intergovernmental conference was also appointed to

		consider amendments to the Rome treaty.
	December	The inter-governmental conference produces the Single European Act, a series of treaty amendments designed to speed up decision-making, especially on internal market measures. It is signed by all member states.
1986	**January**	Spain and Portugal become members of the EC.
1987	**April**	Turkey applies to join the EC.
	July	The Single European Act comes into force.
1988	**February**	Delors I package, which set the guidelines for expanding EC budgets, but with tighter control over agricultural spending, over the five years 1988–92, agreed.
1989	**June**	Third direct elections to European Parliament. Austria applies to join the EC.
	July	G7 summit asks EC to co-ordinate Western aid to Poland and Hungary. This aid is subsequently extended to other East European countries, and negotiations follow to conclude trade and association agreements with the former Soviet "satellites".
	November	Breach of the Berlin Wall heralds the collapse of communism in Eastern Europe.
	December	Negotiations begin between the EC and the EFTA states to form a European Economic Area (EEA).
1990	**July**	Capital movements liberalised throughout the Community. Madrid summit conference approved in principle a plan to introduce economic and monetary union in three stages, with Mrs Thatcher reserving the UK position. Cyprus and Malta apply for EC membership.
	October	German unification: territory of former East Germany joins EC, as integral part of West Germany.
	December	Two inter-governmental conferences, on economic and monetary union and on political union respectively, begin work. Rome EC summit approves programmes of food aid and technical assistance to the Soviet Union.
1991	**July**	Sweden applies for EC membership.

	September	Following the failed Soviet coup, EC mission visits the former Soviet Union and the newly independent Baltic states to discuss an enhanced aid programme. EC-sponsored peace conference opens on Yugoslavia.
	November	Agreement reached to set up European Economic Area on January 1st 1993.
	December	At Maastricht summit, agreement is reached on the Treaty on European Union. This included detailed arrangements for EMU, with a single currency, to be in force no later than 1999, with an opt-out provision for the UK, and for gradual progression towards a common foreign and security policy.
1992	February	Delors II package proposes increasing EC budget by 30% over five years.
	March	Finland applies for EC membership.
	May	Switzerland applies for EC membership.
	June	Denmark narrowly rejects Maastricht Treaty in referendum; Jacques Delors is reappointed for two more years, from January 1993, at Lisbon summit; reform of CAP narrowly agreed by Council of Ministers.
	November	Blair House agreement aligns EC and US proposals on the agricultural sector of the Uruguay round of the GATT negotiations.
	December	Switzerland turns down EEA in a referendum; Edinburgh summit adopts reduced Delors II budget package, spreading it out over seven years instead of five, and approves establishment of European Investment Fund.
1993	February	Negotiations begin on accession of Austria, Finland and Sweden.
	April	Negotiations begin on accession of Norway.
	May	In second referendum the Danish people vote in favour of the Maastricht treaty.
	July	Adoption of the TACIS programme to provide technical assistance to the independent states of the former Soviet Union.

	August	After many delays, the UK finally ratifies the Maastricht treaty.
	October	Germany, the last state to do so, deposits its ratification of the Maastricht treaty after a court challenge fails.
	November 1	Maastricht treaty comes into force: the European Community becomes the European Union.
	December	Brussels summit approves an action plan based on the European Commission's White Paper on growth, competitiveness and employment.
	December	Uruguay round negotiations successfully concluded in Geneva.
1994	**January**	European Economic Area agreement comes into force, linking the EU and five member states of EFTA, but excluding Switzerland and, temporarily, Liechtenstein.
	March	Accession negotiations successfully completed with Austria, Finland, Norway and Sweden.
	June	Fourth direct elections to the European Parliament. Partnership and Co-operation Agreement signed with Russia at Corfu summit. The UK vetoes nomination of Jean-Luc Dehaene as president of the European Commission.
	July	Jacques Santer nominated as commission president to succeed Jacques Delors.
	November	Norway rejects EU membership in referendum.
	December	Essen summit gives go-ahead for first 14 priority projects for Trans-European Networks.
1995	**January**	Austria, Finland and Sweden join the EU. New commission under Jacques Santer takes office. Pact on Stability in Europe between the EU and the states belonging to the Organisation on Security and Co-operation in Europe (OSCE) signed in Paris.
	April	Liechtenstein accedes to the EEA.
	May	Commission produces white paper on steps that the countries of Central and Eastern Europe should take to prepare for membership of the EU.
	July	EU member states sign convention establishing Europol (the European Police Office). First EU ombudsman, Jacob Söderman, elected.

	November	Euro-Mediterranean ministerial conference at Barcelona adopts declaration regulating future relations, including financial aid and progress towards free trade areas, between the EU and 12 Mediterranean states.
	December	EU and the United States sign a new transatlantic agenda and joint action plan. Customs union between Turkey and the EU approved by European Parliament. Madrid summit confirms introduction of a single currency (euro) on January 1st 1999.
		During the year Bulgaria, Estonia, Latvia, Lithuania, Romania and Slovakia apply for membership of the EU.
1996	**January**	Czech Republic applies for EU membership.
	March	Inter-governmental conference to review the Maastricht treaty and to prepare for further enlargement opened in Turin. EU bans UK beef exports, but offers financial aid to help combat BSE outbreak. The UK begins systematic policy of non-co-operation in effort to secure the lifting of the ban.
	June	The UK ends non-co-operation after EU stipulates conditions for the eventual lifting of the ban. Slovenia applies for EU membership.
	October	EU emphatically rejects the extra-territorial provisions of the Helms-Burton Act regarding trade with Cuba, and threatens counter-measures against the United States.
	December	Dublin summit agrees on stability pact to impose economic and financial disciplines on member states joining the single currency, reinforcing confidence that EMU would be successfully launched in January 1999.
1997	**May**	Newly elected Labour government in UK announces "fresh start" in relations with EU, and ends British opt-out from the Social Chapter.
	June	Signing of the Amsterdam Treaty, containing modest amendments to the Rome and Maastricht treaties.

	July	Commission adopts "Agenda 2000" policy statement, preparing the ground for further EU enlargement, and setting long-term targets for financial and agricultural reforms.
	December	At Luxembourg summit the way is cleared for membership negotiations to begin in March 1998 with Cyprus, the Czech Republic, Estonia, Hungary, Poland and Slovenia.
1998	May	Agreement is reached at special Brussels summit for 11 member states to participate in a single currency, under EMU, from January 1st 1999. Wim Duisenberg is appointed as the first president of the European Central Bank. At EU-US summit President Clinton agrees to ask the US Congress to exclude the EU from sanctions under the Helms-Burton Act.
	September	Malta reactivates its application for EU membership.
	December	European Parliament refuses to approve final accounts of the 1996 budget, precipitating a crisis with the commission.
1999	March	Entire Santer commission resigns in anticipation of being censured by the Parliament. At Berlin summit Romano Prodi is nominated as successor to Santer. The summit also approves budgetary perspectives for 2000–06.
	May	Treaty of Amsterdam comes into force. Foreign ministers propose a stability pact for south-east Europe, following the Kosovo conflict.
	September	New commission, led by Romano Prodi, takes over, following its approval by the European Parliament.
	October	Special summit meeting on justice and home affairs calls for the creation of an area of "freedom, justice and security" within the EU.
	December	Helsinki summit decides to open accession negotiations with Bulgaria, Latvia, Lithuania, Malta, Romania and Slovakia.
2000	March	Special Economic Summit in Lisbon inaugurates a ten-year programme to make the EU "the most

		competitive and dynamic knowledge-based economy in the world".
	September	Denmark votes in referendum by 53.3% to 46.7% not to adopt the euro.
	October	Convention draws up a draft Charter of Fundamental Rights for the EU.
	December	European Council in Nice agrees treaty amending the Union's institutional provisions to facilitate the admission of up to 12 new member states.
2001	January	Greece becomes the 12th country to join the euro.
	June	Irish referendum rejects the Nice treaty by 53.87% to 46.13%.
	December	Laeken summit adopts wide-ranging proposals to combat terrorism in the wake of the September 11th attacks on the United States. It also establishes a Convention on EU reform in preparation for the 2004 IGC.
2002	January–February	Euro notes and coins replace national currencies in the 12 member states of the Eurozone.

Suggestions for further reading

There is a vast literature on the EU, much of it of a highly specialist nature. The European Commission itself produces a stream of pamphlets and documentation of various kinds, much of which is available (often free of charge) from the information offices of the European Union in London, Edinburgh, Cardiff and Belfast. There are similar offices in all the major EU capital cities, as well as in other major centres including New York, Washington, New Delhi, Ottawa and Canberra.

The historical background to the creation of the Community is described in fascinating detail in Jean Monnet's memoirs and his biography, and placed in a wider context by two other well-known authors.

Duchêne, François, *Jean Monnet: The First Statesman of Interdependence*, W. W. Norton, New York and London, 1994.

Grosser, Alfred, *The Western Alliance: European-American relations since 1945*, Macmillan, London, 1980.

Monnet, Jean, *Memoirs*, Collins, London, 1978.

Stirk, Peter M.R., *A History of European Integration since 1914*, Pinter, London and New York, 1996.

Among the large number of books written about particular aspects of the Community's affairs, the following may be mentioned.

Bainbridge, Timothy, *The Penguin Companion to European Union*, Penguin Books, Harmondsworth, 2nd edition, 1999.

Bond, Martin, Smith, Julie and Wallace, William (eds), *Eminent Europeans: Personalities who shaped contemporary Europe*, Greycoat Press, London, 1996.

Edwards, Geoffrey and Spence, David (eds), *The European Commission*, Cartermill, London, 1994.

Edwards, Geoffrey and Wiessala, Georg (eds), *The European Union: Annual Review of the EU*, Blackwells, Oxford, yearly.

Emerson, Michael, *Redrawing the Map of Europe*, Macmillan, London, 1998.

Grant, Charles, *Delors: Inside the House that Jacques Built*, Brealey, London, 1994.

Hix, Simon, *The Political System of the European Union*, Macmillan, London, 1999.

Jacobs, Francis, Corbett, Richard and Shackleton, Michael, *The European Parliament* (3rd edition), Cartermill, London, 1995.

Jenkins, Roy, *European Diary 1977–1981*, Collins, London, 1989.

Leonard, Dick and Leonard, Mark (eds), *The Pro-European Reader*, Palgrave-Macmillan, London, 2001.

Leonard, Mark, *Network Europe: The New Case for Europe*, Foreign Policy Centre, London, 1999.

March Hunnings, Neville, *The European Courts*, Cartermill, London, 1996.

Mathijsen, P.S.R.F., *A Guide to European Union Law*, Sweet and Maxwell, 7th edition, London, 1999.

Nugent, Neill, *The Government and Politics of the European Union* (4th edition), Macmillan, London, 1999.

Pinder, John, *The European Union: A Very Short Introduction*, OUP, Oxford, 2001.

Siedentop, Larry, *Democracy in Europe*, Columbia University Press, New York, 2001.

Wallace, Helen and Wallace, William (eds), *Policy-making in the European Union*, OUP, Oxford, 2000.

Westlake, Martin, *The Council of the European Union*, Cartermill, London, 1995.

Young, Hugo, *This Blessed Plot: Britain and Europe from Churchill to Blair*, Macmillan, London, 1998.

Index